CENSUS OF INDIA 1891

Census of India 1871-1951, 9 Sets In 384 Bindings (9788121258876) Rs. 700000

Census of India 1891, 28 Vols. In 49 Bindings (978-81-212-7129-5) Rs. 125000

1. General Report (9788121269834) Rs. 1450
2. General Tables For British Provinces And Feudatory States (9788121269810) Rs. 2710 (Vol. I)
3. General Tables For British Provinces And Feudatory States (9788121269797) Rs. 950 (Vol. II)
4. Assam - Report (9788121269773) Rs. 2390 (Vol. I, V.1)
5. Assam - Tables (9788121269759) Rs. 2210 (Vol. II, V.2)
6. Assam - Provincial Tables (9788121269735) Rs. 1310 (Vol. II, V.3)
7. The Lower Provinces of Bengal and their Feudatories - The Report (9788121269711) Rs. 1660 (Vol. III)
8. The Lower Provinces of Bengal and their feudatories - The Administrative Tables (9788121269698) Rs. 4200 (Vol. IV)
9. The Lower Provinces of Bengal and their feudatories - The Caste Tables (9788121269674) Rs. 2600 (Vol. V, Pt. 1)
10. Lower Provinces of Bengal - The Provincial Tables (9788121269650) Rs. 1980 (Vol. V, Pt. 2)
11. Berar or the Hyderabad Assigned Districts (9788121269636) Rs. 3360 (Vol. VI)
12. Bombay and Its Feudatories - Report (9788121269612) Rs. 4010 (Vol. VII, Pt. 1)
13. Bombay And Its Feudatories - Imperial Tables (9788121269599) Rs. 790 (Vol. VIII, Pt. 2)
14. Imperial Series - Burma Report (9788121269575) Rs. 2320 (Vol. IX-V.1)
15. Imperial Tables - Burma Report (9788121269551) Rs. 3360 (Vol. X-V.2)
16. Provincial Tables Burma Report (9788121269537) Rs. 3510 (Vol. X-V.3)
17. Provincial Tables Burma Report (9788121269513) Rs. 3630 (Vol. X-V.4)
18. The Central Provinces And Feudatories - The Report (9788121269490) Rs. 2290 (Vol. XI, Pt. 1)
19. The Central Provinces And Feudatories - Imperial tables and supplementary returns (9788121268936) Rs. 2010 (Vol. XII)
20. Madras The Report On The Census (9788121269476) Rs. 2870 (Vol. XIII)
21. Madras - Tables I to XVII-C, British Territory (9788121269452) Rs. 3490 (Vol. XIV)
22. Madras - Tables A TO E, British Territory. Tables for feudatory States and A Caste Index (9788121269438) Rs. 2820 (Vol. XV)
23. The North Western Provinces and Outh - Report and Provincial Tables (9788121268912) Rs. 3100 (Vol. XVI, Pt. 1)
24. The North - Western Provinces and Oudh- Imperial Tables (9788121269414) Rs. 2000 (Vol. XVII, Pt. 2)
25. The North - Western Provinces and Oudh- Imperial Caste Tables (9788121269391) Rs. 3020 (Vol. XVIII, Pt. 3)
26. Punjab and Its Feudatories - The Report on the Census (9788121269377) Rs. 2710 (Vol. XIX, Pt. 1)
27. Punjab and Its Feudatories - Imperial Tables and Supplementary Returns for the British Territory (9788121269353) Rs. 1370 (Vol. XX, Pt. 2)
28. Punjab and Its Feudatories - Imperial Tables and Supplementary Returns for the Native States, Together With A Caste Index (9788121269339) Rs. 4910 (Vol. XXI, Pt. 3)
29. Report on The Census of The Districts of Ajmere-Merwara (9788121269056) Rs. 720 (Vol. XXII)
30. His Highness The Nizam's Dominions - Report (9788121269315) Rs. 2240 (Vol. XXIII, Pt. 1)
31. His Highness The Nizam's Dominions - Report (9788121269292) Rs. 2410 (Vol. XXIII, Pt. 2)
32. His Highness The Nizam's Dominions - Imperial And Supplementry Tables and Caste Index (9788121269278) Rs. 3390 (Vol. XXIII, Pt. 3)
33. Baroda - Report (9788121269254) Rs. 3810 (Vol. XXIV, Pt. 1)
34. Baroda - Tables (9788121269230) Rs. 2620 (Vol. XXIV, Pt. 2)
35. Mysore - Report (9788121269216) Rs. 2590 (Vol. XXV, Pt. 1)
36. Mysore - Imperial Tables (9788121269193) Rs. 1600 (Vol. XXV, Pt. 2)
37. Mysore - Tables (9788121269179) Rs. 5320 (Vol. XXV, Pt. 3)
38. Mysore - Supplementary Tables (9788121269155) Rs. 3590 (Vol. XXV, Pt. 4)
39. Mysore- Supplement to the Mysore census report of 1891 being a list of villages in the Mysore province and : comparing the population as per Censuses of 1891, 1881 & 1871 (9788121279024) Rs. 5350 (Vol. XXV, Pt. 5)
40. Rajputana - The Report, Imperial Tables And Supplementary Returns (9788121269131) Rs. 2330 (Vol. XXVI, Pt. 1)
41. Rajputna - The Provincial Tables and Remarks (9788121269117) Rs. 550 (Vol. XXVI, Pt. 2)
42. Central India (9788121269094) Rs. 2000 (Vol. XXVII)
43. Kashmir State - The Report on the census and Imperial and supplementary Tables (9788121269070) Rs. 2290 (Vol. XXVIII)
44. The Census of Calcutta (9788121269032) Rs. 890
45. Report on the census of Cochin (9788121269018) Rs. 790 (Pt. 1)
46. Report on the census of Cochin - The Final Census Tables with Appendices (9788121268998) Rs. 910 (Pt. 2)
47. Report on the Census of Coorg (9788121268974) Rs. 730
48. Report on the census of Travancore -Report (9788121274029) Rs. 4220 (Vol. I)
49. Report on the census of Travancore -Appendix (9788121268950) Rs. 5300 (Vol. II)

Owing to the antiquity and rarity of this book, certain pages are regrettably absent, and readability is compromised due to the blurring of the original text. If you possess any insights regarding the availability of these missing sections, kindly inform us. Your assistance is crucial in ensuring the completion of this significant work for the benefit of future generations.

CENSUS OF INDIA, 1891

BOOK-44

REPORT

THE CENSUS OF CALCUTTA

H. E. J. T. MAGUIRE

GYAN

Published by

Gyan Publishing House
5, Ansari Road
Daryaganj, New Delhi-110002
Phone: 011-47034999, 9811692060
E-mail: books@gyanbooks.com

Distribution Network
gyanbooks.com
India, USA, Canada, UK, Australia

ISBN: 978-81-212-7129-5 (Set) 28 Vols. In 49 Bindings
978-81-212-6903-2 (PB) Book-44

First Published, 1891

2nd Impression 2024

Printed at: Gyan Press, Delhi.

CENSUS OF INDIA 1891

REPORT

ON

THE CENSUS OF CALCUTTA.

Taken on the 26th February 1891.

BY

H. F. J. T. MAGUIRE,

CENSUS OFFICER.

CALCUTTA:

PRINTED AT THE BENGAL SECRETARIAT PRESS.

1891.

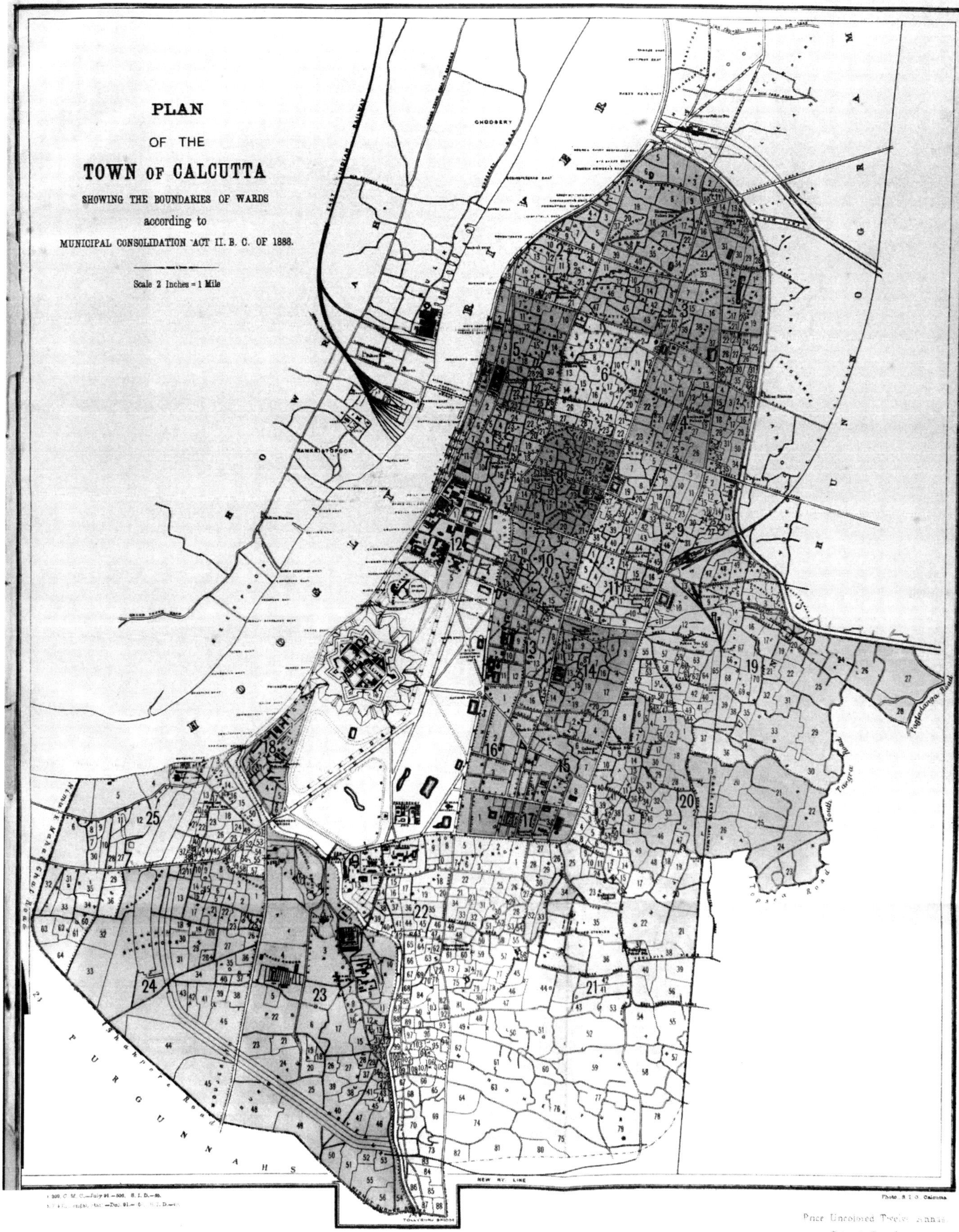

Price Uncolored Twelve Annas
,, Colored One Rupee

REPORT

ON

THE CENSUS OF CALCUTTA.

Taken on the 26th February 1891.

THIS report will be divided into two parts. The first part will relate to the preliminary arrangements up to and including the enumeration on the night of February 26th, 1891. The second part will deal with the results of the census after the completion of abstraction and tabulation.

Preliminary.

PART I.

PRELIMINARY ARRANGEMENTS.

2. The work which was under my charge was the census of the town of Calcutta as defined by Bengal Council Act II of 1888, that is to say, the area bounded by a line drawn along the southern and western bank of the Circular Canal from the river Hooghly to the south of Beliyaghatta, till it meets the Pagladanga road; thence along the eastern edge of the Pagladanga road to a point where it meets the Chingrahatta road; thence along the southern edge of the Chingrahatta road to a point where it meets the South Tangor road; thence along the eastern edge of the South Tangor road to a point where it meets the Topsea road; thence along the eastern edge of the Topsea road to its junction with the Tiljullah road; thence westward to the South-Eastern Railway, then southward along the western edge of the line of the Railway, and westward along the south of the new embankment to the Russapuglah road; thence along the eastern edge of the Russapuglah road to its junction with the road leading to the Tollyganj bridge; thence along the southern edge of this road and its continuations, the Sharpore road, the Goragachee road, and the Taratollah road, to Nimuck Mehal Ghât, where it joins the Hooghly; and thence along the left bank of the Hooghly to its junction with the Circular Canal. The accompanying map shows more conveniently than words can the difference between the area of the old town and that of the new.

Area of operations.

3. For the purposes of the Municipal Act (1) Fort William, (2) the Esplanade, and (3) that part of Hastings north of the south edge of Clyde Row which has hitherto been excluded from the municipality, were excluded from the above area. But for the purposes of the census these portions of the town are included in it.

4. The census of the port was also taken under the supervision of the census officer. The port census was taken of the water population of the river Hooghly within the following boundaries:—

On the north.—A line drawn from the boundary pillar at the Cossipore Gun Foundry Ghât to a point on the opposite side at Ghoosery.

And on the south.—A line drawn from a masonry pillar placed at the mouth of the Budge-Budge khal to a pillar on the Howrah side of the river Hooghly, bearing north-west of the first-named pillar. It will be observed that the area both of the town and the port is much larger than at the time of the preceding census, but the deductions to be drawn from this fact belong rather to the second part of the report.

5. The preliminary arrangements for the census commenced on August 1st, 1890, when Mr. George, who had performed similar duties at the preceding census, commenced with a small establishment to have plans prepared for the several blocks. This was the first step towards the taking of the census. The preparation of the plans in the old area of the town which had been surveyed in recent years, and maps of which were available on a scale of 99 feet to an inch, afforded no difficulty. It was only necessary to have the maps copied on tracing paper. For the added area maps had to be otherwise prepared. For this purpose the maps of the survey of Panchannagram estate and of a survey of the land adjoining Kidderpur docks were employed. But it was necessary first to have them enlarged, and then tested on the ground, as they did not contain sufficient details. This work was in progress at the time when I was appointed to assist the Chairman in the work.

Survey, and preparation of plans.

6. I took charge on November 17th, 1890. At this time the plans for wards I to XVIII were all but ready, the plans for wards XIX to XXII were from a fourth to a half ready, while those for the remaining wards had not been commenced. The plans for wards XIX to XXII were checked while they were on a smaller scale, and enlarged afterwards, while those for wards XXIII to XXV were enlarged before they were checked, so that they were ready for work as soon as they had been checked.

7. As soon as the plans had been prepared, copies of them had to be made for each block. These copies were made by carbon paper from the plans. A large staff, chiefly composed of apprentices who wished to be appointed enumerators, was employed for this work, and it was completed on December 20th for the town wards, and on January 26th for the wards of the added area.

8. In the old municipal area it was decided to follow the blocking of the previous census in order to facilitate comparison with the results of that census. In the added area the blocking had to be done by the surveyors. The blocking had been put in hand before I joined in accordance with the instructions of the Provincial Superintendent which applied rather to rural than urban circumstances, and the blocks were in many cases too small. Even when I attempted to revise the blocking, I had to follow statistics given by the surveyors, which were statistics of buildings, not of houses; and as the arrangements for the suburbs were altogether so backward, I thought it better to allow a slight extra expenditure than by changes at the last moment to risk the success of the census. A general revision of the added area blocks should be made at the next census, but owing to the scattered nature of most of the outlying portions, these blocks will always contain fewer houses than the blocks of the old town.

Blocking.

9. As the block plans for each ward became ready, it was possible to commence the numbering of the houses and the preparation of certain registers required for municipal purposes. These registers were in the following forms :—

Numbering and registration of houses.

Register of Houses in Ward No. ————, Enumerator's Block No. ————.

1	2	3	4	5	6	7	8	9	10	11	12
Serial No. of House in Block.	Name of Street.	No. of House in Street.	Pucca or kutcha.	How many storeys.	Whether inhabited, uninhabited, or in course of building.	Residential or rented.	If rented, whether occupied as a whole or let out in portion.	Any verandah over roadway? Hanging or supported on pillars?	Name of occupier.	Name of owner.	REMARKS.

Register of Conservancy ——— *Ward No.* ————, *Enumerator's Block No.* ————.

1	2	3	4	5	6	7	8	9	10	11		12		13		14
Serial No. of House in Block.	Name of Street.	No. of House in Street.	Whether House is or is not connected with the sewer.	Is there a privy on the premises?	Is the privy connected with the sewer?	Is the Privy connected with water-supply? If connected, with filtered or unfiltered supply.	1. Is there a reservoir supply cistern? & Is there a flushing cistern as well?	Is night-soil service performed?	Is there a cowshed?	NUMBER OF COWS AND BUFFALOES.		IS THERE A STABLE.		NO. OF HORSES INCLUDING PONIES.		REMARKS.
										Cows.	Buffaloes.	Ticca.	Private.	Ticca.	Private.	

Register of Drainage and Water Connections in Ward No. ————, *Enumerator's Block No.* ————.

1	2	3	4	5	6	7	8	9
Serial No. of House in Block.	Name of Street.	No. of House in Street.	Whether house is or is not connected with the water-supply? If connected, state whether with filtered or unfiltered supply.	No. of drainage pits inside House.	How many water taps in House?	Is there a reservoir? What is its approximate size?	Is there a well in the House?	REMARKS.

House enumerators were then appointed, and to some four and to some five of the blocks were allotted, and instructions were given to them in the following letter:—

Under Section 196 *of Act II* (*B.C.*) *of* 1888.

1.—You are appointed to be an Enumerator in the area bounded N. by E. by S. by and W. by which contains blocks Nos. of Ward No. Your proceedings will be under the control and supervision of who is the supervisor of the Circle in which the area lies.

2.—A plan of each of the blocks in your charge is made over to you. You will begin by numbering the houses in each, commencing at the right-hand top corner and proceeding from east to west to the western side and working then back and forwards from west to east and from east to west till the houses are all numbered. If you find any house not entered on the plan you are to note its position on the plan and number it also. You are to observe that each 'bari' or collection of houses in one compound is to be considered as one house. When you have given a house its number in the block, you will paste up a label on it thus— Ward No. Block No. House No. and also note the number on the plan of the block in which it is situated.

3.—You will then proceed to fill up the three registers which are given to you block by block.

4.—In the register of houses you will enter in column 1 the number assigned to the house as above, in the block. In column 2 you will enter the name of the street if there is a name. If there is no name, you will note such particulars as are necessary to identify it, as for instance a lane running from No. so and so in one street to No. so and so in another street, or from so and so's house in one street to so and so's house in another street.

5.—You will similarly note in column 3 whatever number is attached to the house by the Municipal authorities, or if there is no number, then note that there is no number. Columns 4 to 9 do not require any explanation. In column 10 you will enter the name of each head of a family occupying the house. A separate line will be given for each family. In cases where any occupier is a respectable European or English-knowing native, you should enter in column 12 the word *P.S.*, meaning that he is to have a private schedule for enumerating his family.

6.—As to the other registers you will only have to ask for the information required by the headings of the columns, and enter it in the registers.

7.—It is expected that the work of your sub-circle will be finished within a month.

8.—You are to be subject to whatever instructions the supervisor may give you, and in any difficulty will apply to him for advice or assistance. You must at all times have your books ready to be checked by him or any of the superior census officers.

The only point in these instructions which requires remark is the definition of "house," which is a point on which authorities are not agreed. The term "bari" or compound, meaning all the houses in one enclosure, is, however, well understood by the natives, and seemed a more convenient unit for the enumeration of houses than the tenement or holding of each occupier would have been. The number of occupiers, which is also necessary, was obtained from the house register. The municipal numbering would not, as will be seen below, have been a safe guide to the total number of houses in the town.

Appointment of supervisors.

10. At the same time supervisors were appointed. Municipal servants were selected with the sanction of departmental heads and the Chairman's approval. The following number of supervisors were appointed in each ward:—

In Ward	I	... 2		In Ward	XIII	... 1
,,	II	... 1		,,	XIV	... 1
,,	III	... 2		,,	XV and XVI	... 1
,,	IV	... 2		,,	XVII	... 1
,,	V	... 2		,,	XVIII	... 1
,,	VI	... 2		,,	XIX	... 3
,,	VII	... 1		,,	XX	... 2
,,	VIII	... 2		,,	XXI	... 3
,,	IX	... 2		,,	XXII	... 4
,,	X	... 1		,,	XXIII	... 2
,,	XI	... 1		,,	XXIV	... 2
,,	XII	... 1		,,	XXV	... 2

11. In Wards XII and XVII two specially appointed Census Superintendents were appointed to supervise in addition to their other duties. These wards were so small that it was not thought necessary to appoint a man who would require to be paid. In Ward VII the Health Inspector failed to do the work properly, and a special supervisor had to be appointed, and special men were also appointed in Wards XX and XXIII. The supervisors were to receive a bonus of Rs. 25 for satisfactory work. The specially appointed men were given Rs. 30 for the job.

House enumerators.

12. In all 99 house enumerators were appointed. They were to receive Rs. 10 each for the job, and five annas for contingencies, *i.e.*, paste and a cooly to paste labels on. The difficulties attendant on the employment of these men and getting the work done by them were very great. Although candidates for employment came in crowds, many did not seem to have any real wish to do the work indicated in the appointment letter, which was thought to be derogatory. Many of them, therefore, became ill. Many received bad news from home, and went away. Some had given wrong addresses, and went away with plans and registers, and could not be found at all. Then the supervisors at first were very backward in reporting the defection of the enumerators. At last, however, things improved, and by the 15th December the registers began to come in. There was, however, considerable delay in their completion, and some few had not been finished or checked before the census enumeration had to be taken in hand. The supervisors were directed to test 20 per cent. of the entries in these registers, and they have certified that they did this. Although I was unable to test the accuracy of this work in any complete way, I have incidentally found reason to believe that the registers were for the most part correctly prepared.

Enumerators in Wards XIX to XXV.

13. In Wards XIX to XXV, which were formerly in the Suburban Municipalities, no house enumerators were appointed. The men who were appointed to do the actual enumeration at the census were also expected to number the houses and prepare the registers. They were to receive Rs. 10 for each block. As I have already stated, the blocks in these wards were generally smaller, and the houses in them were almost always fewer than in the blocks of

the old town. The work of the preparation of the registers was also much less because in many parts of the added area there is no water connection, and very little drainage. In the last of these wards the plans and registers were distributed to the enumerators on 26th January, just one month before the census.

Appointment of enumerators.

14. Meanwhile the appointment of enumerators for the other wards had been going on, and a commencement was made in training the enumerators by giving them test schedules, explaining what they had to do, and correcting their attempts. The total number of enumerators was 890. One hundred and five assistant enumerators were also appointed in the larger blocks, and 91 Municipal servants assisted in the wards where they lived.

Preliminary enumeration.

15. The preparation of the preliminary record of the census was to have commenced on February 9th, but owing to delays in the receipt of the house registers the indent for schedules was delayed, and then the work was further kept back by the Saraswati Puja, so that regular work did not begin generally until 16th February. The next few days were spent by the Superintendents and myself in constant visits to the wards, for the purpose of checking work and preventing mistakes.

Household schedules.

16. On February 23rd the distribution of household schedules commenced. The entries in the house registers as to the houses at which these schedules were to be left were not always carefully made, and demands for them were also put forward by some who were not intended to receive them On this account the supply ran short, and some of the schedules were not distributed till the day of the census, and in some few cases arrangements had to be made for having them filled up after the night of the final census.

Number of schedules.

17. The total number of ordinary schedules used was 146,890, and of private schedules 6,370 for Europeans and 7,525 for natives. Seven hundred and eight books of 12 schedules for boats were also used.

Final enumeration.

18. The preliminary arrangements being thus far ready, an order was issued to all supervisors to the following effect :—

To all Supervisors.

The final census will be taken from 8 P.M. on February 26th.

Before that time you should see that the preliminary work has all been finished, and that each man has sufficient space in his registers for further entries, if needed.

All your enumerators should be directed to attend at your office at 7 P.M., having each a pen and some red ink and a lantern.

You should also direct all your sirkars and any municipal servants in the ward to attend. If any enumerator fails to attend, you must appoint one of these men to work in his place.

The enumerators should then each be directed to read carefully the instructions as to the final enumeration.

They should then go to their respective wards and commence at 8 P.M. precisely to test the preliminary enumeration according to the rules.

In difficult blocks a constable will accompany each enumerator. In other blocks municipal peons should be sent with them. In large blocks your sirkars and respectable residents should assist. One or more of the registers should be made over to these assistants, and the first house in it pointed out during the day of the 26th.

The enumerators should instruct the inhabitants to be present in their houses on the night of the 26th, and to have a light burning in each house. But any one found in a block outside a house must be enumerated, unless he says that he has already been enumerated elsewhere.

You (the supervisors) should be on duty all night, and should visit all the blocks and sub-blocks in your circles to see that the work is being carefully and properly done. On the morning of the 27th, the enumerators are to go round their blocks in order and collect private schedules, and pin them into their books in the proper order.

They will then bring their books to you, when you should cause them to total up the number of persons, and enter them in the enumerator's khatiyan at page 4 of the schedule book. Only the general total need be filled up ; the details of Hindus, &c., may be left blank for the present.

On receipt of the books you are to fill in form M, which is sent herewith, and return it with the registers to this office as soon as possible. In column 2 of form M the word "village" is to be changed to "block."

The registers for each block should be tied up separately. I expect to receive all the registers by March 2nd.

The Commissioner of Police kindly arranged to supply police assistance, and it may be convenient to print here the circular order which he also issued about the census:—

CIRCULAR MEMO.

No. 8A.

(CENSUS.)

The Inspectors of the following sections will depute constables as detailed below to assist the census enumerators on the night of the 26th instant.

2. Before leaving the thana each Inspector will explain to the men selected, that their duty is to accompany such enumerator or enumerators, as they may be told off to, and to see that the enumerator is not interfered with in the execution of his duty, and to advise persons inclined to be troublesome that they are bound by law to give the information required.

3. Steady and reliable men are to be selected for this work:—

Town Sec.	Constables.	Town Sec.	Constables.	Subn. Sec.	Constables.
A	15	J	10	F	10
B	12	K	10	G	10
C	20	L	2	H	15
D	12	M	10	I	20
E	10	N	12	J	15
F	12	O	4	K	15
G	12	P	2	L	15
H	12	Q	4	M	10
I	18	R	3	N	5

4. The Superintendent, Reserve Force, will depute for this duty 10 constables to Section F Suburbs, 5 men to Section G Suburbs, and 10 men to Section I Suburbs.

5. All native officers and constables detailed for this duty will have a cooked meal in the afternoon, and will be ready for duty at 6 P.M., on being applied for by the census officers.

6. All parades are excused for Thursday the 26th instant, and the following day.

7. The Superintendent, Reserve Force, will direct 2 European constables to report themselves for duty at 7 P.M. at each of the following thanas:—

Bow Bazar, Puddopooker, Taltollah, and Fenwick Bazar.

8. On the night of the census, Inspectors and native officers will move about their sections, rendering assistance to the enumerators generally, and preventing or restraining all attempts to obstruct, insult or annoy them in the performance of their duty. The police will be responsible that no obstruction, unnecessary annoyance, or breach of the peace takes place.

9. These orders also apply to the Suburban Sections beyond the amalgamated portions. Sections A and B will detail 15 men each, Section E will detail 20 men, and Sections C and D will detail 10 men each for this duty. The Superintendent, Reserve Force, will also send 5 men to Section C and 5 men to D, to be placed at the disposal of the Census officers.

A general proclamation was also issued through the police to the effect that every one was to be in his house by 7 P.M. on the night of February 26th, 1891, and to keep a light burning there.

19. The Chairman and I drove along the chief streets between 9 and 11 P.M., stopping on the way to see how the work was being done, or to enquire if the enumerator had yet visited the inhabitants. But few wayfarers were to be seen, and in most houses there were lights burning. As there are so many high houses in Calcutta in which different families live on the different flats, one cannot see much of the actual enumeration by a necessarily hasty visit of this sort. But from what could be seen and the enquiries which we made, it seemed that the work was everywhere in progress. It was reported that the work generally was completed by 2 A.M., but in some cases it continued till 4 or even 5 A.M. Some complaints were made by Europeans and Eurasians that they were awakened to deliver schedules or give information, but these complaints were probably due for the most part to the sleepfulness of their darwans.

Collection of household schedules.

20. The household schedules should have been collected on the following day in the morning, but in many cases there was delay in this matter. As the enumerators had many of them been up till a very late hour on the previous night, this delay was at least excusable, and it obviously does not affect the correctness of the census. For a few days I continued to receive information from private

sources and through the press of cases in which the census had been omitted. There were also complaints that household schedules had not been given for certain families. The last class of complaints were due to jealousy, some persons thinking themselves slighted by not receiving these schedules. I enquired (for the most part personally) into complaints of omission of census, and where they were found to be true, prepared or caused to be prepared schedules for the persons who were omitted. But I may say that the general rarity of these complaints and the facts elicited in the course of my enquiries in the neighbourhood of the omissions tended to a belief in the general correctness of the census.

Census of the Fort.

21. The census of the Fort was arranged for by the Station Staff Officer, Captain P. K. Mockler, who was kind enough to relieve me of all responsibility in the matter. The actual enumeration was done (except for officers who received household schedules) by regimental writers. The enumeration of the native troops at Alipore lines was in a similar way carried out by the regimental agency under the Quartermaster, Captain Davidson. The regularity of military life renders census taking among soldiers a comparatively easy matter.

Census of the port.

22. All previous censuses of the port in recent years have been under the immediate superintendence of Mr. G. A. Robertson of the River Police. This officer gave me the benefit of his experience, but was unable to take any very active part in supervising the actual work. The blocks into which the river was divided were suggested by him, and are noted for future guidance. One boat and two enumerators had afterwards to be added to the list given in the following instructions. They worked between Baboo Ghât and Prinsep's Ghât:—

Census of the Port.

1. The census of the port will be taken on February 26th and the following days up to March 15th. The census will extend to the present limits of the port, that is to say, to the part of the Hooghly bounded on the north by a line drawn from the boundary pillar at the Cossipore Gun Foundry Ghât to a point on the opposite side at Ghoosery, and on the south by a line drawn from a masonry pillar placed at the mouth of the Budge-Budge khal to a pillar on the Howrah side of the river Hooghly bearing north-west of the first-named pillar.

2. For the purposes of the census three supervisors have been appointed, and the river between the northern boundary as above stated on the north and a line drawn from Matiabruz Ghât to the end of the Botanical Gardens has been divided into three circles and 44 enumerators' blocks as follows:—

CALCUTTA SIDE.				HOWRAH SIDE.		
From	To	Enumerators ashore.	Enumerators in boats.	From	To	
FIRST CIRCLE.						
Cossipore Gun Foundry	Chitpore Canal ...	1	2 enumerators in 1 boat.	Boundary pillar	Sulkea Ghât ...	2 enumerators in 1 boat.
Chitpore Canal ...	Buttotollah Ghât ...	1				
Buttotollah Ghât ...	Rajah's Ghât ...	1				
Rajah's Ghât ...	Ruth Ghât ...	1				
Ruth Ghât ...	Ahireetollah Ghât ...	1				
Ahireetollah Ghât ...	Nimtollah Ghât ...	1	Do.	Sulkea Ghât ...	Nimuckgola Gh.	Do.
Nimtollah Ghât ...	Prossonno Coomar Gh.	1				
Prossonno Coomar Ghât	Juggernath Ghât ...	1				
		8	4 & 2 B			4E & 2B.

CALCUTTA SIDE.				HOWRAH SIDE.		
From	To	Enumerators ashore.	Enumerators in boats.	From	To	
SECOND CIRCLE.						
Juggernath Ghât ...	Meerbohur Ghât ...	1	2 enumerators in 1 boat.	Nimuckgola Ghât	Coal depôt ...	2 enumerators in 1 boat.
Meerbohur Ghât ...	Hooghly Bridge, N.	1				
Hooghly Bridge, South	Armenian Ghât ...	1				
Armenian Ghât ...	No. 4 Jetty ...	..	Do.	Coal depôt ...	Seebpore ...	Do.
No. 4 Jetty ...	No. 8 Jetty ...	..				
No. 8 Jetty ...	Colvin Ghât ...	1	Do.			
Colvin Ghât ...	North Baboo Ghât...	1				
		5	6 & 3 B			4 E & 2 B.
THIRD CIRCLE.						
Baboo Ghât ...	No. 4 Esplanade ...	2	2 enumerators in 1 boat.	Seebpore ...	East of the Botanical Gardens.	2 enumerators in 1 boat.
No. 4 Esplanade ...	Prinsep's Ghât ...	2				
Prinsep's Ghât ...	Tolly's Nullah ...	2	Do.			
Tolly's Nullah ...	P. & O. Co. ...	...				
P. & O. Co. ...	Matiabruz ...	...	1 enumerator in 1 boat.			
		6	5 & 3 B			2 E & 1 B.

For the lower part of the port no preliminary enumeration seems to be necessary.

3. Thirteen boats will be required for the use of these enumerators, and on the night of census, four steam-launches will be required and 12 extra boats.

4. Vessels and boats in port may be divided into two classes—

(1) Vessels which will be censused by the master or other person in charge;
(2) Vessels which will be censused by the paid enumerators.

5. In vessels which will be enumerated by the master or other person in charge, the schedules will be distributed beginning from February 19th. They will be distributed by the port authorities, who should see that a sufficient number are supplied to each vessel. A list of these schedules, containing opposite to each the receipt of the person to whom it is delivered, will be kept by each person entrusted with the duty of delivering the schedules.

6. On the morning of February 27th, these schedules will be collected by the same persons who had made them over, who should see that all schedules are duly accounted for.

7. Masters of sea-going vessels, leaving the port on the 25th or 26th, should fill up the schedules on the night of the 26th, and make them over to the pilot if he is still on board. The pilot will then give the master or person in charge an enumeration pass in the prescribed form. If the vessel has left the Sandheads before the night of the 26th, the schedules should be made over at the first British port touched, with instructions that they are to be forwarded to the Census Officer, Calcutta.

8. The pilots should ask all vessels (including native sea-going vessels) arriving at the Sandheads between February 26th and March 15th if they have been censused. If they have already received schedules, he should collect them. If they have not received them, he should give them a sufficient number of schedules, and let them be filled in on the way up the river.

9. As to the vessels and boats which will be censused by the paid enumerators, the operations may be divided into three stages—

(1) Preliminary enumeration;
(2) Actual enumeration;
(3) Supplementary enumeration.

10. (1) As to *preliminary enumeration*, each enumerator will be provided with 300 schedules bound in books twelve of 24 and one of 12 schedules. He will also be provided with 300 white and 300 green tickets. On these tickets will be printed the words "Block No. Boat No. ." On February 19th each enumerator will commence at the north end of his block and proceed to enumerate all the persons in all the boats which he finds there, entering the particulars of each person in the books of schedules. As he completes the work of each boat he will paste on a white ticket in a part of the boat where it is not likely to be washed off, and deliver a green ticket to the person in charge of the boat.

On the morning of February 26th the books already filled up should be returned to the supervisors, who will previously have tested them from time to time, so as to ensure their correct preparation.

11. (2) *Actual enumeration.*—The enumerators will take the books remaining to them and other fresh ones, if necessary, a supply of red tickets with 'checked' printed on them, and a brass file apiece. They will commence at 7 P.M. on the night of February 26th, and visit all the boats in their respective blocks. A steam-launch will be despatched from Matiabruz to Budge-Budge and back, to enumerate all boats found in that part of the river.

12. In the case of boats which have been already censused, the enumerators will take the green ticket from the person in charge and place it on the file, and will enquire if there has been any change in the persons on board since the former enumeration. If there has been a change they will note this on the back of the green ticket, and if there is any new person on board they will write his name and other particulars in one of the forms with them, giving the number of block and boat to identify the boat. All entries on the night of February 26th will be made in red ink. When the census of a boat has been checked, a red ticket will be pasted over the white one.

13. If a boat is found not to have been previously censused, the enumerator will take down all the particulars of those on board and paste a red ticket on it. To such boats a fresh number in red ink will be given in the block where they are found.

14. (3) *Supplementary enumeration.*—During February the 27th and 28th and March 1st the enumerators will remain at their blocks, and will census all boats which may be found in the port after the night of the 26th, and which have not been enumerated elsewhere. Three boats will be placed across the river at the northern and southern limits of the port, and three more at the southern end of the Botanical Gardens. These boats will stop all boats coming up and down the river, and see if they have been enumerated before or not. Each boat that has been enumerated will be known by its having a red ticket. Such boats will be allowed to pass, but others must be duly censused. This supplementary census will cease at sundown on March 1st.

15. The supervisors will bring their enumerators and their supplementary schedules and green tickets to the Census Office on March 2nd. The original schedules will then be compared with the results of the second census as obtained from the green tickets. The entries for the boats which have been found in port will be allowed to stand or be corrected, while the entries of those whose green tickets have not been found will be erased.

The census schedules supplied for the use of ships were ordinary household schedules and required to be supplemented by the following circular:—

To all Masters of Sea-going Vessels.

1. The bearer of this is an officer entrusted with the duty of obtaining from you certain necessary particulars as to the officers, crew and passengers of the vessel under your command. He will make over to you a sufficient number of forms in which you will please record the required particulars according to the instructions endorsed on them.

2. You are requested to observe, further, that you should enter or cause to be entered first your own name, then the names of your crew, then after drawing a cross line in column 1 of the form, the names of your passengers.

3. You should not, if possible, allow any of your crew to go on shore between the hours of 8 P.M. on the night of the 26th and 6 A.M. on the morning of the 27th. If any one is obliged to go on shore, you should furnish him with a certificate saying "censused on board ," giving the name of your ship and signing it. Any one going on shore should be directed to show this certificate to any one wishing to enumerate him there.

4. If you are leaving the port before the morning of the 27th for another port in British India or Burmah, you should fill up the forms on the night of the 26th, and deliver them to the Customs or other authority who may ask for them at the first port touched or to the pilot on board, if you are still in the river on the morning of the 27th.

5. If you are in the port on the morning of the 27th, you should deliver up the schedules duly filled up to the officer who calls for them.

6. When you give up the schedules, you will receive an enumeration pass which you should keep carefully on board your vessel till 25th March and produce when required.

In future censuses some such instructions should be printed on special schedules for the sea-going population.

Cost of the census.

23. The following statement gives the cost of the census up to final enumeration and the collection of the schedules:—

	Rs.	A.	P.
Pay and conveyance allowance of special officer ...	4,600	0	0
Establishment	5,027	13	4
Surveying	3,522	12	5
Pay of supervisors	1,000	0	0
Pay of enumerators	10,369	0	0
Printing	740	7	0
Contingencies	1,187	3	3
Total ...	26,447	3	0

The cost of the census of the port was as follows:—

	Rs.	A.	P.
Printing	44	8	0
Boat hire	413	0	0
Supervisors	150	0	0
Enumerators	459	0	0
Contingencies	26	2	0
Total ...	1,092	10	0

Comparison of cost with that of the previous census.

24. The cost of taking the census of 1881 in the town and suburbs is stated to have been Rs. 19,744. It does not clearly appear whether this sum includes the census of the port or not. Part of the present increase in expenditure is due to the fact that at the last census only the special allowance of the census officer was debited to the cost of census, while on this occasion his whole pay has been so debited. The preliminary work of this census has been estimated to have continued up to March 15th, while in 1881 it was considered to have closed on the night of the census. For these reasons there is an increase of Rs. 3,100 in the item "Pay of the census officer." At the last census the pay of the Superintendent was shown under a lump sum with that of the supervisors and enumerators. This time I have shown the pay of the Superintendent and two Assistant Superintendents under the head of Establishment. The increased cost under the head of Establishment and the expenses shown under surveying were chiefly due to the necessity for the general survey of the added area. In 1881 no such survey was made. It may also be stated that a good deal of the work in connection with the numbering of houses at the previous census was done by the municipal staff without any extra charge. Considering the additional work done and the way in which the census officer's pay has been debited, the present census may be said to have been a little cheaper than the previous one.

Suggestions for the future.

25. I think it advisable to add a few suggestions as regards future censuses. In the present census I have necessarily followed the lines of the former censuses of 1876 and 1881, partly because the shortcomings of the system hitherto employed had not come within my experience, and partly because, even if they had, there was no time to introduce a new one.

Survey of the added area.

26. There are certain preliminary matters which must necessarily receive attention in connection with the work now done. In the first place, the whole of the added area should be surveyed on a large scale. In the next place, all streets should be named and all houses numbered. I would suggest in this connection a general renumbering of houses. The system (if indeed it can be called a system) on which the houses were numbered in 1881 is thus described by Mr. Beverley in his report:—"It may be premised that all the land and all pucka premises in the town are distinguished by the consecutive series of numbers that run through them. Thus No. 14 in the street may be a pucka house standing in its own compound, or one of a row of pucka shops or warehouses, while No. 15 represents a piece of land without any pucka building standing upon it. The premises or land may in time be subdivided, and the different portions be separately assessed, in which

Naming and numbering of streets.

case each portion must bear a separate assessment number; but, instead of disturbing the arrangement, and altering all the numbers in the street, the new number is introduced as a broken or fractional number. Thus, suppose the plot of land No. 15 as above to be subdivided into four portions separately assessed, these portions would be numbered respectively 15, 15-1, 15-2 and 15-3. The occurrence of broken numbers may thus considerably increase the total of pucka numbers in the street, and unless the broken numbers are marked on the ground (which is not always the case), it is only by a reference to the assessment books that their existence can be ascertained.

"Again, the plot of land No. 15 may be covered with kutcha huts, and besides the assessment on the land, each of those huts is liable to assessment. The huts then are ordinarily distinguished in the assessment books by letters following the pucka number as 15-2G, 15-2H; and when letters of the alphabet are exhausted, a number is affixed to the letter as 15-2 Z23. But huts of course are constantly being pulled down and removed, and new huts have new numbers given them, so that neither the series of letters nor that of the following numbers can be relied on as complete. The hut 15-2A may be still in existence, but 15-2B and 15-2C may have disappeared; 15-2 D2 may be found, but 15-2 D1 may have been removed, and so on. Lastly, it must be explained that these letters and numbers have been assigned without reference to any systematic arrangement, and that the numbers themselves were not affixed to the huts."

27. At that time instructions were given to revise the orders of the numbers and to mark them on the ground plans and on the houses. It also appears that the clumsy method of numbering huts by letters was abandoned, and that instead the number was thus given, 15-H 1, 2, and so on—H representing 'hut.' But it must be said that either the instructions to revise the order of the numbers were then imperfectly carried out, or they have been changed since, as they do not now always follow in regular order. Also numbers were either not attached to all houses, or they have since been removed. Very many huts in bastis have no numbers attached to them. And it must be remembered that numbers are given not to houses but to holdings, and that a holding seems to mean whatever land is held by one man, or even a group of men in the same ward, so that to find out all the huts under one number is still a matter of much difficulty. Furthermore, especially in the added area, many houses have no ascertainable number at all. Now it is no doubt convenient for collection purposes to have holdings numbered as they are at present, because then the Collector knows that he has to collect so much from each number. But for all other purposes it seems to me that the numbering should follow the local order of the houses. A register of rate-payers can show the numbers of the houses for which each rate-payer is assessed. I therefore propose that new numbers be affixed on some system. Perhaps the best would be to commence at the north-east corner of each street, and assign odd numbers to the right-hand and even numbers to the left-hand houses in each street.

Maintenance of conservancy and other registers.

28. When the registers of conservancy, water-pipes, and so on, are made over to the departments concerned, some arrangement should be made for keeping them up to date in future. I understand that in some wards there are already registers giving information of the sort contained in these registers, but they are not always correct nor properly kept up. The preparation of these registers is not part of regular census work, and the importance of having such information up to date is apparent.

Supervision of the census.

29. As to the way in which the actual work of the census should be done in future, I must first say that the plan of appointing municipal servants as supervisors, which I introduced, has not been altogether satisfactory. It is true that my principal idea, that the employment of persons known already as municipal servants and familiar to the people would prevent idle rumours and opposition to the work, has proved to be correct. It is also true that good work was done by some supervisors. But many of them were ignorant of Bengali, and as they were serving more than one master, it was often difficult for me to control them and to get them to do exactly what I wished.

Enumeration in the past.

30. The chief difficulty, however, in taking the census here is the selection and management of the enumerators. The work of going round from house to house is thought derogatory, and the pay is not high enough to attract good men. Hence almost every candidate was given a trial at least, and it was practically necessary to allow time for each bit of work to be done twice over, so that failure in the first instance might be remedied. Now it is desirable in census work that the interval between preliminary and final enumeration should be as short as is compatible with the due completion of the registers, for the longer this interval is, the greater is the margin of error. It is also a truism that the shorter time a temporary establishment is employed, the cheaper it is. It is required, therefore, to appoint a better class of men as enumerators yet so as not to materially increase the cost of the census. To this end the following plan is suggested. It is estimated that in Calcutta one enumerator can take down the particulars of 1,000 persons in one day. I would therefore give each enumerator an area containing about 10,000 persons, and to provide for unforeseen delay allow him 14 days for the work of preliminary enumeration.

and in the future.

31. As, prior to the preliminary enumeration, these men would have to prepare plans of the area in which they are to work, and a register of families in order to form a correct estimate of the number of schedules which would be required, they would have to be employed altogether for a month or six weeks. For this work I would give them Rs. 50 each and an assistant on Rs. 10. With the class of men who could be obtained for this pay, it ought not to be necessary to have any special establishment for supervision, but Municipal Inspectors would be instructed to assist and to report as to the way in which work was being done. On the night of the census additional enumerators would have to be appointed, but help would be forthcoming from the Municipal offices, and if early orders are passed, the resident Government clerks could assist. At the late census a holiday was given to such clerks in order that they might help us, but this permission was communicated to me too late to be of any use. Anyhow, it is easy to get men in Calcutta to do the necessary checking for the night at a rupee for sixty or seventy houses, and the preliminary enumerators who would be responsible for the results could easily supervise the checking in their allotted area.

A proposal to do away with household schedules.

32. In this connection it is necessary to add that the present system of private or household schedules is very unsatisfactory. Not only are half the complaints after the census due to vanity hurt by exclusion from the privilege of these schedules, but there is a danger that this vanity may prompt those possessed by it to pay the enumerators for the said privilege. It must also be stated that those who do obtain the schedules prove themselves in many cases unworthy of the distinction.

33. There will always be some people who make bad jokes in their census papers, describing themselves, for instance, as 'Heathen Chinese' or 'very much married,' or 'born in Timbuctoo,' and there are others who leave the age column blank. Perhaps this sort of misplaced wit is intended to lighten the routine of the abstracting census clerks, and I hope they are grateful for it. But there are others who leave all the columns blank, and others who say in general terms that there are so many children or so many servants. Added to these sorts of errors which require another visit to the houses for their rectification, the schedules being loose sheets are liable to get lost and mislaid, and when pinned on, frequently tear off. The only remedy that I can see for these evils is to do away with private schedules altogether. The enumerator should go round to the houses of that class of persons who have hitherto received them, and take down the particulars of those likely to be at home on the night of the census. If anyone likes to write these particulars himself, there is nothing to prevent him, but the enumerator will see that the columns are correctly filled up. Then if anyone wishes, a ticket may be given, and the master of the house may note on it any changes which have occurred since the preliminary census, and leave it on the night of the census with the darwan to give to the enumerator, who will correct his register accordingly.

34. To the other advantages of this plan may be added the fact that the enumerators could with the help of their assistants abstract and tabulate the returns themselves. It is very much easier for him who made the entries to abstract them than for another.

Accuracy of the census.

35. This is not properly the place to discuss the accuracy of the census, which can only be properly judged by results. I have naturally been at a disadvantage in following Mr. Beverley, who conducted the two preceding censuses in 1876 and in 1881, and who, as Chairman of the Municipality, had already acquired local knowledge which I have had to acquire for myself. The labyrinthine nature of most of the bastis and of a considerable part even of the masonry-built streets and lanes and the large barracks many stories high, and containing in each room four, five or even more inhabitants, place great difficulties in the way of a completely accurate enumeration. At the same time, I have already said that the omissions actually brought to light have been very few, and though many persons have been ready to say that the census was incomplete, very few have been able to put forward cases in which it actually failed, and such cases when put forward have proved more often than not to have been based on incorrect information.

PART II.

THE RESULTS OF THE CENSUS.

36. It has not hitherto been the practice in Calcutta census reports to deal at all with the mode in which the published tables are obtained from the abstraction books.

Preparation of the statistics.

But as I have necessarily given a great deal of attention to the subject, and as I think that the present system is much in need of improvement, I propose shortly to describe how these tables are prepared, and to suggest a new method of preparing them.

37. After the census schedules had been received in the office they were first examined to see if any houses had been omitted, and to check any incorrect entries. To this end I appointed a staff of enumerators who had proved themselves efficient to read through the books. Any errors discovered by them were corrected by myself at first, and later by some of the more capable among those who had been reading the books. In some cases it became necessary to send out the books again with enumerators to supply omissions. But this was not very satisfactory, as in many cases the entries referred to people who had already left Calcutta. One master of a vessel, for instance, returned 37 natives, whose particulars he was unable to give as none of the Europeans on board were sufficiently acquainted with their language to interrogate them, and the ship had sailed before I received the schedules.

Correction of the schedules.

38. When the schedules had been corrected and brought as far as possible into conformity with the rules, they became ready for abstraction. The entries are abstracted into eleven sheets. The first is for civil condition by religion and age; the second is for education by religion and age; the third is for occupations; the fourth for castes and sub-castes; the fifth for mother-tongue; the sixth for district of birth; the seventh for infirmities; the eighth and ninth for religions and races of Christians; the tenth for education by caste; and the eleventh for civil condition by age and caste In all the tables the sex is distinguished. All the sheets are ruled so as to give space for the entry of the necessary particulars required in the tables. The abstractors then enter the particulars of the individuals by strokes in this manner //// = 5. In Calcutta the unit of abstraction was a block. This means that all the sheets for one block were kept together after abstraction, and one total for each block only is carried to the tabulation register. The theory which underlies the system is that the sheets are to be worked separately and independently, and that comparison of all of them will show by a general agreement the correctness of the results. But, as a matter of fact, in the earlier work at least there was no correspondence between the figures in the different sheets at all, and there was no means even of guessing which set of figures was correct. The abstractors either put strokes at random, or left out names, or left out whole books of schedules, or did the same book twice over. It then appeared necessary to prepare one set of figures on which absolute reliance could be placed. But although the best men were selected for this work, the results even so obtained were not always correct. A comparison with the results of the previous census, however, enabled me to detect at once the probability of error, and I then myself examined the figures of doubtful blocks. But even when the total figures corresponded, there was often found to be discrepancy under the minor heads; and if a single stroke had been misplaced in age or sex or caste, it was sometimes necessary to look through the whole sheet before the mistake could be rectified. In cases, therefore, where I was not satisfied about the figures, I caused Sheets I, II and XI to be prepared together—one man reading and three men writing—and they were instructed at the end of each fifty persons to compare their several results and see that they corresponded. It might be thought that this system would lead to fudging; but in the first place those employed were, as a rule, too stupid to fudge, and in the next I was able, by constant personal supervision, to see that they did not. The great danger of the present system of abstraction is that the men get into careless habits by going on too quickly and having nothing to recall them to attention,

Abstraction.

while when they stop at every fiftieth name this tendency is counteracted. It is, of course, very true that the method is a slow one; but no work of this kind could properly be said to be slow "if it were done when 'tis done."

A new method of abstraction suggested.

39. Nevertheless, so endless are the possibilities of error in the present system, and so difficult is it to put one's finger on the exact point where error has occurred, that I cannot believe the system to be the best attainable. It seems to me essential that there should be some way of identifying the people who have been censused in the different sheets; so that when one compares, for instance, age periods in two different sheets, one could ascertain the person in whose case a difference has occurred, and rectify it by a reference to the original schedule. For this purpose I had thought of noting the serial numbers of persons in the abstraction sheets, but I found that they took up so much room and were so confusing that I could not expect the abstractors to carry out the method properly. But if the serial numbers were written on counters, and large sheets of paper were prepared with spaces ruled according to the information required, and each abstractor was given the counters of a block and told to distribute them over these spaces, I believe that the work would be done much more correctly than it is at present. The form of the work would be more interesting, and if there were any differences they could be corrected at once by a comparison of the counters. Moreover, with this system, the work is ready for tabulation at once, the abstractor having merely to count the counters and enter them in the register. I believe that if the system I have already suggested for carrying out the enumeration were adopted, and the abstractors were instructed to tabulate their returns on this method, the work would be done much more efficiently, and at a far lower cost.

Census history of Calcutta.

40. This is the first census which has been taken of Calcutta since its area and population were so largely increased by Bengal Council Act II of 1888. Before another census is taken, the term "added area," which in the present report has such an important signification, will be little more than a memory, along, it may be hoped, with the absence of drainage and water connection which it might now be said to imply. It is desirable, therefore, to sketch briefly for the last time from a census point of view the growth of the city from the little settlement at Sutanuti to its present position as the capital of British India. Up to the year 1686 the present site of Calcutta was occupied by small hamlets, built, as is usual in this part of Bengal, on the rising ground which forms the river bank. In that year the English under Job Charnock, being driven down the river by the Dutch, settled at Sutanuti. In 1696 the settlers received permission to defend themselves, and the first Fort William was built. The early progress of the town was not very rapid, as in the year 1710 an observer states that the population was from 10,000 to 12,000, while its area seems to have extended from Baranagar to the Salt Lakes. In the year 1742 the Indian inhabitants of the town seem to have so far appreciated the benefits of British rule that they commenced at their own expense to dig the Mahratta Ditch in order to repel the invaders of that name. The ditch was never finished, but continued for a long time to be in its unfinished state the boundary of Calcutta on the north and east. In the year 1752 Mr. Holwell, who himself considerably enlarged Calcutta, made an estimate of the population there. This estimate gives a total of 409,056. It was based on observation of the number of houses and families in certain areas, and an estimate that each family contained 8 persons. No doubt this last estimate is much too high for Calcutta. The figures given by Mr. Holwell cannot, however, be very well compared with subsequent figures, because in the first place the southern part of the town had not been built, and in the second the out-towns of Baniapukar, Pagladanga, Tengra, and Dollond (Dullanda) seem to have been included in his estimate, though they were not included in the town until the recent amalgamation. At the same time, if Mr. Holwell's estimate was anything like correct, it would somewhat extenuate the atrocity of the Black Hole tragedy to think that it was but a slight exaggeration of the condition of the natives in their daily lives. The great historical events of the years 1756 and 1757 resulted in an improved position for the town, as the land revenue was forgiven to the Company in the year 1758, and Calcutta became a free town.

Mr. Beverley says that modern Calcutta dates from 1757, and indeed from this time the Company became a Company of conquerors rather than of merchants. The interval between 1757 and 1794 was one of steady progress. The travellers who visited the country remark not only on the neatness and elegance of the European part of the town, but also on the extreme want of sanitation and cleanliness in the native part. In spite of not unfrequent epidemics the population seems to have continued to increase. In 1782 it was estimated at 500,000. In 1789-90 a traveller put the population of the Black Town alone at 600,000. It will be seen that all these estimates are very vague, nor is it clear to what area they refer. If they include the Suburbs and Howrah they need not necessarily have been much over the mark.

Establishment of municipal government.

41. The year 1794 was an important one in the history of Calcutta, as in that year there was a commencement of municipal government by certain persons who were called Justices of the Peace. At the same time the boundaries of the town were for the first time fixed. These boundaries, which are published in an appendix, continued to mark the Municipality of Calcutta up to the year 1888.

Census of 1821.

42. It seems that the first regular census of Calcutta was taken in 1821 by certain assessors appointed to revise house-rate assessments. This census gave a total population of 179,917. Males and females were apparently not distinguished. In the same year the Justices estimated the population at 230,552. But this was only an estimate based, like Mr. Holwell's, on the probable number of persons inhabiting each house. In 1831 the Superintendent of Police took a census and obtained a total of 187,081. It has been suggested that the censuses of 1822 and 1831 did not include females. But the next census which was taken in 1837 gave a total population of 229,714, of whom 144,911 were males and 84,803 females; so that the former censuses can hardly have been of males only. But in both these censuses the enumeration was very likely imperfect.

And of 1831.

Census of 1850.

43. In 1850 another estimate was made by Mr. Simms, who surveyed the town in that year, with a result of 361,369, and in the same year the Chief Magistrate also took a census which gave a total of 255,036 males and 160,027 females. It will be observed that this population has remained almost unaltered up to the present time. But it is not certain whether the figures of the 1850 census include those of the Port and the Fort or not.

Censuses of 1866 and 1872.

44. It appears that until the year 1866 no further census was taken. In that year the numbers given were males 231,345 and females 146,576. This census is generally thought to have under-estimated the population. In it were included the populations of the Fort (3,878) and Port (15,384). In the census which was taken in connection with the general census of 1872 the population was given as 447,601, of whom 299,857 were males and 147,644 females. These figures include the Fort (2,483) and the Port (16,623). Much doubt has been thrown on the accuracy of this census, and the results certainly seem not to have been compiled very carefully, while the destruction of all records very soon after the census was calculated to raise suspicion. It is known that the figures, which were the largest ever obtained, were to some extent vitiated by the inclusion of the figures of a previous test census. It is also likely that the carelessness of abstractors was not sufficiently guarded against.

Census of 1876.

45. In consequence of the general belief in the inaccuracy of the census of 1872, another census was taken in 1876 under Mr. Beverley's direction. The figures obtained on that occasion were—

	Males.	Females.	Total
Town	262,455	146,581	409,036
Fort	2,408	395	2,803
Port	17,643	53	17,696
Total ...	282,506	147,029	429,535

Of 1881.

46. The last census prior to the present one was taken in 1881, and the figures then were—

	Males.	Females.	Total.
Town	257,778	143,893	401,671
Fort	3,002	346	3,348
Port	28,037	163	28,200
Total ...	288,817	144,402	433,219

Census of the Suburbs in 1872.

47 As to the added area, I do not find that there is any record of a census before that of 1872. In that year the population of the Suburbs is stated to have been 257,149, of whom 151,011 were males and 106,138 were females. The boundaries of the Suburban Municipality at that time are given in an appendix. They were modified by a notification, dated 10th September 1877, and it was of the population within the revised boundaries that the census of 1881 was taken. This census gave a population of 147,205 males and 104,234 females. The Suburban Municipality was divided into six wards, which comprised respectively the following thanas :—

And in 1881.

The contents of the Suburban Municipality.

I.—Cossipur, Chitpur, and Ultadanga.
II.—Maniktala and Beliyaghatta.
III.—Entally and Baniyapukar.
IV.—Ballyganj and Tollyganj.
V.—Bhawanipur and Alipur.
VI.—Watganj, Ekbalpur, and Garden Reach.

The "added area."

48. The added area is formed of parts of Chitpur, Ultadanga, Maniktala Beliyaghatta, and Entally thanas, and of the whole of all the other thanas except those known as Garden Reach and Tollyganj. A small portion in the south-eastern corner was added from the South Suburban Municipality. The added portion can easily be distinguished in the map. The old eastern and southern boundary was generally the Circular Road as far as Zeerut Bridge, and after that Tolly's Nulla as far as Hastings Bridge. In Ward III, however, the boundary went beyond the Circular Road in order to follow the Mahratta Ditch which there bent outwards in order to include Halsibaghan, the garden of the celebrated Omichand. This part extends over Blocks 2, 3, 5, 17, and 21 of Ward III. Unfortunately there is no accurate information as to the total area thus added to the former area of the town, and I have not been able to find any record of the blocks into which the Suburbs were divided at the last census, without which the population of the added area cannot be distinguished from that of the rest of the Suburbs, except in Wards XX, XXII, XXIII and XXIV, which correspond to the thanas known as Baniyapukar, Bhawanipur, Alipur, and Ekbalpur, respectively. Ward XIX corresponds very nearly to thana Entally. The figures for these thanas are given in Mr. Beverley's report. At the time of the last census their population appears to have been 86,202. Their population as now ascertained is 95,755.

49. At the time of the amalgamation, estimates were made of the population of those wards a part of whose area only was added, which were as follows :—

Added area in Ward I	3,024
" " in Wards III, IV and IX ...	11,500
" " in Ward XXI	10,423
" " in Ward XXV	27,920

The present population in the added area of Ward I is 6,934, in that of Ward III 8,057, in that of Ward IV 9,078, and in that of Ward IX 10,363. The other above-mentioned wards will be dealt with further on. It seems that the estimates made at the time of the amalgamation were considerably below the mark.

Area of the town.

50. The area of the old town at the time of the last census was said to be 5,037 acres, of which 1,283 were occupied by the Esplanade, Fort William, and Tolly's Nulla. The added area was estimated at the time of amalgamation to be 8,455

acres, but there has been no separate survey of this area. The Surveyor-General has, however, been kind enough to have the area of all the wards calculated by planimeter for me, and the present area of the town appears to be 18·53 square miles, excluding the Fort and maidan. This area is divided into twenty-five wards, the limits of which are printed in an appendix. They are generally conterminous with police sections, but this is not the case with the added area in Wards I, III, IV and IX. The jurisdiction of the High Court and of the Calcutta Police Court has not been extended to the added area.

51. The population of the town on the night of 26th February 1891 has been found to be—

	Males.	Females.	Total.
In the old town ...	287,032	149,361	436,393
In the added area ...	128,007	85,001	213,008
In the Fort ...	3,119	349	3,468
In the Port ...	26,516	73	26,589
In the canals ...	2,072	30	2,102
GRAND TOTAL ...	446,746	234,814	681,560

Density of population.

52. In Table II will be found the total population of each ward and its relative density, while in Table III there is a comparison between the population now and that of the census of 1881. It will be seen that the density of the population is still greatest in Ward VIII (226 to the acre), while Ward V now occupies second place with 161 to the acre, and other wards which are thickly populated are VI (159), X (154), XIII and XIV (147), XI (125), II (122), IV (108), and IX (107); while in Wards XXI and XXIII the population is only 11 to the acre.

Variation in population of Wards.

53. The population has been found to have especially increased in Ward VI. It has also increased considerably in Wards I and IV; and all the wards except XVII either vary very little or show an increase on the figures of 1881. In general the figures may be said to confirm the conclusion arrived at from previous censuses that the population of Calcutta varies to a very small degree. At the same time it must be remembered that a large number of people came to Calcutta to bathe in the Ganges shortly before the census, and though most of these had left before the night of the 26th, some probably remained. There was also a meeting held on the day of the 26th to protest against what is known as the Age of Consent Bill, and this will account for some of the increase in the numbers. Had it not been for these extraneous reasons, I do not believe that there would have been any increase in the total population. There has, however, no doubt been a real increase in the population of Wards I, IV and VI. The increase in the former wards is a natural result of expansion, as it will be observed that the density of the population is still less than in the neighbouring Wards, II and V. The large increase in Ward VI is more difficult to explain. But partly a considerable share of the population which was removed from Wards VIII and IX to make way for the Central Road must have migrated there, and partly a larger proportion of the visitors may have found shelter in the lodging houses in Baranusi Ghose's and Machua Bazar Streets; for it was in these streets and their neighbourhood that the increase chiefly occurred. The decrease in Ward XVII appears to be due to the removal of large bastis between Camac Street and Elysium Row. The proportional difference is considerable, but the numbers are insignificant.

54. With regard to the "added area," the estimate made at the time of amalgamation as to the added population in Wards I, III, IV and IX is so manifestly inaccurate that no useful result can be attained by comparing the figures. In Ward XIX the population is now 33,147. The population of thana Entally in 1881 is given as 26,929, and the increase is even greater than the figures show, inasmuch as a small portion of what was included in that thana has been excluded from the Municipality. In Ward XX the population has increased from 18,895 to 23,020, and in Ward XXII from 38,002 to 42,591. In Ward XXIII the increase is smaller, the figure being 14,288 as against 13,438. On the other hand, the population in Ward XXIV has decreased from 15,869 to 15,350. The figures in Wards XXI and

XXV cannot be accurately compared with any figures for 1881. In that year thanas Tollyganj and Ballyganj returned a population of 24,423, but part of the area of these thanas has been excluded from the Municipality and part of the south suburban area has been added to Ward XXI, and the former population of each part cannot be distinguished. The population of the part of these thanas which was added was estimated at 10,423, but no estimate was made of the part which was taken from the South Suburban Municipality. It was estimated that the population of the added area in Wards XXIV and XXV had a population of 43,789, and as the population of Ward XIV which corresponds to Ekbalpur thana of the last census was 15,869, that would leave 27,920 for the population of Ward XXV. This estimate seems to be more correct than those for other wards.

55. The increase in Wards XIX, XX, XXI, and XXII is no doubt a true one. The reason for the increase is the same as has been given for the increase in Wards I and IV, namely, that the expansion of the population naturally follows the direction in which there is most space for it. The population in the other three wards would no doubt show a similar increase had it not been for the building of the Kidderpur docks which caused the clearance of many crowded bastis.

Variations in Fort and Port.

56. The population of the Fort has remained nearly stationary.

The population of the Port has decreased from 28,200 to 26,588. The figures at the last census showed a very large increase on those of the census of 1876. The area of the Port has been considerably increased by the addition of that part of the river between Paikpara Point and Budge-Budge. But the population in the boats of this area only amounted to 374 at this census. From the way in which the returns were prepared, I am unable to give separately the figures for sea-going ships and boats, but the falling off in the number of Europeans points to an imperfect enumeration of the ships in the Port. It is a fact that several ships failed to return their schedules. The case of some of these was reported to me by the Port Commissioners, but when I sent to enquire about them several had already left the Port, and there were no doubt others which went away and never returned the schedules. It is of course impossible to estimate what the population on board these ships was, but it would probably account for the total decrease in the population of the Port. The census in the rest of the Port seems to have been sufficiently accurate. I may note that at the last census Mr. Robertson, who was in charge of the Port census, was able personally to see that ship schedules were collected. I myself saw that they had been distributed in some of the vessels, but had to depend on the Port authorities for their collection, and, as I have said, it was too late to remedy the failure when it came to my knowledge.

Canals.

57. The population in the suburban canals at the time of the last census was 3,007. The population of those parts included in the Municipality is now 2,102. But the canal area included in the suburbs at the last census was larger than that now included in the Municipality, and especially it included Dhappa toll-house where many boats do congregate.

58. Upon the whole, therefore, it would appear that the population of the more crowded portions of Calcutta is still more or less stationary, if I am right, that is, in attributing a great part of the increase to the abnormal number of visitors on account of the Age of Consent meeting and the Ardhadaya Jog. Nevertheless, there is distinctly a tendency to expansion in the less crowded wards and in the suburbs.

59. Calcutta is essentially a trading city, and that its trade is still growing may be judged from the fact that its total imports and exports, which in 1880-81 amounted to 66 crores, had risen in the year 1890-91 to 77 crores. Some account must be made for the depreciation in exchange which increases the rupee value of imports, even if it has not increased prices generally. But that there has been a considerable expansion there is no doubt. This circumstance, however, influences chiefly the day population. The increased cost of living in Calcutta, and the increased facilities given by railways and tramways, have caused and enabled a larger population to live in their native villages and come in daily to perform their duties in the city. The difference

between the street crowds of Barabazar by day and its emptiness by night is very striking, and it is only by taking a day census in Calcutta that it would be possible to really gauge its progress. Yet it is to be noted that the actual population of Calcutta is apparently decreasing if it were not supported by immigration, as the deaths there still considerably exceed the births.

HOUSE ACCOMMODATION.

House accommodation.

60. The summary of the results of the house registers which is printed as Table II shows that there were in Calcutta at the time of the census 26,070 pakka houses, of which 23,739 were inhabited, and 47,351 kacha houses, of which 43,789 were inhabited. I have already explained (paragraph 9 *supra*) that these figures were obtained from a census of houses. On previous occasions such figures have been tested by reference to municipal assessment registers, but I have endeavoured to show that these do not form a sound basis for purposes of enumeration. If the suggestion made elsewhere is adopted, and houses are numbered without reference to taxation, the number can, on the occasion of the next census, be readily compared with that now obtained.

61. The difficulty in comparing such figures will always be the uncertainty of the meaning of the word "house" which at some times has been taken to mean a municipal number which may include over 100 houses if by that term we understand compounds, while at other times it has been taken to mean a tenement, and may be a floor or part of a floor in a large house, or one of a row of shops such as honeycomb the road frontage of the houses in Barabazar. It may be noted that at the census of 1881 Mr. Beverley adopted practically the same definition as I have done, and that the results in those wards whose figures can be easily compared are extraordinarily similar. In Ward II, for instance, there are now 2,644 inhabited houses as against 2,677 in 1881, and in Ward V there are 2,731 as against 2,729. In many parts of the town there is no room for any new houses. Out of the total population of 649,401, 244,068 persons are housed in masonry houses, and the rest in tiled huts. In table XIX will be found information regarding conservancy and the number of cattle and horses in the town. But the enquiries as to the latter probably suggested taxation, and the results seem lower than might have been expected.

RELIGIONS.

Religions.

62. Of the total population of the town, 428,762 are Hindus; there are 189,226 Muhammadans, 26,406 Christians, 2,145 Buddhists, 493 Jains, 1,387 Jews, 166 Zoroastrians, 108 Sikhs, and 708 Brahmos. The total figures cannot usefully be compared with those of the census of 1881 owing to the changes of jurisdiction. But in those wards which have remained unchanged since that year, the general proportions of the castes have remained the same as before. The Hindus form in most wards the bulk of the population, and are more evenly distributed than the adherents to any other religion. Muhammadans, on the other hand, seem to live for the most part in Wards VIII, IX, X, XIII, and XIV, in which wards also the highest proportion of the Christian population is found. The Christians in these wards are mostly Eurasians and natives, the Europeans being found rather in the more southern wards—XV, XVI, and XVII. There is also a considerable Christian population in Ward XIX. The Brahmos, whose numbers appear to have increased, are more evenly distributed than most of the smaller religions, but occur chiefly in Wards VI, VIII, and IX. The number of Brahmos may also be larger than that shown, as many of them returned their religion as Hindu and named Brahmo as their sect. The great bulk of the Buddhists is to be found in Wards VII and X. There has been some difficulty about the Jains, because their castes in many cases bear the same names as Hindu castes, and great care was required to prevent the tabulators from confusing the two religions on this account. It may be that the attention paid to this matter may account for the increase in the number of Jains which appears at the present census. Jews and Zoroastrians are chiefly to be found in the commercial centres of Wards VII and VIII. Fewer Sikhs have been shown as such than in the previous census. They also in many cases returned

their religion as Hindu and only stated that they were Sikh by sect. Four male and two female "theists" have been grouped with Brahmos, and forms of modern unbelief have been treated, as in 1881, as Christian sects.

SEX AND AGE.

63. The returns for the old town in regard to sex may thus be compared with those for 1881 :—

Sexes' comparative statement.

	Males.	Females.	Total.
1881	257,778	143,893	401,671
1891	287,034	149,359	436,393

The female river-population is so small that it is unnecessary to discuss it, ınd. the figures for the suburbs cannot be usefully compared because, as has ›een already said, the population in 1881 of the area afterwards added to the own cannot be ascertained. It may be observed that the males still very argely exceed the females, but that the added area figures, which give 128,007 nales and 85,001 females, show a much more even distribution of the sexes. n many parts of the "added area" the conditions are much more rural than n the town.

64. The population of the town by age groups is here given :—

Ages.

	Males.	Females.	Total.
Under 1	5,258	4,486	9,744
1	4,063	3,391	7,454
2	5,261	5,106	10,367
3	5,996	5,447	11,443
4	5,599	4,864	10,463
Total 0—4	26,177	23,294	49,471
5—9	25,083	22,399	47,482
10—14	30,315	18,477	48,792
15—19	33,612	19,068	52,680
20—24	48,843	22,562	71,405
25—29	54,031	24,574	78,605
30—34	55,623	25,513	81,136
35—39	37,114	16,326	53,440
40—44	41,509	20,070	61,579
45—49	17,662	9,116	26,778
50—54	20,199	12,383	32,582
55—59	7,617	5,287	12,904
60 and over	17,254	15,293	32,547
Total	415,039	234,362	649,401

65. The proportion which these figures bear to one another may be compared with the figures given for the town and suburbs together at the census of 1881 which are taken from Mr. Beverley's report—

Ages.	Both sexes.	Males.	Females.
Under 1	10,852	5,628	5,224
1	7,966	4,044	3,922
2	9,386	4,618	4,768
3	10,770	5,365	5,405
4	9,651	5,068	4,583
Total under 5 ...	48,625	24,723	23,902
5—9	47,228	24,859	22,369
Total under 10 ...	95,853	49,582	46,271
10—14	45,549	27,749	17,800
15—19	51,297	33,052	18,245
Total under 20 ...	192,699	110,383	82,316
20—24	79,078	53,387	25,691
25—29	90,952	63,975	26,977
30—34	94,579	65,767	28,812
35—39	54,062	37,854	16,208
Total between 20 and 40 ...	318,671	220,983	97,688

Ages.		Both sexes.	Males.	Females.
40—44	... ...	67,230	44,631	22,599
45—49	... ...	25,964	16,842	9,122
50—54	... ...	34,569	20,083	14,486
55—59	... ...	10,756	6,174	4,582
Total between 40 and 60	...	138,519	87,730	50,789
60 and upwards	... ...	34,603	16,814	17,789
Unspecified	... ...	166	112	54
GRAND TOTAL	...	684,658	436,022	248,636

Except that there is now in the earlier ages a larger surplus of males over females, the two results are remarkably similar. It will be observed that both the first two age-periods give nearly the same numbers, after which the population under each increases gradually up to the 30—34 period, after which it falls off again; but more people are shown in the group 40—44 than in the group 35—39, and more are said to be aged 50—54 than 45—49. It will also be observed that the proportion between the sexes, which had in the middle periods been about two to one, returns to comparative equality in the last three. And also the number of children stated to be under one year is greater than that stated to be of one year, and the number of those stated to be of two years is greater than that of those stated to be of one year; and those of three years are more than those of four. This state of figures can be very simply explained. The age of a native child is of very little importance, especially among the lower classes, and they do not take the trouble to consider and state it accurately. Thus a child is called an infant long after the first year of its life has past, in much the same way as among us the youngest of a family is called "baby" long after the days of babyhood are over. Then in the next stage a child is said to be two—three years of age and then three—four years of age. Therefore there is a double likelihood of a careless enumerator recording a child's age as three if he takes the choice of one of the two figures, instead of enquiring more particularly as to the exact age. The increased proportion of males to females is supported by the municipal birth statistics, which gave in 1889 4,626 males and 4,151 females. It is of course considered to be more likely that female births have remained unreported than that male births have, and also that females have been omitted from enumeration than males. But in view of the fact that the figures remain alike at each recurring census, and that there is not in Calcutta any known reason for concealment of female births, it seems quite as probable that there is here some physical law by the operation of which male births exceed female births. It may also be said that if there was any general concealment of female births there would be even fewer reported than is the case at present. The greater number of children of three and four years makes it probable that children of these ages accompany their parents when they come to Calcutta.

66. The variations in the general age-periods are due to the natural increase in immigration, at first for the purposes of education and then for labour up to the age of thirty-four. After that apparently the labourers gradually go home. But in the uncertainty which prevails as to age, the age groups which contain round numbers naturally claim a larger population than the others. The return to equality in the proportion between the sexes in the more advanced periods appears to show that the men for the most part return to their former homes, while the older women have no longer any ties to draw them there nor any means of going.

CONJUGAL CONDITION.

Conjugal condition.

67. I propose in discussing the conjugal condition of the town to leave out of consideration the population of the Port and the Fort where the conditions as regards conjugal condition are altogether abnormal. The population of the native infantry lines at Alipur (1,002) and of the two jails (3,319) might also be

[e]xcluded; but this would cause confusion, while the Port and Fort figures have [a]ll along been separated from the others.

68. The returns for the town show the following to be the conjugal [c]ondition of its inhabitants:—

		Males.	Females.	Total.
Single	...	126,525	57,338	183,863
Married	...	271,861	105,726	377,587
Widowed	...	16,653	71,298	87,951
Total	...	415,039	234,362	649,401

These figures yield the following percentages on the total populations:—

		Male.	Female.	Total.	On each sex.	
					Male.	Female.
Single ...	...	19·5	8·8	28·3	30·5	24·4
Married ...	...	42·0	16·3	58·3	65·5	45·2
Widowed	...	2·5	10·9	13·4	4·0	30·4
Total	...	64·	36·	100·	100·	100·

At the last census the percentages were on the total population—

		Male.	Female.	Total.	On each sex.	
					Male.	Female.
Single ...	...	20·5	7·9	28·4	32·2	21·7
Married	...	40·3	15·5	55·8	63·2	42·7
Widowed	...	2·9	12·9	15·8	4·6	35·6
Total	...	63·7	36·3	100·	100·	100·

Although the figures obtained at the last census cannot be compared, the percentages may, because the character of the population of the present Muni[c]ipality is sufficiently similar to that of the town and suburbs together at the last census.

Religions compared as to their conjugal condition.

69. The subject should be dealt with for each religion separately. But it is only necessary to deal with the three larger religions, Hinduism, Muhammadanism, and Christianity, because the numbers of those professing other religions are too small to admit of their illustrating any general law.

70. The figures, then, for the three main religions are—

Hindus.

		Males.	Females.	Total.	Percentage on total population.			On each sex.	
					Males.	Females.	Total	Males.	Females.
Single	...	80,868	33,609	114,477	18·9	7·8	26·7	29·7	21·5
Married	...	179,521	66,505	246,027	41·9	15·5	57·4	66·0	42·6
Widowed	...	12,043	56,216	68,259	2·7	13·2	15·9	4·3	35·9
Total	...	272,432	156,330	428,762	63·5	36·5	100·	100·	100·

Muhammadans.

	Males.	Females.	Total.	Percentage on total population.			On each sex.	
				Males.	Females.	Total.	Males.	Females.
Single ...	36,284	16,547	52,831	19·2	8·7	27·9	29·	26·0
Married ...	85,307	34,023	119,330	45·1	18·0	63·1	67·8	54·0
Widowed ...	4,000	13,065	17,065	2·1	6·9	9	3·2	20·0
Total ...	125,591	63,635	189,226	66·4	33·6	100·	100·	100·

Christians.

	Males.	Females.	Total.	Percentage on total population.			On each sex.	
				Males.	Females.	Total.	Males.	Females.
Single ...	8,028	6,500	14,528	30·4	24·7	55·1	58·6	51·2
Married ...	5,149	4,435	9,584	19·5	16·8	36·3	37·6	34·8
Widowed ...	513	1,781	2,293	1·9	6·7	8·6	3·8	14·
Total ...	13,690	12,716	26,406	51·3	48·2	100·	100·	100·

71. As to these statistics, it must be remembered that they are prepared according to statements made by or on behalf of the persons interested, and that no strict enquiry is made as to the validity of the tie which they call marriage. It must also be remembered that a very large number of women who have left their husbands and come to Calcutta find it convenient to believe their husbands to be dead and return themselves as widows, while men in similar circumstances consider themselves to be still married. But again most of the Muhammadan women of marriageable age are (whatever life they may be leading) united by the tie called nikah to some man, while, except among the lower castes, a Hindu woman once widowed must remain so to the end. These considerations will account for the comparatively large proportion of Hindu widows. The large proportion of widows to widowers is explained in the same way, and also by the fact, elsewhere stated, that the widows have no longer any home to return to in their old age. The late age at which Christians marry is illustrated by the large number of single in both the sexes.

72. It may be considered that the number of married women shown in the returns fairly represents the actual number of married couples living together at the time of the census. The small proportion that these couples bear to the total population points to the polyandry which exists in all great cities and especially it would seem in Calcutta, from the large increase of those who are on this occasion returned as prostitutes. At the same time there are many among the higher classes who lodge in Calcutta during the week and return on occasional Sundays to their homes in the neighbouring districts.

Conjugal condition by age.

73. As the conjugal condition of the population by age is given in Table VI, it is not necessary here to deal with it at any length. It appears that of children up to nine years of age, among the Hindus 441 males and 1,238 females were married, and 44 males and 139 females were widowed, while 31,745 males and 27,562 females were unmarried. Among Muhammadans the figures are, married 233 males, 411 females; widowed 10 males, 23 females; unmarried 15,583 males, 13,074 females. There are no married Christians in this age-period, but there are two widowers and one widow. It may be that these figures were to some degree affected by the Age of Consent Bill agitation which may have led some people to return young married children as unmarried; but the figures are not much less than those of 1881, and the numbers may correctly represent the disfavour into which these marriages are gradually falling. It may be noted that marriages of very young children are proportionally more common among Muhammadans than among Hindus.

74. An examination of the other figures shows only that women appear to marry earlier than men, which is a fact generally known. The abnormal nature of the population makes it little useful to discuss the variations of civil condition among the other age groups.

EDUCATION.

Educational statistics.

75. In the census of 1881 the educational returns were classified by religions only. They are now classified by ages also. The instructions directed that all persons under instruction, from the child learning at its mother's knee up to the candidate M.A., should be shown as learning. It was also directed that if the person enumerated knew English, he was to be shown as knowing it as well as the vernacular he knew best, but for those who were learning, no such language was to be shown. But many who were really learning were recorded as knowing English and Bengali, and this has confused the abstractors. The percentage of males under instruction on the total population is 5·, and that of females 1·3. The percentage of males who are returned as able to read and write is 28·5 and of females 7. Thus the percentage of those under instruction and 'literate' on the whole population is 33·5 for males and 8·3 for females. At the last census these percentages were 31·1 and 6·6 respectively. Among the Hindus 39· per cent. of the males and 7·5 per cent. of the females are either learning or literate. Among other religions these percentages are :—

	Males.	Females.
Muhammadans	16·7	1·7
Christians	74·7	70·
Brahmos	77·4	65·4
Buddhists	59·2	25·6
Jews	62·9	36·2

In 1881 these percentages were :—

	Males.	Females.
Hindus	36·9	6·8
Muhammadans	14·2	1·
Christians	79·	67·
Brahmos	85·3	64·6
Buddhists	52·9	12·5
Jews	63·5	29·3

Progress of education.

76. Thus among the chief religions there is a steady increase in the number of those who can read and write. Among Christians the percentage is slightly lower, owing probably to the increase in the number of Native Christians already noticed. A slight numerical alteration affects the percentages so much in the other religions that a detailed comparison is unnecessary. But it may be observed that in every religion the percentage of educated females is higher than it was ten years ago.

77. I have said that there has perhaps been some confusion as to those who are shown as 'learning,' as their number has considerably fallen off, but it must also be remembered that in the last decade the number of good schools in the country has much increased, so that the need to resort to Calcutta for education is less. Unfortunately education by age-periods was not abstracted in 1881, or a comparison with the figures of the ages 0—14 would form a good basis for an opinion on this subject.

LANGUAGE.

Mother-tongues—Indian languages.

78. In table VIII the inhabitants of Calcutta are classified according to the language found in their schedules as their mother-tongue. It appears that of the total population of 681,560, the Bengali language is the mother-tongue of 375,528, while either Hindi or Urdu is returned for 247,645. The only other Indian language much spoken is Uriya, which is the parent-tongue of 23,899 persons.

Character of population judged by mother-tongues.

79. The character of the various populations speaking these languages may be judged by the fact that of the Bengalis 153,043, or about 40 per cent., are females, while among the speakers of Hindi and Urdu, the percentage is little more than 25, and among those who speak Uriya, it is less than 10.

Other Asiatic languages.

80. Of those who speak Asiatic languages from beyond India, nearly half are returned as speaking Persian. But it may be noted that among Mussalmans many who rarely or never speak any other language than Bengali return their parent-tongue as Urdu, Persian, or even Arabic. In the same way Jews often return their parent-tongue as Hebrew, though, perhaps, they do not speak it much.

Non-Asiatic languages.

81. Of the non-Asiatic languages, English naturally occupies the first place, German being second, and French third, but as to French, I am inclined to believe that in some cases the abstractors have thought the word Firingi, which rather signifies Portuguese, to mean French. There are, however, 242 persons returned as born in Chandernagore, and they may have returned French as their parent-tongue. Four persons are returned as speaking Gaelic, 42 as speaking Irish, 58 as speaking Scotch, and nine as speaking Welsh. In 1881 no one was returned as speaking these languages; but whether this circumstance is due to the editing of the return, or whether the Celtic languages are now more spoken, I am unable to say.

BIRTH-PLACES.

Birth-places.

82. The following statement shows the birth-places of the inhabitants of Calcutta :—

		Males.	Females.	Total.
Calcutta	...	104,137	103,028	207,165
The 24-Parganas	...	29,342	26,133	55,475
Total	...	133,479	129,161	262,640
The rest of Bengal	...	226,480	84,798	311,278
,, rest of India	...	50,749	18,385	69,134
,, rest of Asia	...	1,634	526	2,160
Elsewhere	...	2,530	1,364	3,894
Unspecified	...	167	128	295
Total	...	415,039	234,362	649,401

Calcutta and the 24-Parganas.

83. It is convenient to group together those returned as born in Calcutta and the suburbs, as it seems that in the census of 1881 persons born in the suburbs were often returned as born in the 24-Parganas. At the present census the returns seem to have been made more correctly. At the last census the percentage of those born in Calcutta and the 24-Parganas was 38·7 on the whole population. This percentage is now just 40. But Mr. Beverley's calculation was made on the whole of Calcutta, including Port and Fort, while mine is made on the figures of the town only. And there are comparatively few Calcutta-born persons in the Fort and Port, so that in this respect the state of the town seems to continue as before.

Other districts in Bengal.

84. The other districts which most largely contribute to the population are—

Hooghly	...	...	...	52,696
Gaya	...	...	...	32,412
Burdwan	...	...	...	26,271
Midnapur	...	...	...	24,985
Patna	...	...	...	20,867
Cuttack	...	...	...	20,176
Nadiya	...	...	...	16,958
Shahabad	...	...	...	16,731
Saran	...	...	...	12,833
Dhaka	...	...	...	12,561

85. Curiously enough, these ten districts were at the last census the only ones which contributed more than 10,000 each to the population, though they

then came in a different order. So far as the figures can be compared, the Bengal districts show a falling off, due no doubt to railway facilities, while Behar districts keep nearly the same proportion, except Gaya, which has risen from fifth to second place.

Birth-place statistics prove the general correctness of the returns.

86. It has sometimes been said that the disproportion of males to females in Calcutta censuses is due to concealment of female population; but these figures make it clear that there is no such concealment. The population born at and near the metropolis is almost equally balanced as regards the sexes, while as we move further away the disproportion increases. Thus, of the Hooghly-born 36 per cent. are females, while of Gaya-born this percentage is only 23, and of the natives of Cuttack only 10.

87. Of those who come from the rest of India, the great majority (about 74 per cent.) come from the North-West Provinces, but it seems that there are fewer immigrants from the rest of India than there were in 1881. Of the other countries in Asia, China and Nepal claim the largest share of the population.

88. In the 1881 report the figures for the Town and Fort are put together, and this largely influences the results in comparing the birth-places of Europeans. The total number of British-born was returned as 3,631 in 1881 for Town and Fort. It is now 3,827. But in 1881 there were more Irish and Scotch than there are now, which might easily be explained by the presence of a regiment in which these nationalities preponderated.

CASTES, TRIBES AND NATIONALITIES.

Statistics required for imperial purposes.

89. The Census Commissioner has prescribed a very elaborate system of arranging the castes according to their traditionary occupation. The returns to be submitted to him will also show the civil condition of each caste in four age groups, and their relative condition as regards education and their sub-castes. But for the purposes of the present report it has appeared sufficient to print the total number of males and females in each caste only. The information to be obtained will be very interesting when dealt with province by province; but in Calcutta the caste tie is greatly relaxed, and the present bears no relation to the traditionary occupation. Up-country Brahmans, for instance, will carry burdens on their heads—a degradation they would never be permitted to submit to in their native village.

Difficulty of preparing caste statistics.

90. It was difficult to get the caste and sub-caste recorded intelligently and abstracted correctly. Then in certain cases the caste is given in the column for sub-caste, and the sub-caste in the column for caste. Added to these there is a constantly recurring difficulty in names so similar as Teli and Tili, Kumar and Kamar. I did all I could to overcome these difficulties; and, though I cannot say that the work has been done in a perfect manner, the total number of Hindu castes has risen from 89 to 126, and only 1,632 have been shown as 'unspecified' against 5,344.

Chief castes.

91. The following castes claim the largest share of the population:—

	Males.	Females.	Total.
Brahmans	41,546	20,162	61,708
Kaisths	37,474	21,313	58,787
Chamars	18,060	6,428	24,488
Kaibartas	12,967	10,397	23,364
Gwalas	14,043	5,888	19,931
Subarnabarniks ...	10,666	8,960	19,626
Baisnabs	6,940	9,821	16,761
Tantis	8,225	7,911	16,136
Kahars	11,244	2,852	14,096
Gandabaniyas	9,057	5,025	14,082
Telis	7,054	3,643	10,697

92. All these castes, except Gandabaniyas, were among the first thirteen in 1881. On that occasion Sadgops and Mehtars also exceeded 10,000.

Now Sadgops fail to reach this number by four, while Mehtars are a good deal fewer. It is possible that Mussalman Mehtars have taken the place of Hindus. But it is among the lower castes that the greatest confusion occurs.

Mussalmans.

93. Out of 189,226 Mussalmans, 173,332 are returned as Shaikhs. There are also 11,101 Pathans.

Christians.

94. Of the Christians in the town, it appears that 5,131 males and 4,287 females are non-Asiatic, 4,771 males and 5,032 females are Eurasian, and 3,788 males and 3,397 females are Asiatic.

Port and Fort.

95. In the Fort 1,041 males and 192 females are non-Asiatic, and in the Port and Canals there are 1,243 non-Asiatic males and 16 females.

Europeans and Eurasians.

96. It appears from the report for 1881 that there was considerable confusion in the returns for Europeans and Eurasians, and hence it is not very useful to compare the present results with the former. I do not propose to discuss the nationality question. It is extremely difficult to say exactly under what nationality certain persons should be classed. It is a tradition in some old Eurasian families that they are of true British descent. And one meets problems such as one laid before me by one of my supervisors, who asked how the son of a German father by a Creole mother born in Calcutta was to describe himself. Looking at the man, I said he had better call himself an Eurasian; but I am not sure that I was right. The rule is that people are to be recorded according to their own descriptions, and therefore there is considerable room for doubt as to the results. Nevertheless the probabilities are in favour of the correctness of the present return, which shows a larger proportion of Eurasians than the former one. It will be observed that a large number of those returned as Europeans must have been born in India. There is still sufficient prospect of profit to induce members of old Indian families to try their fortune where their forefathers did.

Native Christians.

97. The number of Native Christians has considerably increased. I am not aware if this is due to actual conversion in Calcutta, or to the fact that converts are better cared for here.

Sects of Christians.

98. Among the sects of Christians the chief are the Churches of England and Ireland, and Protestants, which mean to a certain extent the same thing. People were specially requested in the schedules to note the denomination of Protestants to which they belonged, but people did not always read the instructions. Some people call themselves Protestants who would decline to classify themselves under any Church. And there are among Eurasians and natives many who only know themselves as Protestants as opposed to Roman Catholics and Baptists. Next to Protestants come Roman Catholics, and the Church of Scotland and Baptists are next in number. Among the curiosities of this return are to be found five Quakers, one of whom gives his religion as Rationalist, two members of the Salvation Army, seven Unitarians, two Agnostics, one Positivist, one Freethinker, one Specialist, and 23 of no religion. The last class appears to be composed of Hindu families who have lost their own religion and have failed to find any other. There appears to have been a falling off in those recorded as unbelievers since the census of 1881. But the schedule instruction provided the use of the word 'unsectarian' Christian, a term so colourless that even Professor Huxley might almost be persuaded to allow himself to be called by it. As 149 persons are shown under this class, it may be considered that many whose religious belief was not very strong have placed themselves in it.

OCCUPATIONS.

Difficulty of obtaining correct statistics of occupations.

99. Of all the parts of a census, there is none so difficult as that of occupations. It is the most difficult in enumeration, in abstraction, in tabulation, and in compilation. In the English census, which is for the most part a census of occupations, an elaborate classification is printed on each schedule,

so that those who read it with sufficient intelligence can have no difficulty in recording themselves correctly. But such a system would hardly be possible in India, for few would read such a long statement, and fewer still would understand it. At the present census matters have been somewhat complicated by the instruction that those who had no occupation of their own, but depended on others for their livelihood, were to be classed as dependent on the occupation of those who supported them. Many, however, were recorded as 'dependent' simply or dependent on some person, *e.g.*, Shyam Lal (dependent). It might be that one could find out who Shyam Lal was, or it might be that he did not live in the same house. There is also the difficulty that women often have a right of maintenance in a joint-family, and such would write 'joint-family' (dependent), and it was necessary to see who was the head of the joint family and what his business, and this was not always possible. A further difficulty occurred from the instruction on European household schedules that instead of writing, *e.g.*, banker (dependent), (banker) should be written, and this instruction was not at once understood by the abstractors.

100. Moreover, I at first received instructions that no information was required about dependents, and accordingly caused only the entries for workers to be abstracted. Afterwards I heard that for provincial purposes dependents were not to be distinguished from workers, and finally I was ordered to show workers and dependents separately. But as workers had been abstracted first separately, so dependents had also to be abstracted separately, and it was not easy to be sure that all the people were accounted for. These considerations will account for a great part of those shown as of 'unspecified' occupation. Many also state themselves to be of no occupation, and some being thieves or pimps may not wish to state theirs.

Compared with results in 1881.

101. Nevertheless it may be noted that, while in 1881 101,089 males and 183,962 females are shown as of unspecified occupation, the numbers now are 29,349 males and 40,879 females.

Classification by age-periods.

102. In 1881 the occupations were arranged according to religions. They are now arranged by ages. In certain cases children of 0—4 are shown as having occupations. In some cases where this was obviously absurd I have amended the returns. In more doubtful ones I have left them as they were. The enumerator may have omitted the word 'dependent,' or the abstractor may have put a stroke in a wrong column, or, what is just as likely, the head of the family may have returned the boy as following his own occupation.

Arrangement of occupations.

103. The arrangement of occupations is that prescribed by the Census Commissioner. This arrangement is not the same as that adopted at the last census, and the large number of persons shown as unspecified on that occasion renders the figures useless for purposes of comparison.

Discussion of the returns. Class A.

104. The first class is that of Government and municipal servants. There has been some difficulty about Government clerks. Some of them stated the office in which they worked, but so many more did not do so that I thought it would be more misleading to classify some of the clerks of an office under a separate heading and some under 'Government clerks' than to join them all under one heading. There are 6,353 Government clerks according to the returns.

One Honorary Magistrate has returned himself as such, and one Municipal Commissioner seems to consider this position as his means of livelihood. Only 122 census enumerators have returned themselves as such, but perhaps some were returned as municipal sirkars, of whom there seems to be a very large number.

The next order is the Army, which shows a total of 2,604. The number in 1881 was 2,616.

Class B.

105. After this follows the class of dealers in live-stock. There are 36 cattle-dealers and 21 buffalo-dealers, but these groups merge in group 76—milk-sellers—the two occupations being usually combined.

The next sub-order is agriculture. Land occupants not cultivating are returned at 4,125, of whom 26 are aged 0—4 and 132 5—14. Estate agents number 968, cultivators are naturally few (1,203), and are for the most part immigrants who cultivated before leaving their own districts. There are 1,501 gardeners, including two females.

106. The next class is composed of personal, domestic and sanitary servants. There are 2,607 male and 159 female barbers, and 3,658 washermen and 467 washerwomen. Cooks number 6,381 males and 1,212 females. There are also—

Class C.

	Males.	Females.
House-servants (unspecified) ...	19,403	...
House-bearers	3,108	179
Table-servants	3,929	19
Maid-servants	...	14,165
Nurses	...	1,080
Coachmen	6,443	...
Grooms	6,063	1
Door-keepers	7,218	9

Five persons are shown as Sanitary Inspectors, but more of these Inspectors are included in group 5. It appears that 5,402 males and 1,332 females are employed as sweepers and scavengers.

107. The next class is of those who prepare and supply material substances. Those who keep cows and buffaloes and supply milk and butter are 2,511 males and 526 females. There are 1,446 male and 38 female butchers, and 1,421 fishermen and 544 fisherwomen.

Class D.

Passing next to vegetable food, 1,343 males and 870 females deal in grain (rice mostly), 1,757 males and 487 females prepare or sell flour and dâl or pulse. And there are 3,427 male and 129 female confectioners.

Next, drink, condiments, and narcotics are classed together. No one is classed as a seller of country spirits, probably because in Calcutta those who sell these sell imported wines also. Four hundred and thirty-two males and 20 females are returned as selling imported wines, and 594 males and 18 females as selling tari or toddy. Under this group are included grocers or *mudis*, who should rather perhaps be grouped with grain-dealers (group 83). Of these, there are 6,664 males and 366 females. One thousand two hundred and twenty males and 202 females sell betel leaf, and 1,121 males and 35 females tobacco. There are 130 male vendors of opium and 20 of ganja.

108. The next orders are light, fuel and forage providers, and those engaged in building. One thousand two hundred and ninety-three males and 121 females are engaged in supplying grass and fire-wood. And there are 5,536 male and 141 female masons.

After a sub-order of those engaged in preparing vehicles follow what are called supplementary requirements. These are paper, books, watches, toys, ornaments, and the like. Among those who provide these appear 1,145 male and 25 female stationers. Six thousand and seventy-five males and five females are engaged in the various processes of printing. And there are 2,079 male and one female book-binder. But the native word 'daftari' has been translated 'book-binder,' while a 'daftari,' though he binds books, does many other things as well.

109. Next follow the dealers in textile fabrics: 4,227 males and 112 females deal in woollen cloth, and 2,398 males and 93 females are returned as engaged in the manufacture of jute. There are two large jute mills in Ward XIX. There are 6,010 male and 180 female tailors.

In the next order of those who work and deal in metals, there are 4,901 male and 28 female workers in gold and silver, 1,598 male and 23 female workers in tin (but this is not really tin always, but an amalgamation of brass and zinc), and 1,601 male and 190 female blacksmiths.

There are not many dealers in glass, stone, or earthenware. But there are 5,673 male and 4 female carpenters; 158 males and 245 females are returned as chemists and druggists. Of these, 3 males and 12 females are under 14. These probably merely sit in shops and help to sell. One may infer that the females are old women who sell simples to the credulous.

Among the dealers in leather there are 1,200 male and 8 female tanners, and 10,461 male and 50 female boot-makers. But these two classes cross each other, as most of the Chamars are both tanners and boot-makers.

Class E.

110. The next class is the commercial, the most important, if not the most numerous of all. There seems to be some confusion between groups 346 (bank managers) and 351 (bank clerks), as the former exceed the latter, but many native bankers no doubt transact their own business without any clerk. Four thousand four hundred and thirty-three males and 114 females are returned as general merchants, and 7,857 as clerks of merchants. The shop-keepers shown in group 356 as otherwise unspecified are no doubt nearly all *mudis* (group 109). Of these, there are 5,347 males and 205 females. There are 1,934 male and 82 female hawkers; 4,198 males and 15 females are returned as general brokers.

111. Among those engaged in the transport of commerce, it appears that 1,192 males and 1 female are engaged as drivers, firemen, &c., on the railway, but this number must include porters also. There are 4,965 cart-owners and 3,833 hackney-carriage drivers and stable boys. Then of those engaged in nautical transport, there are 217 captains and 1,355 sailors, and there are 22,084 boatmen and 3,706 dock khalashis. But some sailors in native ships have no doubt been shown as boatmen.

The next groups are the Postal and Telegraph services. There are 800 postal runners and messengers.

Class F.

112. Here follow the learned professions. The first is religion, which forms the occupation of 3,929 males and 123 females. Some children under 4 of both sexes are returned under this head. Such have a family interest in the priesthood and perform certain duties in ceremonies; 2,142 males and 214 females are employed in education; 3,895 males and 29 females are returned as private secretaries and private clerks; and 3,442 males and 29 females as general writers. Most of these are persons who go from shop to shop and keep the accounts of several of them.

113. There are 74 barristers, advocates and pleaders, 61 solicitors, and 1,039 mukhtars. In 1881 there were more pleaders and fewer mukhtars, while possibly the distinction has now been more carefully drawn.

114. Under the head Medicine 1,081 males and 324 females are shown as practitioners by diploma; whila 163 males and 46 females are shown as kabirajes. No other group claims a large number of workers, until we reach the large class of indefinite labourers, under which are found 33,075 males and 2,316 females.

Class G.

115. The number of those stated to be unspecified has already been referred to. Prostitutes number 20,126. This number appears to exceed considerably the number returned at the previous census. Probably the present number represents with fair accuracy those unfortunate women who depend on sexual intercourse for their livelihood. Some European females may have felt ashamed of their calling and returned themselves otherwise, but among the native women no such feeling prevails. In 1881 the Contagious Diseases Act was still partially in force, and may have caused some concealment.

116. In the remaining classes are included 1,329 males and 1,615 females who live on house-rent and the dividends on stocks and shares. There are 3,737 male and 2,914 female beggars, 972 male and 95 female pensioners, and 2,860 male and 53 female convicted prisoners.

General result.

117. The result of this census, therefore, which, as a census of occupations, is the most complete that has ever been taken of Calcutta, is to confirm former indications that the population is mainly composed of Government servants, of those who are engaged in commerce, and of those who supply the wants of the two former classes.

INFIRMITIES.

Lunatics.

118. The number of insane persons shown in the returns is 433, of whom 318 are males and 115 females. Of these 227 males and 66 females were in the asylum

at Bhawanipur. The excess of males is due to the fact that insane females are kept quietly at home, while it is not so easy to detain males. At the last census there were 551 lunatics in the town and suburbs, but I believe that since that time arrangements have been made for accomodating a larger number of these unfortunate people in or near the districts where they are found.

Blind.

119. At this census the abstraction sheets show 171 males and 141 females to be blind. In 1881 961 persons in the town and suburbs were returned as 'blind,' but it is not very clear whether in these were included those blind of one eye or not. It may also be observed that at the last census no fewer than 652 of the blind were aged 40 and over, while those of this age-period are now only 127, whence it may be inferred that these persons have died and have not been replaced.

Deaf mutes.

120. The number of deaf mutes now shown is 206—107 males and 99 females. At the last census there were 190 in the town and 175 in the suburbs. Of this number, 151 were over 40—now there are only 87.

Lepers.

121. The number of lepers in 1881 is shown to be 286 males and 101 females. The present returns show 115 males and 58 females. In the case of lepers there were at the last census 198 aged 40 and over, while now there are only 82.

Possible errors in the returns relating to infirmities.

122. It must be said that the duty of abstracting entries relating to infirmities is one very likely to be neglected because the entries are so few, and they occur after such long intervals. But I see no reason to think that this duty was performed more carelessly in this than in the last abstraction. Also I observed that at the time of the last census there is mention of some special charity of Prince Ghulam Muhammad, which may have attracted not only lepers, but the blind and deaf as well.

123. There were also in the liberties of the late King of Oudh in Garden Reach a vast crowd of mendicants of all sorts. Where these men have gone on the death of their patron is not known to me; but even had they remained there, they would be outside the limits with which this report deals. And it must be said that in Calcutta, unless the infirm are attracted by some special occasion or charity, there is no great place for them.

COST OF COMPILATION.

Cost of compilation.

124. The cost of compiling the returns has been as follows:—

		Rs.	A.	P.
Pay of special officer	...	4,025	0	0
Establishment	...	8,918	11	0
Contingencies	...	299	3	0
Cost of map and printing the report ...	...	......		
Total	...	......		

Cost as compared with that of the previous census.

125. This total slightly exceeds the total expenditure in 1881, which was Rs. 13,747. By obtaining the use of the Town Hall I was able to save house-rent. Although I have completed the work more than a month sooner than it was finished in 1881, the fact that my whole pay was chargeable to the Municipality has caused an excess of Rs. 1,275. In contingencies is included a charge of Rs. 221-0-9 for forms supplied by Government, and at the census of 1881 these forms were supplied free. It may be mentioned that the present tables and report do not by any means represent all the work that has been done. A very elaborate table has been prepared, showing the civil condition of each caste in four age-periods; another shows all the sub-castes recorded under each caste, and another the state of education of each caste. The labour involved in the preparation of all these tables far exceeded that which can have been necessary to prepare the statistics recorded in 1881.

CONCLUSION.

General conclusions.

126. It appears, therefore, from what has been stated that the condition of Calcutta is still one of progress, but that this progress affects the day population more than that which may be found on any given night. It is also clear that such expansion as has been observed has taken place in Ward VI, which was previously the least densely populated ward in the heart of the town, and in other wards where there was more room for expansion. It is further shown that the main population of Calcutta is not home-born but imported, and that the immigrants are generally of the male sex only, which accounts for a disproportion of males to females by almost two to one. Then the general result is to show that the birth statistics are correct in showing a large proportion of male to female births. It is very well known that birth registration in Calcutta has lately improved, and the question is one with which the Health Officer may deal better than I can. But I may perhaps be right in pointing out that in paragraph 111 of Mr. Beverley's report, in which he argues the incorrectness of the Calcutta birth-rate by analogy with the birth-rates of England, he appears to me to be arguing on false premises. For instance, when he says that "it has been ascertained, as might indeed be expected, that the birth-rate depends on the proportion of married women between the ages of 20 and 40," he surely forgets that he is deducing Indian conclusions from English premises. The age of child-bearing begins much earlier in India and naturally closes earlier. Nor, so far as I know, is there any reason to believe that women are so prolific in India as they are in England, while the number of still-born births here seems very considerable. Further, for reasons already given, I think that Mr. Beverley was in error in taking as perfectly accurate the ageing of the children in the early years of their lives. If proper allowances be made on the lines suggested in paragraph 65 of this report, I believe that the figures of both censuses will tend rather to confirm the general accuracy of the birth statistics than to disprove it.

The birth-rate in Calcutta.

Close correspondence of results between this and the last census.

127. It only remains to note what a close resemblance there is between the results of this census and the last. Going through the figures ward by ward, block by block, age-period by age-period, caste by caste or birth-place by birth-place, one finds everywhere slight differences but perfect uniformity—such complete uniformity, indeed, that in any striking difference one expected to find a mistake, and the expectation was generally correct.

General accuracy of the census.

128. I do not pretend that the census of 1891 is a perfectly accurate one. Considering the difficulties in the way and the men with whom I had to work, it has sometimes been a matter of surprise that any census was taken at all or any returns prepared which could be accepted as accurate. It is therefore gratifying to find that the actual result by its close parallelism with the former proves the correctness of both.

Expressions of gratitude.

129. It is fitting to close a report with an expression of gratitude to those who have helped one. A feeling of literary honesty tells me that I ought to begin by acknowledging my indebtedness to Mr. Beverley's reports of the censuses of 1876 and 1881. But if I were to attempt to thank all those who helped me in the work, I should scarcely know where to end.

MUNICIPAL OFFICE;
CALCUTTA,
The 6th July 1891.

H. F. T. MAGUIRE,
Census Officer.

CENSUS OF CALCUTTA, 1891.

TABLE I.—ABSTRACT *of the population of* CALCUTTA *on February 26th*, 1891.

	Males.	Females.	Total.
THE TOWN	415,039	234,362	649,401
FORT WILLIAM	3,119	349	3,468
THE PORT	26,516	73	26,589
CANALS	2,072	30	2,102
GRAND TOTAL ...	446,746	234,814	681,560

Table II.

Ward No.	Area in acres.	Houses. Masonry. Occupied.	Houses. Masonry. Unoccupied.	Houses. Others. Occupied.	Houses. Others. Unoccupied.	Total Males.	Total Females.	Total population.	Number of persons per acre.
1	2	3	4	5	6	7	8	9	10
I	409	1,599	184	2,528	232	21,491	15,394	36 885	90
II	217	1,220	93	1,444	41	16,178	10,436	26,614	122
III	403	1,786	162	2,546	124	21,020	15,411	36,431	90
IV	320	1,255	64	2,361	92	20,633	14,195	34,828	108
V	243	1,375	72	1,356	62	26,411	12,769	39,180	161
VI	262	1,816	152	1,685	145	25.370	16,287	41,657	159
VII	217	1,708	384	365	175	16,226	4,420	20,646	95
VIII	224	1,343	107	1,721	432	35,315	15,466	50,781	226
IX	460	1,945	86	2,373	348	31,976	17,496	49,472	107
X	147	825	19	725	5	15,880	6,788	22,668	154
XI	166	1,175	99	1,192	217	12,715	8,046	20,761	125
XII	211	438	8	49	5	5,583	500	6,083	28
XIII	192	805	76	988	10	21,829	6,537	28,366	147
XIV	198	1,065	85	1,358	46	18,579	10,628	29,207	147
XV	179	372	113	898	130	8,897	4,321	13,218	73
XVI	153	194	2	46	1	3,725	895	4,620	30
XVII	128	89	1	310	3	2,259	1,028	3,287	25
XVIII	108	90	6	166	3	3,238	1,582	4,820	44
XIX	1,062	634	139	3,676	198	20,043	13,104	33,147	31
XX	800	680	42	3,386	110	13,621	9,399	23,020	28
XXI	2,022	591	153	3,323	326	13,018	9,813	22,831	11
XXII	838	1,610	134	4,408	468	24,232	18,359	42,591	50
XXIII	1,241	387	52	1,987	139	9,854	4,950	14,804	11
XXIV	921	184	17	2,296	96	8,297	7,043	15,340	16
XXV	729	553	81	2,602	145	17,356	9,477	26,833	36
Total for Town ...	11,850	23,739	2,331	43,789	3,562	413,746	234,344	648,090	54
Fort William and Esplanade.	1,283	...	...	...	...	4,412	367	4,779	3
Port	...	...	...	...	...	26,516	73	26,589	...
Canals	...	...	...	...	...	2,072	30	2,102	...
Grand Total...	...	...	...	...	...	446,746	234,814	681,560	...

TABLE III.—*Variation in the enumerated Population since last Census.*

WARD No.	TOTAL. 1891.	TOTAL. 1881.	TOTAL. Variation.	MALES. 1891.	MALES. 1881.	MALES. Variation.	FEMALES. 1891.	FEMALES. 1881.	FEMALES. Variation.
1	2	3	4	5	6	7	8	9	10
I Old town	29,951	25,487	+ 4,464 or 17·54%	17,153	14,271	+ 2,882	12,798	11,216	+ 1,582
Added area	6,934	3,024	+ 3,910 or 129·27%	4,338	...	...	2,596	...	...
II	26,614	25,682	+ 932 or 3·63%	16,178	15,680	+ 498	10,436	10,002	+ 434
III Old town	28,374	25,527	+ 2,846 or 11·12%	16,424	14,253	+ 2,171	11,950	11,274	+ 675
Added area	8,057	...	...	4,596	...	...	3,461	...	...
IV Old town	25,750	20,572	+ 5,178 or 25·17%	15,268	11,954	+ 3,314	10,482	8,618	+ 1,764
Added area	9,078	...	...	5,365	...	...	3,713	...	...
V	39,180	36,318	+ 2,862 or 7·88%	26,411	24,324	+ 2,087	12,769	11,994	+ 775
VI	41,657	32,824	+ 8,833 or 26·9%	25,370	19,649	+ 5,721	16,287	13,175	+ 3,112
VII	20,646	20,769	— 124 or ·59%	16,226	16,122	+ 104	4,420	4,647	— 228
VIII	50,781	47,323	+ 3,458 or 7·3%	35,315	31,606	+ 3,709	15,466	15,717	— 251
IX Old town	39,109	39,241	— 132 or ·33%	24,689	23,925	+ 764	14,420	15,316	— 896
Added area	10,363	...	...	7,287	...	...	3,076	...	...
X	22,668	21,627	+ 1,041 or 4·8%	15,880	14,398	+ 1,482	6,788	7,229	— 441
XI	20,761	20,516	+ 245 or 1·1%	12,715	12,126	+ 589	8,046	8,390	— 344
XII	6,083	5,785	+ 298 or 5·1%	5,583	5,220	+ 363	500	565	— 65
XIII	28,366	26,051	+ 2,315 or 8·8%	21,829	19,646	+ 2,183	6,537	6,405	+ 132
XIV	29,207	26,063	+ 3,144 or 12·6%	18,579	15,452	+ 3,127	10,628	10,611	+ 17
XV	13,218	11,840	+ 1,378 or 11·6%	8,897	7,594	+ 1,303	4,321	4,246	+ 75
XVI	4,620	4,968	— 348 or 7%	3,725	3,933	— 208	895	1,035	— 140
XVII	4,598	6,125	—1,527 or 24·8%	3,552	4,596	— 1,044	1,046	1,529	— 483
XVIII	4,820	4,953	— 133 or 2·6%	3,238	3,029	+ 209	1,582	1,924	— 342
XIX	33,147	26,929	+ 6,218 or 23·1%	20,043	16,065	+ 3,978	13,104	10,864	+ 2,240
XX	23,020	18,895	+ 4,125 or 21·8%	13,621	10,792	+ 2,829	9,399	8,103	+ 1,296
XXI	22,831	...	...	13,018	...	...	9,813	...	...
XXII	42,591	38,002	+ 4,589 or 12·07%	24,232	21,035	+ 3,197	18,359	16,967	+ 1,392
XXIII	14,804	13,438	+ 1,366 or 1·16%	9,854	9,012	+ 842	4,950	4,426	+ 524
XXIV	15,340	15,869	— 519 or 3·2%	8,297	8,117	+ 180	7,043	7,752	— 709
XXV	26,833	...	...	17,356	...	...	9,477	...	...
Total population of Calcutta ...	649,401	...	...	415,039	...	...	234,362	...	...
Fort William ...	3,468	3,348	+ 120 or 3·55%	3,119	3,002	+ 117	349	346	+ 3
Port of Calcutta and Canals ...	28,691	28,200	...	28,588	28,037	...	103	163	...
GRAND TOTAL ...	681,560	...	...	446,746	...	...	234,814	...	...

NOTE.—Table III differs from Table II in that the population of the Presidency Jail is included in the Fort and Esplanade in Table II, while in Table III it is included in Ward XVII.

Table IV.—

Ward No.	Total population.			Hindus.			Muhammadans.			Christians.		
	Total.	Males.	Females.	Total.	Males.	Females.	Total.	Males.	Females.	Total.	Males.	Females.
1	2	3	4	5	6	7	8	9	10	11	12	13
I	36,885	21,491	15,394	30,995	17,457	13,638	5,874	4,027	1,847	15	6	9
II	26,614	16,178	10,436	25,482	15,180	10,302	1,116	989	127	4	3	1
III	36,431	21,020	15,411	27,658	15,813	11,845	8,601	5,161	3,440	127	17	110
IV	34,828	20,633	14,195	26,612	15,452	11,160	7,732	4,942	2,790	371	188	183
V	39,180	26,411	12,769	36,711	24,236	12,475	2,112	1,958	154	55	32	23
VI	41,657	25,370	16,287	34,043	20,138	13,905	7,284	5,098	2,186	177	70	107
VII	20,646	16,226	4,420	13,925	10,946	2,979	5,294	4,356	938	561	419	142
VIII	50,781	35,315	15,466	22,153	15,449	6,704	24,696	17,636	7,060	2,628	1,338	1,290
IX	49,472	31,976	17,496	31,513	20,277	11,236	16,479	10,900	5,579	1,280	677	603
X	22,668	15,880	6,788	8,515	6,265	2,250	8,872	6,556	2,316	4,320	2,360	1,960
XI	20,761	12,715	8,046	17,997	11,121	6,876	1,172	839	333	1,559	735	824
XII	6,083	5,583	500	3,498	3,440	58	1,470	1,453	17	978	577	401
XIII	28,366	21,829	6,537	14,366	11,801	2,565	10,896	8,408	2,488	2,931	1,519	1,412
XIV	29,207	18,579	10,628	10,609	7,134	3,475	15,709	10,015	5,694	2,715	1,340	1,375
XV	13,218	8,897	4,321	5,144	3,749	1,395	6,536	4,349	2,187	1,520	791	729
XVI	4,620	3,725	895	2,088	1,918	170	1,517	1,206	311	982	579	403
XVII	4,698	3,652	1,046	2,662	2,107	555	1,210	980	230	616	365	251
XVIII	4,820	3,238	1,582	3,072	2,221	851	1,401	837	564	347	180	167
XIX	33,147	20,043	13,104	20,491	12,720	7,771	10,488	6,494	3,994	2,159	824	1,335
XX	23,020	13,621	9,399	9,798	6,327	3,471	12,643	6,984	5,659	563	299	264
XXI	22,831	13,018	9,813	11,919	7,077	4,842	10,303	5,547	4,756	550	356	194
XXII	42,591	24,232	18,359	34,741	19,477	15,264	6,829	4,220	2,609	990	510	480
XXIII	14,804	9,854	4,950	10,602	6,763	3,839	3,744	2,761	983	287	161	126
XXIV	15,340	8,297	7,043	6,029	3,611	2,418	8,931	4,514	4,417	380	172	208
XXV	26,833	17,356	9,477	18,139	11,753	6,386	8,317	5,361	2,956	291	172	119
Total population of Calcutta ...	649,401	415,039	234,362	428,762	272,432	156,330	189,226	125,591	63,635	26,406	13,690	12,716
Fort William ...	3,468	3,119	349	1,441	1,333	108	597	555	42	1,251	1,052	199
Canals	2,102	2,072	30	1,152	1,122	30	946	946	...	4	4	...
Port of Calcutta ...	26,589	26,516	73	12,782	12,736	46	12,404	12,396	8	1,336	1,320	16
Total of Port and Canals	28,691	28,588	103	13,934	13,858	76	13,350	13,342	8	1,340	1,324	16

Religions.

Brahmos.			Buddhists.			Jains.			Jews.			Parsis.			Sikhs.			Ward No.
Total.	Males.	Females.	Total.	Males.	Females.	Total.	Males.	Females.	Total.	Males.	Females.	Total.	Males.	Females.	Total.	Males.	Females.	
14	15	16	17	18	19	20	21	22	23	24	25	26	27	28	29	30	31	
...	...	...	...	...	...	1	1	...	...	...	...	...	...	...	...	...	...	I
8	4	4	...	...	...	4	2	2	...	...	...	...	...	...	...	...	...	II
35	20	15	...	...	...	2	2	...	...	...	...	8	7	1	...	...	...	III
91	39	52	...	...	...	...	...	...	...	...	...	22	12	10	...	...	...	IV
1	1	...	1	1	...	294	179	115	6	4	2	...	...	...	...	...	...	V
138	57	81	...	...	...	15	7	8	...	...	...	...	...	...	...	...	...	VI
...	...	...	85	69	16	60	51	9	638	320	318	83	65	18	...	...	...	VII
154	92	62	616	544	72	13	6	7	521	250	271	...	...	...	...	...	...	VIII
174	111	63	10	5	5	16	6	10	...	...	...	...	...	...	...	...	...	IX
43	26	17	850	639	211	13	5	8	48	24	24	7	5	2	...	...	...	X
17	11	6	9	4	5	...	...	...	7	5	2	...	...	...	...	...	...	XI
1	1	...	112	97	15	...	...	...	12	6	6	12	9	3	...	...	...	XII
4	3	1	57	43	14	...	...	...	101	47	54	11	8	3	...	...	...	XIII
...	...	...	98	43	55	27	19	8	...	...	...	...	...	...	49	28	21	XIV
...	...	...	1	1	...	2	...	2	15	7	8	...	...	...	...	...	...	XV
...	...	...	20	16	4	...	...	...	13	6	7	...	...	...	...	...	...	XVI
...	...	...	72	71	1	37	28	9	1	1	...	...	...	...	...	...	...	XVII
...	...	...	...	...	...	...	...	...	...	...	...	...	...	...	...	...	...	XVIII
...	...	...	2	2	...	...	...	...	7	3	4	...	...	...	...	...	...	XIX
5	5	...	...	...	...	...	...	...	11	6	5	...	...	...	...	...	...	XX
6	2	4	38	26	12	...	...	...	7	4	3	8	6	2	...	...	...	XXI
15	13	2	9	9	...	7	3	4	...	...	...	...	...	...	...	...	...	XXII
6	4	2	164	164	...	1	1	...	...	...	...	...	...	...	...	...	...	XXIII
...	...	...	...	...	...	...	...	...	...	...	...	...	...	...	...	...	...	XXIV
10	4	6	1	1	...	1	1	...	...	...	...	15	11	4	59	53	6	XXV
708	393	315	2,145	1,735	410	493	311	182	1,387	683	704	166	123	43	108	81	27	Total population of Calcutta.
...	...	...	...	...	...	...	...	...	...	...	...	...	...	...	179	179	...	Fort William.
...	...	...	...	...	...	...	...	...	...	...	...	...	...	...	...	...	...	Canals.
...	...	...	54	54	...	1	1	...	12	9	3	...	...	...	...	...	...	Port of Calcutta.
...	...	...	54	54	...	1	1	...	12	9	3	...	...	...	...	...	...	Port and Canals.

TABLE V.—AGES BY RE

WARD No.	TOTAL POPULATION.			AGE					
	Total.	Males.	Females.	Under 1 year.		1 Year.		2 Years.	
				Males.	Females.	Males.	Females.	Males.	Females.
1	2	3	4	5	6	7	8	9	10
I	30,995	17,457	13,538	309	261	185	181	253	272
II	25,482	15,180	10,302	198	182	128	110	156	151
III	27,658	15,813	11,845	325	241	150	152	238	265
IV	26,612	15,452	11,160	206	176	254	184	260	233
V	36,711	24,236	12,475	114	128	152	112	169	184
VI	34,043	20,138	13,905	304	280	214	233	302	295
VII	13,925	10,946	2,979	119	81	28	22	55	36
VIII	22,153	15,449	6,704	174	117	103	78	123	147
IX	31,513	20,277	11,236	252	220	191	148	222	216
X	8,515	6,265	2,250	54	43	83	36	56	39
XI	17,997	11,121	6,876	121	145	96	68	128	122
XII	3,498	3,440	58	3	3	3	1	2	...
XIII	14,366	11,801	2,565	42	52	38	27	73	70
XIV	10,609	7,134	3,475	56	53	82	66	104	84
XV	5,144	3,749	1,395	24	17	31	25	42	32
XVI	2,088	1,918	170	1	6	2	3	5	7
XVII	2,662	2,107	555	18	4	13	6	17	19
XVIII	3,072	2,221	851	7	30	17	19	38	31
XIX	20,491	12,720	7,771	200	170	151	131	226	228
XX	9,798	6,327	3,471	73	75	109	65	97	93
XXI	11,919	7,077	4,842	128	134	77	58	126	95
XXII	34,741	19,477	15,264	435	371	248	214	316	332
XXIII	10,602	6,763	3,839	105	89	27	30	80	94
XXIV	6,029	3,611	2,418	41	37	38	37	71	80
XXV	18,139	11,753	6,386	158	121	139	60	152	136
Total ...	428,762	272,432	156,330	3,467	3,036	2,509	2,066	3,311	3,261
Fort William ...	1,441	1,333	108	4	4	2	3	3	3
Port and Canals ...	13,934	13,858	76	6	2	3	...	4	...

LIGIONS—PART A.—*Hindus.*

PERIODS.										
3 Years.		4 Years.		Total 0—4.		5—9.		10—14.		WARD No.
Males.	Females.	Males.	Females.	Males.	Females.	Males.	Females.	Males.	Females.	
11	12	13	14	15	16	17	18	19	20	
258	312	258	243	1,263	1,269	1,267	1,145	1,380	961	I
204	170	176	148	862	761	960	818	1,120	618	II
294	267	203	123	1,210	1,048	1,265	1,150	1,301	848	III
328	218	280	244	1,328	1,055	1,074	1,158	1,419	818	IV
172	195	178	156	785	775	832	752	1,178	661	V
343	341	344	280	1,507	1,429	1,253	1,119	1,542	1,025	VI
65	53	67	43	334	235	276	247	471	181	VII
170	151	153	130	723	623	617	584	963	515	VIII
276	233	248	215	1,189	1,032	1,275	1,061	1,602	922	IX
46	51	65	47	254	216	264	250	386	182	X
147	146	157	149	649	630	817	660	828	526	XI
3	...	5	2	16	6	19	5	59	5	XII
56	59	86	63	295	271	297	232	643	218	XIII
96	92	132	70	470	365	454	398	613	342	XIV
39	27	40	33	176	134	172	140	209	125	XV
8	6	2	4	13	26	22	12	64	8	XVI
15	14	14	21	77	64	80	30	92	65	XVII
28	35	26	42	116	157	120	48	122	76	XVIII
248	213	222	162	1,047	904	830	716	834	557	XIX
83	117	97	98	459	448	381	317	653	296	XX
100	123	102	83	533	493	505	439	512	338	XXI
379	365	363	311	1,741	1,693	1,585	1,500	1,809	1,254	XXII
95	89	77	56	384	358	346	298	465	280	XXIII
74	81	46	68	270	303	311	281	304	227	XXIV
170	160	151	154	770	631	733	679	836	510	XXV
3,692	3,518	3,492	2,945	16,471	14,826	15,755	14,099	19,205	11,558	Total
3	2	3	2	14	15	20	9	50	7	Fort William
5	1	6	...	24	3	41	4	536	5	Port and Canals.

TABLE V.—AGES BY RE

WARD No.	AGE 15–19. Males.	15–19. Females.	20–24. Males.	20–24. Females.	25–29. Males.	25–29. Females.	30–34. Males.	30–34. Females.	35–39. Males.	35–39. Females.
	21	22	23	24	25	26	27	28	29	30
I	1,431	1,083	1,987	1,162	2,179	1,432	2,161	1,483	1,514	1,033
II	1,263	811	1,750	857	2,002	1,102	2,042	1,243	1,361	943
III	1,514	961	1,943	1,049	1,694	1,245	2,047	1,367	1,179	884
IV	1,491	859	1,896	968	1,716	1,036	1,872	1,172	1,192	823
V	1,606	896	2,690	1,375	3,626	1,787	3,772	1,711	2,946	1,191
VI	1,872	1,064	2,509	1,207	2,451	1,345	2,369	1,640	1,851	1,194
VII	798	225	1,376	350	1,848	414	1,712	265	1,160	285
VIII	1,239	458	2,039	557	2,327	748	1,928	849	1,617	465
IX	1,816	949	2,768	1,063	2,734	1,233	2,567	1,191	1,556	714
X	574	179	844	240	897	221	962	245	608	146
XI	1,010	600	1,392	655	1,462	673	1,555	761	963	533
XII	258	3	627	5	625	3	591	8	434	4
XIII	923	208	1,694	286	1,885	264	2,030	291	1,239	154
XIV	578	304	845	364	972	367	1,022	322	567	215
XV	229	113	406	144	613	193	665	134	334	95
XVI	115	12	288	25	350	12	375	12	204	15
XVII	105	69	315	65	401	49	343	67	204	43
XVIII	124	89	313	45	405	69	320	74	219	62
XIX	874	643	1,400	720	1,656	814	1,758	884	1,193	538
XX	608	269	802	336	884	341	694	367	497	174
XXI	532	360	741	453	871	449	864	518	587	344
XXII	1,750	1,218	2,069	1,336	2,117	1,464	2,201	1,525	1,440	1,042
XXIII	437	317	963	445	907	385	948	384	651	302
XXIV	224	191	332	219	443	251	470	229	316	150
XXV	899	506	1,509	637	1,507	632	1,535	681	1,025	412
Total ...	22,270	12,387	33,898	14,563	36,572	16,529	36,803	17,423	24,857	11,761
Fort William ...	74	5	267	15	286	19	228	14	177	5
Port and Canals ...	1,541	4	2,149	17	2,231	6	2,242	15	1,244	...

LIGIONS—PART A.—*Hindus.*

PERIODS.										
40—44.		45—49.		50—54.		55—59.		60 and over.		WARD NO.
Males.	Females.	Males.	Females.	Males.	Females.	Males.	Females.	Males.	Females.	
31	32	33	34	35	36	37	38	39	40	
1,646	1,207	791	657	802	813	333	332	703	961	I
1,395	1,042	698	494	778	654	354	242	595	717	II
1,418	1,124	623	415	759	737	256	242	604	775	III
1,274	906	637	511	685	693	335	403	533	758	IV
2,843	1,193	1,333	523	1,341	667	447	313	837	631	V
1,697	1,042	880	698	978	805	450	455	779	882	VI
1,190	258	643	165	570	156	179	53	389	145	VII
1,621	661	674	293	817	375	267	107	617	469	VIII
2,101	1,149	717	440	928	476	349	252	775	754	IX
667	186	230	73	284	111	85	47	210	154	X
1,046	640	394	272	470	359	180	162	355	405	XI
349	5	140	2	164	5	71	...	87	7	XII
1,434	220	472	105	476	135	216	42	297	139	XIII
678	249	275	96	327	175	101	71	237	207	XIV
375	109	147	28	185	54	57	25	181	101	XV
231	21	76	14	115	5	26	3	39	5	XVI
183	32	107	14	87	20	27	8	87	29	XVII
122	89	120	39	101	37	52	19	87	47	XVIII
1,237	668	550	309	585	415	208	153	548	450	XIX
589	249	249	122	278	195	105	77	228	220	XX
705	423	354	227	385	305	151	121	337	372	XXI
1,674	1,307	798	643	978	871	357	344	958	1,167	XXII
688	271	301	169	319	181	117	117	237	332	XXIII
360	123	171	66	153	123	78	66	179	189	XXIV
1,266	597	466	220	523	339	201	166	483	376	XXV
26,783	13,771	11,846	6,595	13,088	8,706	5,002	3,820	10,382	10,292	Total
84	7	53	...	44	6	16	2	20	4	Fort William.
1,148	14	684	5	698	3	766	...	554	...	Port and Canals.

TABLE V.—RELIGION *by* SEX *and*

WARD No.	TOTAL MUHAMMADANS.			Infant.		1		2	
	Total.	Males.	Females.	Males.	Females.	Males.	Females.	Males.	Females.
1	2	3	4	5	6	7	8	9	10
I	5,874	4,027	1,847	32	34	25	19	36	36
II	1,116	989	127	5	2	2	1	3	2
III	8,601	5,161	3,440	114	103	51	39	117	102
IV	7,732	4,942	2,790	68	48	69	45	88	76
V	2,112	1,958	154	5	...	...	3	...	4
VI	7,284	5,098	2,186	60	42	24	24	51	41
VII	5,294	4,356	938	13	8	9	5	13	9
VIII	24,696	17,636	7,060	200	103	178	157	181	116
IX	16,479	10,900	5,579	117	104	104	80	149	149
X	8,872	6,556	2,316	50	30	56	36	62	34
XI	1,172	839	333	3	2	2	2	5	3
XII	1,470	1,453	17	...	...	...	...	...	...
XIII	10,896	8,408	2,488	39	40	27	23	47	48
XIV	15,709	10,015	5,694	75	63	127	124	109	133
XV	6,536	4,349	2,187	36	33	48	32	55	59
XVI	1,517	1,206	311	11	5	7	6	7	13
XVII	1,210	980	230	...	4	4	1	7	8
XVIII	1,401	837	564	11	15	11	9	18	24
XIX	10,488	6,494	3,994	96	90	70	60	80	86
XX	12,643	6,984	5,659	133	123	169	126	182	173
XXI	10,303	5,547	4,756	120	91	136	120	129	122
XXII	6,829	4,220	2,609	71	47	43	43	70	64
XXIII	3,744	2,761	983	28	21	13	32	23	13
XXIV	8,931	4,514	4,417	99	87	64	71	121	121
XXV	8,317	5,361	2,956	72	54	69	35	70	86
Total ...	189,226	125,591	63,635	1,458	1,149	1,308	1,093	1,618	1,522
Fort William ...	597	555	42	4	1	1	...	3	...
Port and Canals ...	13,350	13,342	8	2	...	2	...	3	...

AGE—PART B.—*Muhammadans.*

AGE PERIODS. 3		4		Total 0—4.		5—9		10—14		WARD NO.
Males.	Females.	Males.	Females.	Males.	Females	Males.	Females.	Males.	Females.	
11	12	13	14	15	16	17	18	19	20	
49	50	42	34	184	173	260	220	244	135	I
4	2	5	3	19	10	23	10	34	3	II
139	93	131	101	552	438	503	416	490	269	III
80	70	93	76	398	315	309	313	351	182	IV
2	4	5	2	12	13	11	11	40	11	V
70	47	60	38	265	132	242	198	256	150	VI
19	19	20	16	74	57	142	76	272	70	VII
196	116	209	123	964	615	666	580	1,164	588	VIII
173	155	148	144	691	632	766	575	834	471	IX
46	62	47	49	261	201	289	264	470	163	X
7	6	15	3	32	16	25	34	66	32	XI
...	...	...	...	...	...	9	1	26	...	XII
57	50	65	81	235	242	278	186	501	188	XIII
174	132	141	128	626	580	571	596	807	486	XIV
64	62	75	54	278	240	300	240	330	188	XV
12	14	6	4	43	42	39	42	39	26	XVI
8	3	5	10	24	26	18	11	39	28	XVII
20	16	15	27	70	91	74	72	75	54	XVIII
146	96	94	96	486	428	436	364	542	303	XIX
203	182	172	180	859	784	729	637	685	508	XX
145	133	105	104	635	570	666	587	535	408	XXI
86	65	61	75	331	294	392	305	398	255	XXII
23	23	22	22	109	111	125	106	212	92	XXIII
114	123	115	96	513	498	605	516	435	444	XXIV
97	76	63	69	371	320	314	290	444	231	XXV
1,934	1,589	1,714	1,535	8,032	6,888	7 794	6,650	9,298	5,284	Total.
2	...	1	...	11	1	4	4	16	6	Fort William.
2	...	11	...	20	...	29	...	427	1	Port and Canals.

TABLE V.—RELIGION *by* SEX *and*

WARD No.	AGE 15—19. Males.	15—19. Females.	20—24. Males.	20—24. Females.	25—29. Males.	25—29. Females.	30—34. Males.	30—34. Females.	35—39. Males.	35—39. Females.
	19	20	21	22	23	24	25	26	27	28
I	295	166	359	200	548	224	743	245	376	114
II	69	10	132	13	161	12	183	14	95	14
III	296	239	513	380	597	388	579	411	347	152
IV	334	194	492	284	594	297	669	284	395	211
V	206	23	264	10	[illegible]	19	298	24	202	14
VI	359	168	516	250	597	264	836	272	511	165
VII	366	78	554	85	793	97	635	114	489	79
VIII	1,276	647	1,990	786	2,280	871	2,626	777	1,815	490
IX	856	384	1,129	630	1,349	571	1,425	651	887	306
X	651	194	883	240	787	228	914	248	625	173
XI	53	40	98	50	122	20	159	36	69	13
XII	81	...	190	1	248	3	323	1	251	4
XIII	806	196	1,005	293	1,264	321	1,306	347	919	154
XIV	948	434	1,278	572	1,214	488	1,209	619	647	346
XV	382	151	527	200	481	185	561	241	434	112
XVI	71	25	156	34	210	27	230	34	111	15
XVII	107	22	128	37	174	26	135	13	104	15
XVIII	62	57	101	49	93	43	110	49	88	22
XIX	432	324	651	424	752	442	855	475	577	239
XX	506	448	587	453	654	514	661	571	424	302
XXI	372	347	472	459	489	454	536	439	350	282
XXII	269	200	434	255	433	259	499	266	291	114
XXIII	205	46	396	90	392	96	431	109	231	57
XXIV	285	395	329	441	435	424	425	397	295	184
XXV	394	193	635	343	646	345	666	327	520	145
Total ...	9,681	4,981	13,819	6,579	15,596	6,618	17,014	6,964	11,058	3,722
Fort William ...	37	6	112	3	119	8	105	5	63	1
Port and Canals ...	1,741	1	2,075	...	1,985	3	2,524	...	1,698	2

Age—Part B.—*Muhammadans.*

PERIODS—*contd.*

40—44.		45—49.		50—54.		55—59.		60 and over.		Ward No.
Males.	Females.	Males.	Females.	Males.	Females.	Males.	Females.	Males.	Females.	
29	30	31	32	33	34	35	36	37	38	
467	148	186	69	196	66	58	23	111	64	I
126	14	51	4	46	10	13	...	37	13	II
522	274	182	53	273	152	56	35	251	233	III
527	239	214	75	284	121	181	116	194	159	IV
263	15	96	6	113	4	94	...	[illegible]76	4	V
631	172	226	75	280	126	104	39	275	115	VI
476	103	186	39	186	68	51	17	132	55	VII
1,958	633	824	230	980	270	214	177	877	396	VIII
1,313	500	421	153	537	276	159	76	533	364	IX
642	193	243	64	305	123	155	69	322	157	X
67	36	37	10	71	23	10	5	30	18	XI
196	1	44	1	57	...	9	4	19	1	XII
963	205	339	51	406	132	114	24	272	149	XIII
1,068	466	269	183	505	310	165	74	608	540	XIV
441	209	145	62	194	131	52	33	224	195	XV
148	21	50	5	53	14	11	9	45	17	XVI
89	25	35	7	29	12	74	2	24	6	XVII
46	32	33	24	30	25	20	17	35	29	XVIII
712	339	247	116	377	187	112	64	315	289	XIX
698	485	248	201	371	308	105	73	457	375	XX
530	351	201	145	259	243	100	89	402	382	XXI
481	218	146	82	252	124	55	43	239	194	XXII
262	104	127	45	114	56	35	19	122	52	XXIII
394	323	179	134	227	201	72	76	320	384	XXIV
470	257	211	87	242	170	164	55	284	193	XXV
13,490	5,363	5,040	1,921	6,387	3,152	2,183	1,139	6,204	4,374	Total.
32	3	20	1	16	3	4	1	9	...	Fort William.
1,058	1	570	...	475	...	467	...	323	...	Port and Canals.

TABLE V.—PART

WARD No.	TOTAL POPULATION.			AGE					
	Total.	Males.	Females.	Under 1 year.		1		2	
				Males.	Females.	Males.	Females.	Males.	Females.
1	2	3	4	5	6	7	8	9	10
I	16	6	9	1	...	...	...	...	1
II	4	3	1	...	...	...	...	...	...
III	127	17	110	...	...	...	...	...	...
IV	371	188	183	4	7	3	7	3	4
V	55	32	23	2	...	2	...	1	1
VI	177	70	107	2	1	...	...	5	...
VII	561	419	142	5	3	5	2	5	3
VIII	2,628	1,338	1,290	30	36	30	19	35	21
IX	1,280	677	603	13	3	8	14	9	12
X	4,320	2,360	1,960	34	47	26	38	52	44
XI	1,559	735	824	13	15	14	11	18	11
XII	978	577	401	7	11	7	9	11	17
XIII	2,931	1,519	1,412	32	21	23	12	29	25
XIV	2,715	1,340	1,375	31	26	26	9	24	60
XV	1 520	791	729	12	11	8	19	15	21
XVI	982	579	403	6	4	5	8	6	4
XVII	616	365	251	6	3	3	3	2	4
XVIII	347	180	167	7	7	6	2	5	5
XIX	2,159	824	1,335	28	30	16	15	20	15
XX	563	299	264	8	9	10	6	9	9
XXI	550	356	194	7	5	4	...	5	6
XXII	990	510	480	15	7	9	11	18	10
XXIII	287	161	126	3	2	2	2	13	4
XXIV	380	172	208	2	6	6	3	8	7
XXV	291	172	119	5	3	2	3	5	2
Total ...	26,406	13,690	12,716	273	257	215	193	293	286
Fort William ...	1,252	1,052	199	10	12	6	9	8	8
Port and Canals ...	1,340	1,324	16	2	1	...	...	2	...

C.—*Christians.*

PERIODS.										
3		4		Total 0–4.		5–9		10–14		WARD No.
Males.	Females.	Males.	Females.	Males.	Females.	Males.	Females.	Males.	Females.	
11	12	13	14	15	16	17	18	19	20	
1	...	...	...	2	1	...	1	...	...	I
...	...	...	...	...	...	...	...	...	...	II
...	...	1	16	1	16	...	6	2	53	III
6	5	2	1	18	24	10	7	11	8	IV
1	...	...	1	6	2	1	3	2	1	V
...	5	3	4	10	10	4	11	2	31	VI
2	2	3	4	20	14	41	20	112	9	VII
50	43	53	38	198	157	87	141	131	86	VIII
19	13	11	15	60	57	87	81	75	44	IX
44	56	53	50	209	235	240	210	275	190	X
22	20	18	15	80	72	77	135	75	80	XI
13	9	10	9	48	55	17	39	23	23	XII
40	22	45	46	169	126	155	160	229	193	XIII
29	38	43	37	153	170	167	142	143	157	XIV
12	14	24	14	71	79	82	73	108	67	XV
8	6	5	6	30	28	43	24	40	40	XVI
3	4	4	3	18	17	20	16	76	31	XVII
5	7	4	6	27	27	21	11	11	10	XVIII
15	26	16	31	95	117	107	230	88	298	XIX
8	8	7	9	42	41	30	41	21	24	XX
15	5	8	4	39	20	34	16	61	16	XXI
14	3	11	10	67	41	37	67	37	51	XXII
4	13	3	1	25	22	4	5	24	11	XXIII
2	3	9	4	27	23	53	10	14	22	XXIV
2	3	3	5	17	16	11	10	12	12	XXV
315	306	336	329	1,432	1,370	1,328	1,459	1,572	1,457	Total.
9	9	8	10	41	48	29	24	10	17	Fort William.
...	1	1	...	5	2	3	2	4	1	Port and Canals.

TABLE V.—PART

WARD No.	AGE									
	15—19		20—24		25—29		30—34		35—39	
	Males.	Females.	Males.	Females.	Males.	Females.	Males.	Females.	Males.	Females.
	19	20	21	22	23	24	25	26	27	28
I	...	...	...	2	1	1	...	...	1	2
II	...	...	...	...	2	...	...	1	1	...
III	1	16	...	5	5	3	4	8	1	2
IV	13	42	16	19	9	13	35	12	14	19
V	3	...	3	1	2	7	3	3	4	1
VI	10	14	6	12	8	5	10	4	6	13
VII	5	7	14	19	48	20	58	11	54	15
VIII	142	126	149	136	105	128	118	88	83	94
IX	31	91	61	61	139	72	56	48	33	34
X	286	234	225	167	265	170	250	165	144	102
XI	55	124	67	88	81	70	84	69	51	33
XII	20	35	67	46	102	59	76	38	64	32
XIII	156	142	126	162	140	119	153	128	77	86
XIV	151	133	112	124	113	156	107	117	91	87
XV	120	128	75	75	58	76	42	41	40	31
XVI	39	52	74	53	69	53	66	37	53	31
XVII	33	32	36	20	43	86	30	19	27	18
XVIII	16	21	17	16	18	10	20	13	7	16
XIX	67	147	73	105	79	93	58	71	63	57
XX	24	23	24	29	40	19	31	18	24	22
XXI	51	11	22	28	32	23	35	16	27	15
XXII	44	48	55	55	64	34	62	45	38	28
XXIII	8	20	6	8	15	20	31	11	10	5
XXIV	15	40	12	29	13	22	3	18	9	15
XXV	16	11	8	11	21	18	26	7	21	8
Total ...	1,306	1,497	1,248	1,271	1,472	1,282	1,358	983	943	766
Fort William ...	99	12	345	27	299	30	118	20	90	10
Port and Canals ...	188	5	191	...	216	2	210	...	178	...

C.—*Christians*—concld.

PERIODS—contd. 40—44 Males.	40—44 Females.	45—49 Males.	45—49 Females.	50—54 Males.	50—54 Females.	55—59 Males.	55—59 Females.	60 and over. Males.	60 and over. Females.	WARD No.
29	30	31	32	33	34	35	36	37	38	
2	2	...	...	...	...	...	...	...	...	I
...	...	...	...	...	...	...	...	...	...	II
1	2	...	2	1	1	1	1	...	...	III
35	15	8	16	14	2	2	2	3	4	IV
2	4	5	1	1	...	...	...	...	...	V
3	3	5	3	2	...	4	1	...	...	VI
22	6	14	3	11	6	6	5	14	7	VII
70	64	49	71	58	55	65	50	83	94	VIII
35	44	27	32	31	17	16	6	26	16	IX
124	178	81	120	89	94	46	41	126	54	X
54	47	32	19	29	29	16	20	34	38	XI
47	25	41	24	36	9	21	7	15	9	XII
104	81	77	49	52	51	30	23	51	92	XIII
107	83	53	40	48	52	27	27	68	87	XIV
57	40	47	25	34	30	15	14	42	50	XV
55	30	42	23	38	14	19	5	11	13	XVI
24	20	29	11	14	10	2	7	13	14	XVII
18	11	5	11	9	6	11	6	8	9	XVIII
62	47	40	43	33	32	26	41	33	54	XIX
13	14	10	11	18	8	10	6	12	8	XX
15	12	16	4	11	10	4	8	9	10	XXI
27	35	16	19	22	27	13	13	28	17	XXII
19	9	8	9	7	1	1	...	3	5	XXIII
11	10	5	6	5	7	3	4	2	2	XXIV
17	6	10	2	5	5	5	4	3	9	XXV
924	788	620	544	563	466	343	291	576	592	Total.
13	4	3	1	5	...	...	4	...	2	Fort William.
174	...	89	1	50	...	28	...	38	...	Port and Canals.

Table V.—Religion by sex *and*

Ward No.	Total Population.			Under 1 year.		1		2	
	Total.	Males.	Females.	Males.	Females.	Males.	Females.	Males.	Females.
1	2	3	4	5	6	7	8	9	10
II	8	4	4	...	...	...	...	...	...
III	35	20	15	1	1	1	1	1	1
IV	91	39	52	4	2	2	4	...	3
V	1	1	...	...	...	...	...	...	...
VI	138	57	81	...	3	...	...	...	3
VIII	154	92	62	4	...	...	...	3	1
IX	174	111	63	...	...	...	1	1	2
X	43	26	17	1	1	1	1	1	1
XI	17	11	6	...	...	...	...	...	...
XII	1	1	...	...	...	...	...	...	...
XIII	4	3	1	...	...	...	...	...	...
XX	5	5	...	...	...	...	...	...	...
XXI	6	2	4	...	...	...	1	...	1
XXII	15	13	2	...	...	...	...	...	...
XXIII	6	4	2	1	...	1	1	...	...
XXV	10	4	6	...	...	...	...	...	1
Total ...	708	393	315	11	7	5	9	6	13

AGE.—PART D.—*Brahmo.*

Age periods.										
3		4		Total 0—4.		5—9.		10 - 14.		Ward No.
Males.	Females.	Males.	Females.	Males.	Females.	Males.	Females.	Males.	Females.	
11	12	13	14	15	16	17	18	19	20	
...	...	...	...	...	...	...	1	...	..	II
2	...	...	2	5	5	1	...	1	2	III
4	2	2	1	12	12	2	...	1	11	IV
...	...	...	...	...	...	...	...	...	...	V
4	1	3	2	7	9	8	6	4	26	VI
4	1	8	1	19	3	6	20	6	4	VIII
2	1	5	12	8	16	25	2	9	11	IX
1	...	1	...	5	3	...	...	1	1	X
...	...	...	...	...	...	2	2	3	..	XI
...	...	...	...	...	...	...	...	...	...	XII
...	...	...	...	...	...	...	...	...	...	XIII
...	...	...	...	...	...	...	...	...	...	XX
...	...	...	...	...	2	...	...	...	...	XXI
1	...	1	...	2	...	1	...	1	...	XXII
...	...	1	...	3	1	...	1	...	...	XXIII
1	...	1	...	2	1	...	1	...	1	XXV
19	5	22	18	63	52	45	33	26	56	Total

TABLE V.—RELIGION BY SEX *and*

WARD No.	15—19.		20—24.		25—29.		30—34.		35—39.	
	Males.	Females.	Males.	Females.	Males.	Females.	Males.	Females.	Males.	Females.
	19	20	21	22	23	24	25	26	27	28
II	...	...	...	2	...	...	3	...	...	...
III	1	2	2	...	3	4	3	...	2	...
IV	...	12	7	5	7	4	2	6	3	...
V	1	...	...	...	...	...	...	...	...	...
VI	7	10	4	4	6	4	9	6	3	5
VIII	25	7	2	7	8	12	10	2	...	1
IX	10	6	13	4	3	4	16	8	11	7
X	2	2	1	2	2	1	6	1	4	1
XI	...	...	1	...	...	...	2	3	1	1
XII	...	...	...	...	...	...	1	...	...	...
XIII	...	...	...	...	2	...	...	1	1	...
XX	2	...	1	...	2	...	...	...	...	...
XXI	...	...	...	1	...	1	1	...	...	...
XXII	2	...	2	...	1	2	...	...	1	...
XXIII	...	...	1	...	...	...	...	...	...	...
XXV	...	...	...	1	...	2	1	...	...	...
Total ...	50	39	34	26	34	34	54	27	26	15

AGE.—PART D.—*Brahmo*—concld.

Age periods—*concld.*										Ward No.
40—44.		45—49.		50—54.		55—59.		60 and over.		
Males.	Females.	Males.	Females.	Males.	Females.	Males.	Females.	Males.	Females.	
29	30	31	32	33	34	35	36	37	38	
1	1	...	...	...	...	...	...	...	...	II
2	2	...	...	...	...	...	...	...	...	III
3	...	1	...	1	1	...	1	...	...	IV
...	...	...	...	...	...	...	...	...	...	V
3	7	1	1	3	3	1	...	1	...	VI
11	3	2	1	2	2	1	...	...	...	VIII
13	4	...	...	2	1	1	...	...	...	IX
1	1	3	1	...	1	1	1	...	2	X
2	...	...	...	...	...	...	...	...	...	XI
...	...	...	...	...	...	...	...	...	...	XII
...	...	...	...	...	...	...	...	...	...	XIII
...	...	...	...	...	...	...	...	...	...	XX
1	...	...	...	...	...	...	...	...	...	XXI
1	...	2	...	...	...	...	...	...	...	XXII
...	...	...	...	...	...	...	...	...	...	XXIII
...	...	...	...	...	...	1	...	...	...	XXV
38	18	9	3	8	8	5	2	1	2	Total.

Table V.—Religion by Sex and

Ward No.	Total Population.			Under 1 year.		1		2	
	Total.	Males.	Females.	Males.	Females.	Males.	Females.	Males.	Females.
1	2	3	4	5	6	7	8	9	10
V	1	1	...	...	...	...	...	...	...
VII	85	69	16	1	...	1	...	1	...
VIII	616	544	72	5	5	3	...	4	1
IX	10	5	5	1	...	1	...	...	...
X	850	639	211	7	3	5	3	5	5
XI	9	4	5	1	...	...	1	...	...
XII	112	97	15	1	...	1	1	...	...
XIII	57	43	14	...	...	...	1	...	...
XIV	98	43	55	1	...	...	1	1	2
XV	1	1	...	...	...	...	...	...	...
XVI	20	16	4	...	...	...	...	...	...
XVII	72	71	1	...	...	...	...	...	...
XIX	2	2	...	...	...	...	...	...	...
XXI	38	26	12	...	1	...	3	...	...
XXII	9	9	...	...	...	...	...	...	...
XXIII	164	164	...	...	...	...	...	...	...
XXV	1	1	...	...	...	...	...	...	...
Total ...	2,145	1,735	410	17	9	11	10	11	8
Port and Canals	54	54	...	...	...	...	...	...	...

Age.—Part E.—*Buddhists.*

Age periods. 3 Males.	3 Females.	4 Males.	4 Females.	Total 0—4. Males.	Total 0—4. Females.	5—9 Males.	5—9 Females.	10—14 Males.	10—14 Females.	Ward No.
11	12	13	14	15	16	17	18	19	20	
...	...	...	...	...	...	...	...	...	...	V
1	...	...	1	4	1	1	1	1	7	VII
3	3	5	1	20	10	12	12	18	3	VIII
...	...	...	...	2	...	...	1	1	2	IX
4	5	6	8	27	24	25	13	43	17	X
...	...	...	...	1	1	...	...	...	...	XI
1	...	1	1	4	2	3	4	4	2	XII
...	...	...	...	...	1	2	1	1	2	XIII
2	3	1	...	5	6	3	7	4	7	XIV
...	...	...	...	...	...	...	...	...	...	XV
...	...	...	2	...	2	4	...	5	...	XVI
...	...	...	...	...	...	2	...	...	...	XVII
...	...	...	...	...	...	...	...	...	...	XIX
...	1	1	...	1	5	2	...	5	..	XXI
...	...	...	...	...	...	...	...	...	...	XXII
...	...	...	...	...	...	...	...	1	...	XXIII
...	...	...	...	...	...	...	...	...	...	XXV
11	12	14	13	64	52	54	39	83	40	Total.
...	...	...	...	...	...	...	...	...	...	Port and Canals.

TABLE V.—RELIGION BY SEX *and*

Ward No.	Age									
	15–19		20–24		25–29		30–34		35–39	
	Males.	Females.	Males.	Females.	Males.	Females.	Males.	Females.	Males.	Females.
	19	20	21	22	23	24	25	26	27	28
V	...	...	1	...	...	...	...	...	...	...
VII	8	3	9	...	9	...	9	...	9	...
VIII	59	7	55	6	77	7	70	5	59	2
IX	...	...	1	...	...	1	1	...	...	...
X	74	18	79	22	101	31	94	19	56	6
XI	...	1	...	1	...	2	1	...	...	...
XII	9	1	19	1	17	2	12	1	9	2
XIII	4	2	7	...	5	2	7	...	2	2
XIV	3	5	6	3	4	8	5	4	5	4
XV	...	...	...	...	...	...	1	...	...	...
XVI	3	2	...	...	...	...	4	...	...	...
XVII	5	1	9	...	12	...	11	...	14	...
XIX	...	...	...	...	...	...	...	...	...	...
XXI	4	...	2	1	...	1	6	2	4	2
XXII	2	...	1	...	1	...	...	...	1	...
XXIII	4	...	68	...	33	...	40	...	3	...
XXV	...	...	...	...	...	...	1	...	...	...
Total ...	175	40	252	34	259	54	262	31	162	18
Port and Canals ...	6	...	13	...	5	...	17	...	8	...

Age.—Part E.—*Buddhists.*

PERIODS—*concld.*

40—44		45—49		50—54		55—59		60 and over.		Ward No.
Males.	Females.	Males.	Females.	Males.	Females.	Males.	Females.	Males.	Females.	
29	30	31	32	33	34	35	36	37	38	
...	...	...	...	...	...	...	...	...	...	V
4	1	3	1	2	1	2	1	8	...	VII
46	3	34	7	45	4	18	1	31	5	VIII
...	1	...	...	...	...	...	..	...	...	IX
48	19	33	8	32	15	17	10	10	9	X
2	...	...	...	...	...	...	...	...	...	XI
12	...	...	...	4	...	...	...	4	...	XII
3	...	4	2	4	2	2	...	2	...	XIII
5	3	...	1	3	1	...	2	...	4	XIV
...	...	...	...	...	...	...	...	...	...	XV
...	...	...	...	...	...	...	...	...	...	XVI
16	...	1	...	1	...	...	...	...	...	XVII
...	...	2	...	...	...	...	...	...	...	XIX
2	1	...	...	...	...	...	...	...	...	XXI
2	...	1	...	1	...	...	...	...	...	XXII
19	...	...	...	...	...	...	...	1	...	XXIII
...	...	...	...	...	...	...	...	...	...	XXV
169	28	78	19	92	23	39	14	56	18	Total.
5	...	...	...	...	...	...	...	...	...	Port and Canals.

Table V.—Religion by Sex

Ward No.	Total Population.			Under 1 year.		1		2	
	Total.	Males.	Females.	Males.	Females.	Males.	Females.	Males.	Females.
1	2	3	4	5	6	7	8	9	10
I	1	1	...	...	...	...	...	...	...
II	4	2	2	...	...	...	...	...	...
III	2	2	...	...	...	...	...	...	...
V	294	179	115	3	1	2	1	2	1
VI	15	7	8	...	...	...	...	...	...
VII	60	51	9	2	1	...	1	1	...
VIII	13	6	7	...	...	...	...	...	...
IX	16	6	10	...	...	...	...	...	...
X	13	5	8	...	...	...	...	...	...
XIV	27	19	8	...	...	...	...	...	...
XV	2	...	2	...	...	...	...	...	...
XVII	37	28	9	...	...	...	...	...	...
XXII	7	3	4	...	1	...	...	...	...
XXIII	1	1	...	...	...	...	...	...	...
XXV	1	1	...	...	...	...	...	...	...
Total ...	493	311	182	5	3	2	2	3	1
Port and Canals ...	1	1	...	...	...	...	...	...	...

and Age.—Part F.—*Jains.*

Age Periods.										Ward No.
3		4		Total 0—4		5—9		10—14		
Males.	Females.	Males.	Females.	Males.	Females.	Males.	Females.	Males.	Females.	
11	12	13	14	15	16	17	18	19	20	
...	...	...	...	...	...	...	...	...	...	I
...	...	...	...	...	...	...	2	1	...	II
...	...	...	...	...	...	...	...	...	...	III
2	2	3	2	12	7	6	13	17	9	V
...	...	...	...	...	...	2	1	...	...	VI
...	...	...	...	3	2	...	...	2	...	VII
2	...	...	...	2	...	1	...	...	...	VIII
...	...	...	...	...	...	2	1	1	2	IX
...	...	...	1	...	1	2	...	1	2	X
...	...	...	...	...	...	...	2	...	1	XIV
...	...	...	...	...	...	...	...	...	...	XV
...	...	1	...	1	...	...		3	1	XVII
...	...	...	...	...	1	...	1	...	...	XXII
...	...	...	...	...	...	...	...	...	...	XXIII
...	...	...	...	...	...	...	...	...	...	XXV
4	2	4	3	18	11	13	20	25	15	Total.
...	...	...	...	...	...	...	...	...	...	Port and Canals.

Table V.—Religion by Sex

Ward No.	Age									
	15—19		20—24		25—29		30—34		35—39	
	Males.	Females.	Males.	Females.	Males.	Females.	Males.	Females.	Males.	Females.
	19	20	21	22	23	24	25	26	27	28
I	...	...	...	...	...	...	1	...	...	...
II	...	...	...	...	...	...	1	...	...	...
III	...	...	1	...	...	...	1	...	...	...
V	33	18	10	18	22	14	24	14	15	10
VI	2	2	2	1	...	3	1	1	...	...
VII	7	...	9	...	3	3	4	...	1	...
VIII	...	3	1	1	...	1	...	...	...	...
IX	...	...	...	...	...	...	2	5	1	...
X	...	1	2	...	...	...	...	2	...	...
XIV	...	...	...	...	5	...	7	3	...	...
XV	...	...	...	...	...	...	...	1	...	...
XVII	7	2	2	1	1	1	3	2	1	1
XXII	...	2	...	...	...	...	3	...	...	...
XXIII	1	...	...	...	...	...	...	...	...	...
XXV	1	...	...	...	...	...	...	...	...	...
Total ...	51	28	27	21	31	22	47	28	18	11
Port and Canals ...	...	...	...	...	...	...	...	...	...	...

and AGE.—PART F.—*Jains*—concld.

PERIODS—*concld.*										
40—44		45—49		50—54		55—59		60 and over.		WARD No.
Males.	Females.	Males.	Females.	Males.	Females.	Males.	Females.	Males.	Females.	
29	30	31	32	33	34	35	36	37	38	
...	...	...	...	...	...	...	...	...	...	I
...	...	...	...	...	...	...	...	...	...	II
...	...	...	...	...	...	...	...	...	...	III
11	11	11	1	10	...	7	...	1	...	V
...	...	...	...	...	...	...	...	...	...	VI
11	2	10	...	1	...	...	1	...	1	VII
2	2	...	...	...	...	...	...	...	...	VIII
...	1	...	...	...	...	...	...	...	1	IX
...	2	...	...	...	...	...	...	...	...	X
7	2	...	...	...	...	...	...	...	...	XIV
...	1	...	...	...	...	...	...	...	...	XV
4	1	2	...	2	...	2	...	...	...	XVII
...	..	...	...	...	...	...	...	...	...	XXII
...	...	...	...	...	...	...	...	...	...	XXIII
...	...	...	...	...	...	...	...	...	...	XXV
35	22	23	1	13	...	9	1	1	2	Total.
...	...	...	...	...	...	...	...	...	...	Port and Canals.

TABLE V.—RELIGION BY SEX

WARD No.	TOTAL POPULATION.			Infant.		1		2	
	Total.	Males.	Females.	Males.	Females.	Males.	Females.	Males.	Females.
1	2	3	4	5	6	7	8	9	10
V	6	4	2	...	...	...	...	...	...
VII	638	320	318	10	7	6	5	7	5
VIII	521	250	271	8	11	5	10	5	9
X	48	24	24	2	1	...	...	1	...
XI	7	5	2	1	...	...	...	...	...
XII	12	6	6	...	...	1	...	...	...
XIII	101	47	54	2	1	1	...	1	1
XV	15	7	8	1	...	...	1	...	...
XVI	13	6	7	...	1	...	...	...	...
XVII	1	1	...	...	...	...	...	...	...
XIX	7	3	4	...	...	...	...	...	...
XX	11	6	5	...	...	...	...	...	...
XXI	7	4	3	...	1	...	...	...	...
Total ...	1,387	683	704	24	22	13	16	14	15
Port and Canals	12	9	3	1	...	...	...	...	...

and AGE.—PART G —*Jews.*

AGE PERIODS.										
3		4		Total 0—4.		5—9		10 – 14		WARD NO.
Males.	Females.	Males.	Females.	Males.	Females.	Males.	Females.	Males.	Females.	
11	12	13	14	15	16	17	18	19	20	
...	...	...	...	...	...	1	...	...	1	V
8	6	9	4	40	27	42	54	48	26	VII
7	8	5	10	30	48	32	30	32	28	VIII
...	1	...	2	3	4	2	5	1	...	X
...	...	...	...	1	...	1	...	...	...	XI
...	...	...	...	1	...	1	...	...	...	XII
1	...	...	2	5	4	...	2	8	6	XIII
...	...	...	...	1	1	2	1	...	...	XV
1	...	...	1	1	2	...	...	...	1	XVI
...	...	...	...	...	...	...	...	...	...	XVII
...	...	1	...	1	...	...	...	1	...	XIX
...	...	...	...	...	...	...	...	1	...	XX
1	...	...	...	1	1	...	1	...	...	XXI
18	15	15	19	84	87	81	93	91	62	Total.
...	...	...	...	1	...	2	...	1	...	Port and Canals.

TABLE V.—RELIGION BY SEX

WARD No.	AGE 15—19		20—24		25—29		30—34		35—39	
	Males.	Females.	Males.	Females.	Males.	Females.	Males.	Females.	Males.	Females.
	19	20	21	22	23	24	25	26	27	28
V	1	1	1	...	...	...	...	...	...	...
VII	24	33	16	37	23	39	23	7	23	13
VIII	15	24	21	6	18	21	15	38	13	16
X	9	7	3	...	...	...	...	2	...	...
XI	2	2	...	...	...	...	...	...	...	...
XII	...	2	...	2	...	...	3	...	...	...
XIII	3	14	8	10	2	12	3	...	...	...
XV	...	3	...	2	...	...	2	...	...	...
XVI	5	...	...	...	...	...	...	1	...	2
XVII	...	...	...	...	...	...	1	...	...	...
XIX	...	...	...	...	...	...	...	3	...	1
XX	...	1	2	...	...	2	...	...	...	...
XXI	...	...	...	...	1	1	...	...	1	...
Total ...	59	87	51	57	44	75	47	51	37	32
Port and Canals ...	...	...	2	...	2	1	...	1	...	...

and AGE.—PART G.—*Jews.*

PERIODS—*concld.*										
40—44		45—49		50—54		55—59		60 and over.		WARD NO.
Males.	Females.	Males.	Females.	Males.	Females.	Males.	Females.	Males.	Females.	
29	30	31	32	33	34	35	36	37	38	
1	...	...	...	...	...	...	...	...	...	V
38	41	10	19	18	14	4	3	11	5	VII
8	14	16	13	12	13	26	13	12	7	VIII
...	6	2	...	4	...	...	...	...	...	X
1	...	...	...	...	...	...	...	...	...	XI
1	2	...	...	...	...	...	...	...	...	XII
10	2	7	...	...	1	1	3	...	...	XIII
...	...	...	...	2	...	...	...	...	1	XV
...	...	...	...	...	...	...	1	...	...	XVI
...	...	...	...	...	...	...	...	...	...	XVII
...	...	...	...	...	...	...	...	1	...	XIX
2	2	1	...	...	...	..	...	...	...	XX
1	...	...	...	...	...	...	...	...	...	XXI
63	67	36	32	36	28	31	20	24	13	Total.
...	...	1	...	...	...	...	1	...	...	Port and Canals.

Table V—Religion by Sex

Ward No.	Total Population.			Infants.		1		2		3		4		Total 0—4.		5—9		10—14		15—19	
	Total.	Males.	Females.	Males.	Females.	Males.	Females.	Males.	Females.	Males.	Females.	Males.	Females.	Males.	Females.	Males.	Females.	Males.	Females.	Males.	Females.
1	2	3	4	5	6	7	8	9	10	11	12	13	14	15	16	17	18	19	20	21	22
III	8	7	1	...	...	...	...	...	...	...	...	...	...	...	...	...	...	1	...	2	1
IV	22	12	10	...	...	...	...	...	...	...	...	...	...	...	...	2	1	1	1	5	3
VII	83	65	18	1	...	...	1	2	...	1	1	...	...	4	2	4	2	2	2	3	...
X	7	5	2	...	...	...	...	...	...	...	...	1	...	1	...	...	...	1	...	...	...
XII	12	9	3	...	...	...	...	...	...	...	...	...	...	...	...	...	...	1	1	2	...
XIII	11	8	3	...	...	...	...	...	...	...	...	...	...	...	...	...	...	1	...	...	...
XXI	8	6	2	...	...	...	...	1	...	...	...	...	...	1	...	1	...	...	...	1	...
XXV	15	11	4	...	..	...	...	...	...	1	...	...	...	1	...	1	...	3	...	...	...
Total ...	166	123	43	1	..	...	1	3	...	2	1	1	...	7	2	8	3	10	4	13	4

Table V—Religion by Sex

Ward No.	Total Population.			Infants.		1		2		3		4		Total 0—4.		5—9		10—14		15—19	
	Total.	Males.	Females.	Males.	Females.	Males.	Females.	Males.	Females.	Males.	Females.	Males.	Females.	Males.	Females.	Males.	Females.	Males.	Females.	Males.	Females.
XIV	49	28	21	1	2	...	1	2	...	1	...	1	2	5	5	3	2	5	1	2	4
XXV	59	53	6	1	1	...	...	...	...	...	...	...	...	1	1	2	1	...	...	5	1
Total ...	108	81	27	2	3	...	1	2	...	1	...	1	2	6	6	5	3	5	1	7	5
Fort William ...	179	179	...	...	...	...	...	...	...	...	...	...	...	...	...	1	...	1	...	42	...

and AGE.—PART H.—*Parsi.*

AGE PERIODS.

20—24		25—29		30—34		35—39		40—44		45—49		50—54		55—59		60 and over.		WARD NO.
Males.	Females.	Males.	Females.	Males.	Females.	Males.	Females.	Males.	Females.	Males.	Females.	Males.	Females.	Males.	Females.	Males.	Females.	
23	24	25	26	27	28	29	30	31	32	33	34	35	36	37	38	39	40	
1	...	1	...	1	...	...	...	1	...	...	...	...	...	...	...	...	...	III
...	...	...	1	...	1	2	...	2	3	...	...	...	...	...	...	...	...	IV
3	4	4	4	16	1	8	...	8	3	6	...	3	...	...	...	4	...	VII
...	1	1	...	...	...	1	...	...	...	1	1	...	...	...	...	...	...	X
1	...	...	1	3	...	...	...	...	1	...	...	...	...	1	...	1	...	XII
...	1	2	2	2	...	...	...	3	...	...	...	...	...	...	...	...	...	XIII
...	...	1	...	2	...	...	..	...	2	...	...	...	...	...	...	...	...	XXI
...	1	2	1	2	1	...	...	2	1	...	...	...	...	...	...	...	...	XXV
5	7	11	9	26	3	11	...	16	10	7	1	3	...	1	...	5	...	Total.

and AGE.—PART I.—*Sikhs.*

20—24		25—29		30—34		35—39		40—44		45—49		50—54		55—59		60 and over.		WARD NO.
Males.	Females.	Males.	Females.	Males.	Females.	Males.	Females.	Males.	Females.	Males.	Females.	Males.	Females.	Males.	Females.	Males.	Females.	
2	4	2	1	1	...	1	1	1	3	1	...	1	...	2	...	2	...	XIV
7	...	10	...	11	3	6	...	1	...	2	...	3	...	2	...	3	...	XXV
9	4	12	1	12	3	7	1	2	3	3	...	4	...	4	...	5	...	Total.
88	...	40	...	34	...	15	...	3	...	9	...	2	...	1	...	...	...	Fort William.

TABLE VI.—CIVIL CONDITION BY RELIGION

WARD No.	TOTAL UNMARRIED.			(1) UNMAR AGE- 0–4.		5–9.		10–14.		15–19.		20–24.	
	Total.	Males.	Females.	Males.	Females.	Males.	Females.	Males.	Females.	Males.	Females.	Males.	Females.
1	2	3	4	5	6	7	8	9	10	11	12	13	14
I	8,665	5,918	2,747	1,263	1,264	1,249	1,066	1,217	269	896	51	550	23
II	6,758	4,972	1,786	854	755	936	754	988	164	798	20	598	23
III	8,345	5,703	2,642	1,204	1,035	1,229	1,033	1,162	243	985	87	552	70
IV	8,417	5,913	2,504	1,328	1,036	1,054	1,077	1,263	263	960	17	589	10
V	7,249	5,286	1,963	779	768	822	716	984	237	869	45	718	31
VI	9,469	6,575	2,894	1,498	1,412	1,224	1,062	1,370	301	931	15	646	25
VII	2,937	2,366	571	334	234	259	230	359	44	389	5	339	4
VIII	5,277	3,919	1,358	717	600	602	550	755	173	645	9	567	9
IX	8,834	6,378	2,456	1,184	1,027	1,246	952	1,262	300	1,022	72	760	21
X	2,105	1,540	565	251	216	262	232	319	76	306	8	206	8
XI	5,601	3,831	1,770	647	624	811	620	745	190	678	81	419	53
XII	564	548	16	16	6	19	5	46	1	97	...	181	...
XIII	2,336	1,733	603	293	268	243	212	402	81	325	19	223	5
XIV	3,026	2,072	954	466	360	436	377	439	165	304	32	189	3
XV	1,228	868	360	174	129	166	135	170	60	112	11	92	5
XVI	294	252	42	13	26	22	8	48	4	58	1	55	3
XVII	607	459	148	77	64	77	28	55	36	57	12	58	2
XVIII	767	526	241	115	157	118	39	92	31	58	7	58	1
XIX	5,638	3 841	1,794	1,044	893	803	647	688	148	343	49	364	27
XX	2,633	1,735	898	454	442	368	342	410	94	196	8	140	4
XXI	3,324	2,300	1,024	533	493	497	386	457	95	309	15	217	12
XXII	10,854	7,359	3,495	1,731	1,581	1,563	1,381	1,603	388	1,114	34	593	22
XXIII	2,814	2,112	702	384	353	343	266	406	65	210	5	361	10
XXIV	1,737	1,117	620	270	300	300	248	245	46	123	10	70	4
XXV	4,998	3,542	1,456	768	631	693	606	682	162	507	15	392	9
Total ...	114,477	80,868	33,609	16,397	14,674	15,342	12,972	16,167	3,636	12,292	628	8,932	379
Fort William ...	302	275	27	14	14	18	7	33	3	33	2	49	...
Port and Canals ...	2,167	2,155	12	21	3	37	4	387	...	461	...	502	3

and AGE—PART A—*Hindus.*

RIED.																
PERIODS.																WARD No.
25—29.		30—34.		35—39.		40—44.		45—49.		50—54.		55—59.		60 and over.		
Males.	Females.	Males.	Females.	Males.	Females.	Males.	Females.	Males.	Females.	Males.	Females.	Males.	Females.	Males.	Females.	
15	16	17	18	19	20	21	22	23	24	25	26	27	28	29	30	
304	10	179	13	87	8	114	16	24	13	15	14	6	...	14	...	I
305	22	196	9	106	14	94	10	35	3	23	3	19	5	25	4	II
220	46	181	49	60	22	70	27	15	6	11	6	6	9	8	9	III
284	4	153	16	156	52	44	10	15	1	21	1	28	15	18	2	IV
472	55	275	24	187	42	100	10	30	11	30	8	10	12	10	4	V
339	20	239	20	133	15	48	8	58	6	37	9	20	1	32	...	VI
309	20	150	3	80	4	81	5	30	7	20	5	3	5	13	6	VII
292	4	152	5	69	...	65	3	15	4	18	...	13	...	9	1	VIII
389	15	228	16	88	7	121	14	25	12	21	12	12	6	20	2	IX
83	16	47	3	28	4	17	3	12	2	4	1	1	...	4	1	X
237	90	124	45	64	39	65	16	14	3	11	5	9	1	7	3	XI
73	...	49	1	30	...	14	1	12	1	6	1	2	...	4	...	XII
93	6	64	4	58	1	20	2	6	1	1	1	1	1	4	2	XIII
130	7	55	...	25	4	14	4	1	2	7	...	1	...	5	...	XIV
47	5	26	1	17	8	41	...	6	2	9	1	4	...	4	3	XV
28	...	10	...	12	...	4	...	...	...	2	...	...	...	...	...	XVI
70	1	40	...	9	...	7	2	5	1	2	...	...	...	2	2	XVII
40	1	19	2	16	...	2	1	1	...	4	1	...	...	3	1	XVIII
230	13	188	7	82	5	41	2	17	1	23	1	4	1	17	...	XIX
72	2	42	4	16	...	16	1	6	1	8	...	5	...	2	...	XX
112	8	77	5	26	4	33	2	13	3	9	1	10	...	7	...	XXI
286	16	176	15	109	24	75	13	30	3	26	6	22	7	31	5	XXII
196	2	97	...	68	...	23	1	10	...	8	...	...	...	16	...	XXIII
48	4	22	3	15	3	14	2	2	...	6	...	...	...	2	...	XXIV
210	8	124	7	76	10	41	2	15	1	16	2	6	1	12	2	XXV
4,869	375	2,913	252	1,607	266	1,164	155	397	84	337	78	182	64	269	46	Total.
74	1	40	...	10	...	...	...	2	...	1	...	...	...	1	...	Fort William.
296	2	102	...	201	...	57	...	51	...	34	...	4	...	2	...	Port and Canals.

TABLE VI.—CIVIL CONDITION BY RELIGION

WARD No.	TOTAL MARRIED.			(2) MAR AGE. 0—4.		5—9.		10—14.		15—19.		20—24.		25—29.	
	Total.	Males.	Females.	Males.	Females.	Males.	Females.	Males.	Females.	Males.	Females.	Males.	Females.	Males.	Females.
1	2	3	4	5	6	7	8	9	10	11	12	13	14	15	16
I	15,740	10,580	5,160	...	5	17	75	159	652	526	883	1,409	860	1,819	829
II	13,152	9,550	3,602	7	6	19	52	130	417	458	677	1,147	580	1,661	561
III	14,121	9,345	4,776	6	13	36	107	134	575	521	769	1,354	844	1,426	706
IV	13,347	8,901	4,446	...	19	18	56	163	528	518	700	1,284	779	1,390	710
V	23,285	18,004	5,281	6	7	4	32	184	383	724	695	1,929	905	3,083	987
VI	18,379	12,666	5,713	6	12	27	54	168	674	895	888	1,808	827	2,036	801
VII	9,676	8,119	1,557	...	1	17	16	109	133	402	192	1,022	285	1,499	306
VIII	13,889	10,902	2,987	6	23	14	32	202	333	563	409	1,444	404	1,995	518
IX	18,110	13,103	5,007	5	4	27	75	221	545	773	768	1,972	840	2,291	814
X	5,509	4,523	976	3	...	2	17	64	104	264	151	623	195	797	139
XI	9,725	6,933	2,792	2	6	6	37	83	327	330	477	959	496	1,190	381
XII	2,777	2,745	32	...	...	...	...	13	4	158	3	438	4	534	3
XIII	11,057	9,738	1,319	2	3	44	20	233	129	593	166	1,355	223	1,763	206
XIV	6,378	4,743	1,635	48	5	16	21	170	155	266	239	645	304	822	273
XV	3,564	2,756	808	2	5	5	5	39	64	115	95	307	132	553	169
XVI	1,689	1,604	85	...	...	...	4	14	3	55	9	224	19	312	8
XVII	1,882	1,552	330	...	...	3	...	35	28	47	52	252	60	316	44
XVIII	2,037	1,575	462	1	...	1	8	30	36	64	78	248	42	349	64
XIX	11,685	8,150	3,535	3	10	27	61	140	387	519	521	996	556	1,350	544
XX	5,927	4,320	1,607	3	4	13	34	141	188	405	233	648	276	788	251
XXI	5,838	4,373	2,065	...	...	6	48	53	222	213	323	508	351	727	324
XXII	17,650	11,093	6,557	8	7	20	116	198	820	597	1,057	1,438	1,034	1,759	1,003
XXIII	5,876	4,272	1,604	...	2	3	32	59	201	211	270	571	307	711	210
XXIV	3,520	2,317	1,203	...	3	11	32	57	171	96	165	258	184	387	210
XXV	10,623	7,657	2,966	2	...	39	69	140	330	379	438	1,083	521	1,250	459
Total ...	246,026	179,521	66,505	66	135	375	1,003	2,929	7,409	9,691	10,258	23,922	11,028	30,808	10,520
Fort William	1,087	1,015	72	...	1	2	2	16	4	41	3	215	15	208	17
Port and Canals	11,220	11,194	26	3	...	4	...	141	5	1,051	...	1,602	6	1,891	...

SEX, *and* AGE.—PART A.—*Hindus.*—continued.

RIED.														
PERIODS.														
30—34.		35—39.		40—44.		45—49.		50—54.		55—59.		60 and over.		WARD No.
Males.	Females.	Males.	Females.	Males.	Females.	Males.	Females.	Males.	Females.	Males.	Females.	Males.	Females.	
17	18	19	20	21	22	23	24	25	26	27	28	29	30	
1,877	672	1,332	432	1,370	314	664	176	654	136	260	54	494	72	I
1,767	456	1,193	254	1,177	241	605	133	661	120	287	43	438	62	II
1,787	644	1,034	350	1,198	356	546	129	642	163	195	46	466	77	III
1,660	632	976	341	1,129	262	551	100	571	162	261	85	390	72	IV
3,391	879	2,668	555	2.592	370	1,203	186	1,140	149	374	54	706	79	V
2,095	891	1,645	614	1,535	274	740	226	818	215	326	97	567	140	VI
1,052	168	1,037	192	1,054	131	560	63	477	48	153	9	287	13	VII
1,707	510	1,491	225	1,461	247	597	99	711	97	202	16	519	74	VIII
2,251	666	1,405	391	1,846	483	640	144	792	136	292	52	588	89	IX
899	143	566	86	615	81	195	18	248	23	77	7	170	12	X
1,400	397	866	223	919	156	356	104	399	93	147	48	276	47	XI
526	7	390	2	314	4	118	...	138	3	57	...	59	2	XII
1,917	212	1,150	105	1,365	116	442	40	435	55	206	7	233	37	XIII
928	245	520	148	603	108	233	31	276	48	75	22	185	41	XIV
620	96	309	75	319	84	131	14	162	28	49	10	145	31	XV
356	9	178	10	224	12	72	6	109	3	24	1	36	1	XVI
289	57	181	36	168	22	92	8	78	12	20	3	71	8	XVII
283	72	188	56	111	62	110	15	89	17	42	5	59	7	XVIII
1,469	546	1,035	295	1,094	245	473	113	472	118	167	58	405	81	XIX
628	267	453	102	526	108	219	51	229	49	88	13	179	31	XX
753	304	580	166	607	141	303	68	320	68	108	22	245	28	XXI
1,921	900	1,253	527	1,116	491	671	233	821	209	284	57	708	113	XXII
814	237	586	111	573	106	252	48	254	28	88	22	200	30	XXIII
433	161	282	96	323	70	154	20	121	40	60	21	135	30	XXIV
1,845	421	896	213	1,143	253	404	84	438	86	173	62	365	30	XXV
32,618	9,589	22,114	5,600	23,671	4,737	10,331	2,099	11,065	2,106	4,015	814	7,926	1,207	Total
177	14	157	4	82	5	48	...	38	5	15	1	16	1	Fort Willam.
2,107	6	1,002	...	1,003	6	582	...	601	3	715	...	492	...	Port and Canals.

TABLE VI.—RELIGION BY CIVIL CONDITION,

WARD NO.	TOTAL WIDOWED.			(3) WI AGE 0—4.		5—9.		10—14		15—19.		20—24.	
	Total.	Males.	Females.	Males.	Females.	Males.	Females.	Males.	Females.	Males.	Females.	Males.	Females.
1	2	3	4	5	6	7	8	9	10	11	12	13	14
I	6,590	959	5,631	...	...	1	4	4	40	10	149	28	279
II	5,572	658	4,914	1	...	5	12	2	37	7	114	10	254
III	5,192	765	4,427	...	...	...	10	5	30	8	105	37	135
IV	4,848	638	4,210	...	...	2	25	3	27	13	142	23	179
V	6,177	946	5,231	...	...	6	4	10	41	13	156	43	439
VI	6,195	897	5,298	3	5	2	3	4	50	46	161	55	355
VII	1,312	461	851	...	...	...	1	3	4	7	28	15	61
VIII	2,987	628	2,359	...	...	1	2	6	9	31	40	28	144
IX	4,569	796	3,773	...	1	2	34	19	77	21	109	36	202
X	911	202	709	...	...	...	1	3	2	4	20	15	42
XI	2,671	357	2,314	...	...	...	3	...	9	2	42	14	106
XII	157	147	10	...	...	...	...	...	...	3	...	8	1
XIII	973	330	643	...	...	10	...	8	8	5	23	16	58
XIV	1,205	319	886	...	...	2	...	4	22	8	33	11	57
XV	352	125	227	...	...	1	...	...	1	2	7	7	7
XVI	105	62	43	...	...	...	...	2	1	2	2	9	3
XVII	173	96	77	...	...	...	2	2	1	1	5	5	3
XVIII	268	120	148	...	...	1	1	...	9	2	4	7	2
XIX	3,168	726	2,442	...	1	...	8	6	22	12	73	40	137
XX	1,238	272	966	2	2	...	1	2	14	7	28	14	56
XXI	2,157	404	1,753	...	...	2	5	2	21	10	22	16	90
XXII	6,237	1,025	5,212	2	5	2	3	8	46	89	127	38	280
XXIII	1,912	379	1,533	...	3	...	...	...	14	16	42	31	128
XXIV	772	177	595	...	...	...	1	2	10	5	16	4	31
XXV	2,518	554	1,964	...	...	1	4	14	18	13	53	34	107
Total ...	68,259	12,043	55,216	8	17	38	124	109	513	287	1,501	544	3,156
Fort William ...	52	43	9	...	...	...	...	1	...	...	...	3	...
Port and Canals ...	547	509	38	...	...	...	...	8	...	29	4	45	8

SEX and AGE.—PART A.—*Hindus.*

DOWED.

PERIODS.

25—29.		30—34.		35—39.		40—44.		45—49.		50—54.		55—59.		60 and over.		WARD No.
Males.	Females.	Males.	Females.	Males.	Females.	Males.	Females.	Males.	Females.	Males.	Females.	Males.	Females.	Males.	Females.	
15	16	17	18	19	20	21	22	23	24	25	26	27	28	29	30	
50	503	105	798	95	593	162	877	103	468	133	663	67	278	195	889	I
36	519	79	778	62	675	124	791	58	358	94	531	48	194	132	651	II
48	493	79	677	85	612	150	741	62	280	106	568	55	187	130	689	III
42	322	59	524	60	430	101	634	71	410	93	530	46	303	125	684	IV
71	745	106	808	91	594	151	813	100	326	171	510	63	247	121	548	V
76	524	35	729	73	565	114	760	82	466	123	581	104	357	180	742	VI
40	88	60	94	43	89	55	122	53	95	73	103	23	39	89	127	VII
40	226	69	334	57	240	105	411	63	190	88	278	52	91	89	391	VIII
54	404	88	509	63	316	134	652	52	284	115	328	45	194	167	663	IX
17	66	16	99	14	56	35	102	23	53	32	87	7	40	36	141	X
35	202	31	319	33	271	62	468	24	165	60	261	24	113	72	355	XI
18	...	16	...	14	2	21	...	10	1	21	1	12	...	21	5	XII
29	52	49	75	31	48	49	102	24	64	40	79	9	34	60	100	XIII
20	87	39	77	22	68	56	137	41	63	44	127	25	49	47	166	XIV
13	19	19	37	8	12	15	25	10	12	14	25	4	15	32	67	XV
10	4	9	3	14	5	3	9	4	8	4	2	2	2	3	4	XVI
15	4	14	10	14	7	7	8	10	5	7	8	7	5	14	19	XVII
16	4	18	...	15	6	9	26	9	24	8	19	10	14	25	30	XVIII
76	257	101	331	76	238	102	421	60	195	90	296	37	94	126	369	XIX
24	88	24	96	28	72	47	140	24	70	41	116	12	64	47	189	XX
32	117	34	209	31	174	65	280	38	156	56	236	33	99	85	344	XXI
72	445	104	610	78	491	184	803	97	417	131	656	51	280	219	1,049	XXII
...	173	37	147	57	191	92	164	39	121	57	153	29	95	21	302	XXIII
8	37	15	65	19	51	23	51	15	46	26	83	18	45	42	159	XXIV
47	165	66	253	63	189	82	342	47	135	69	251	22	103	106	344	XXV
895	6,634	1,272	7,682	1,136	5,895	1,948	8,879	1,118	4,412	1,696	6,522	805	2,942	2,187	9,030	Total
74	1	63	...	10	1	2	2	3	...	5	1	1	1	3	3	Fort William.
44	4	33	9	41	...	88	8	51	5	63	...	47	...	60	..	Port and Canals

TABLE VI.—CIVIL CONDITION BY RELIGION

WARD No.	TOTAL UNMARRIED.			(1) UNMAR AGE-									
				0—4.		5—9.		10—14.		15—19.		20—24.	
	Total.	Males.	Females.	Males.	Females.	Males.	Females.	Males.	Females.	Males.	Females.	Males.	Females.
1	2	3	4	5	6	7	8	9	10	11	12	13	14
I	1,348	922	426	183	171	256	182	185	42	149	9	60	4
II	200	176	24	19	10	23	10	30	1	33	1	31	1
III	2,672	1,739	933	547	426	483	370	364	117	142	10	90	9
IV	2,021	1,342	679	392	302	306	297	307	76	104	...	117	2
V	226	196	30	12	13	11	11	32	4	51	2	32	...
VI	1,637	1,175	462	261	187	235	190	220	65	148	11	102	3
VII	1,211	1,006	205	74	57	141	74	233	43	209	10	149	9
VIII	5,678	4,122	1,556	958	608	654	542	895	288	543	21	401	30
IX	4,693	3,276	1,417	682	624	744	539	690	212	533	12	320	9
X	2,306	1,707	599	261	199	284	249	385	97	341	34	314	12
XI	268	176	92	32	16	24	34	56	23	23	3	19	5
XII	133	132	1	...	...	9	1	20	...	22	...	31	...
XIII	2,719	2,140	579	235	242	270	180	456	104	472	13	247	12
XIV	4,913	3,425	1,488	621	571	566	569	733	289	642	26	482	11
XV	1,912	1,308	604	278	237	293	232	288	106	187	11	157	7
XVI	271	193	78	42	42	38	25	33	10	34	1	20	...
XVII	294	229	65	24	26	18	11	30	18	38	2	52	1
XVIII	450	271	179	70	86	71	64	61	20	17	5	19	1
XIX	2,925	1,950	975	481	413	425	348	450	166	238	23	160	12
XX	4,553	2,862	1,691	850	777	720	617	621	267	335	6	175	8
XXI	3,713	2,312	1,401	635	570	666	575	492	234	227	8	161	7
XXII	2,150	1,390	760	329	292	381	296	297	136	154	15	105	5
XXIII	991	714	277	109	111	123	97	190	55	128	4	111	2
XXIV	3,144	1,853	1,291	500	496	570	504	410	255	194	17	100	5
XXV	2,403	1,668	735	367	306	311	275	402	134	197	10	167	3
Total ...	52,831	36,284	16,547	7,962	6,782	7,621	6,292	7,880	2,762	5,161	254	3,622	158
Fort William ...	113	106	7	11	1	3	4	15	1	22	1	13	...
Port and Canals ...	2,232	2,228	4	11	...	19	...	240	1	702	1	245	...

and AGE.—PART B.—*Muhammadans.*

RIED.

PERIODS.

25—29.		30—34.		35—39.		40—44.		45—49.		50—54.		55—59.		60 and over.		WARD No.
Males.	Females.	Males.	Females.	Males.	Females.	Males.	Females.	Males.	Females.	Males.	Females.	Males.	Females.	Males.	Females.	
15	16	17	18	19	20	21	22	23	24	25	26	27	28	29	30	
58	1	18	2	6	1	2	10	3	4	2	...	...	...	...	...	I
24	1	9	...	4	...	2	...	1	...	...	...	...	...	...	...	II
52	...	10	...	20	...	9	1	4	...	15	...	2	...	1	...	III
66	...	16	...	15	...	6	...	5	...	3	...	...	2	5	...	IV
23	...	13	...	17	...	2	...	3	...	...	...	...	...	...	...	V
52	4	36	2	51	...	26	...	16	...	20	...	4	...	4	...	VI
109	3	42	7	23	1	10	...	6	...	6	...	1	1	3	...	VII
211	38	203	8	193	4	27	8	19	2	10	3	2	1	6	3	VIII
153	9	75	1	29	4	27	...	5	1	7	1	2	2	9	3	IX
61	3	29	2	8	1	13	1	7	...	2	1	1	...	1	...	X
11	1	3	2	5	...	3	1	...	2	...	2	...	2	...	1	XI
24	...	15	...	9	...	2	...	...	...	...	...	...	...	...	...	XII
172	10	140	10	126	1	17	4	3	1	...	1	...	...	2	1	XIII
173	12	79	4	32	5	45	1	10	...	26	...	5	...	11	...	XIV
49	6	32	2	8	2	10	...	3	1	1	...	...	...	2	...	XV
14	...	3	...	3	...	4	...	2	...	...	...	...	...	...	...	XVI
32	3	19	...	9	...	4	4	1	...	2	...	...	...	...	...	XVII
24	1	6	1	...	1	3	...	...	...	...	...	...	...	...	...	XVIII
84	4	40	2	20	2	12	1	6	...	13	1	15	1	6	2	XIX
85	6	39	5	16	3	5	...	5	...	5	1	...	1	6	...	XX
58	1	25	3	27	2	10	1	3	...	5	...	1	...	3	...	XXI
41	10	29	3	27	...	6	1	6	1	7	...	4	...	4	1	XXII
8	5	23	1	10	1	6	...	2	1	3	...	...	...	1	...	XXIII
45	7	21	2	7	2	4	1	1	1	...	...	1	1	...	...	XXIV
74	3	45	3	82	...	9	...	5	1	1	...	...	...	8	...	XXV
1,703	128	970	60	747	30	264	34	116	15	128	10	38	11	72	11	Total.
25	...	10	...	6	...	...	...	...	...	...	...	1	...	...	...	Fort William.
328	1	307	...	209	...	57	1	21	...	60	...	11	...	18	...	Port and Canals.

TABLE VI.—CIVIL CONDITION BY RELIGION,

WARD No.	TOTAL MARRIED.			(2) MAR AGE- 0—4.		5—9.		10—14.		15—19.		20—24.	
	Total.	Males.	Females.	Males.	Females.	Males.	Females.	Males.	Females.	Males.	Females.	Males.	Females.
1	2	3	4	5	6	7	8	9	10	11	12	13	14
I	4,048	2,982	1,066	1	2	3	38	56	92	142	150	295	180
II	872	806	66	...	...	...	...	4	2	35	8	101	11
III	5,178	3,280	1,898	5	11	18	46	125	148	151	221	410	345
IV	5,032	3,419	1,613	6	13	2	15	41	103	227	183	364	268
V	1,826	1,730	96	...	...	...	...	8	6	154	17	231	7
VI	5,005	3.762	1,243	4	5	7	7	36	78	204	137	409	202
VII	3,706	3,246	460	...	...	...	2	36	26	155	66	396	70
VIII	17,100	12,973	4,127	6	7	14	37	237	290	704	542	1,561	695
IX	10,448	7,243	3,205	9	7	22	35	141	235	312	355	782	597
X	5,896	4,695	1,201	...	2	5	15	92	63	306	146	560	210
XI	799	644	155	...	...	1	...	10	8	30	37	78	37
XII	1,294	1,286	8	...	...	...	...	6	...	58	...	159	1
XIII	7,333	6,068	1,265	...	...	7	6	44	77	330	161	743	212
XIV	9,278	6,255	3,023	5	9	5	25	73	193	300	377	786	525
XV	4,033	2,932	1,101	...	3	7	8	42	80	191	136	362	178
XVI	1,184	992	192	1	...	1	17	6	15	36	22	135	33
XVII	828	701	127	...	...	...	...	9	9	69	17	71	35
XVIII	826	532	294	...	5	2	8	13	32	43	51	78	45
XIX	6,558	4,295	2,263	5	15	11	14	92	127	191	273	480	378
XX	6,558	3,847	2,711	8	7	7	20	60	237	167	412	396	405
XXI	5,315	3,028	2,287	...	...	1	12	41	168	137	305	303	409
XXII	3,973	2,648	1,325	2	1	11	8	100	117	106	177	317	234
XXIII	2,431	1,931	500	...	...	2	9	22	36	70	38	282	87
XXIV	4,746	2,504	2,242	13	2	35	11	23	182	90	362	221	403
XXV	5,063	3,508	1,555	4	14	3	15	42	94	194	168	461	301
Total ...	119,330	85,307	34,023	69	103	164	348	1,359	2,418	4,402	4,361	9,981	5,868
Fort Willam ...	471	440	31	...	...	1	...	...	5	15	5	99	3
Port and Canals ...	10,885	10,881	4	9	...	9	...	187	...	1,026	...	1,807	...

Sex and Age—Part B.—*Muhammadans.*

RIED.

PERIODS.

25—29.		30—34.		35—39.		40—44.		45—49.		50—54.		55—59.		60 and over.		Ward No.
Males.	Females.	Males.	Females.	Males.	Females.	Males.	Females.	Males.	Females.	Males.	Females.	Males.	Females.	Males.	Females.	
15	16	17	18	19	20	21	22	23	24	25	26	27	28	29	30	
480	189	697	187	364	84	446	61	175	26	175	22	52	4	96	11	I
137	8	174	11	91	12	122	9	48	3	46	2	13	...	35	...	II
532	356	559	343	313	114	492	152	166	36	228	55	49	15	222	56	III
515	270	629	237	370	188	489	153	191	48	263	49	164	59	158	27	IV
256	17	283	18	185	10	254	12	89	5	105	2	94	...	71	2	V
535	215	785	216	445	129	581	114	196	44	241	70	92	9	227	17	VI
673	75	582	81	455	50	455	52	169	11	170	17	47	4	108	6	VII
2,031	760	2,363	633	1,582	378	1,851	359	766	136	906	97	181	77	771	116	VIII
1,162	525	1,311	578	822	241	1,225	340	392	79	493	95	140	33	432	85	IX
705	183	870	203	697	137	611	108	225	42	293	32	138	31	293	29	X
108	16	153	25	63	7	62	14	37	5	67	6	9	...	26	...	XI
223	2	300	1	238	3	183	1	41	...	53	...	7	...	18	...	XII
1,076	218	1,126	251	772	95	917	112	316	26	370	53	111	15	247	39	XIII
1,029	427	1,099	521	588	250	961	314	335	106	438	114	139	28	497	134	XIV
416	168	516	185	419	77	419	95	137	31	181	66	60	15	192	69	XV
193	27	225	30	106	12	142	17	47	3	51	6	9	5	40	5	XVI
104	21	107	12	88	12	79	11	27	4	22	4	73	...	22	2	XVII
65	38	100	40	85	18	38	21	31	12	28	12	19	5	30	7	XVIII
641	388	775	410	534	202	666	225	233	56	313	84	87	20	267	71	XIX
551	438	598	464	387	220	661	267	231	65	326	109	93	13	362	54	XX
416	409	494	362	305	217	496	180	183	63	231	75	88	19	333	68	XXI
379	226	455	219	249	83	452	128	124	34	215	53	44	7	194	38	XXII
371	80	391	86	211	43	234	58	119	23	101	28	31	6	97	6	XXIII
383	385	397	335	280	142	370	203	164	65	208	61	60	17	260	71	XXIV
555	286	592	254	419	108	413	159	197	43	223	54	158	12	247	47	XXV
13,566	5,717	15,581	5,702	9,968	2,832	12,619	3,185	4,639	966	5,766	1,169	1,948	394	5,245	960	Total.
93	7	93	5	56	...	31	3	20	1	14	1	10	1	8	...	Fort William.
1,578	2	2,191	...	1,455	2	981	...	518	...	394	...	444	...	282	...	Port and Canals.

TABLE VI.—CIVIL CONDITION *by* RELIGION,

WARD NO.	TOTAL WIDOWED.			(3) WIDO AGE 0—4.		5—9.		10—14.		15—19.		20—24.	
	Total.	Males.	Females.	Males.	Females.	Males.	Females.	Males.	Females.	Males.	Females.	Males.	Females.
1	2	3	4	5	6	7	8	9	10	11	12	13	14
I	478	123	355	...	...	1	...	3	1	4	7	4	16
II	44	7	37	...	...	...	...	...	...	1	1	...	1
III	751	142	609	...	1	2	...	1	4	3	8	13	26
IV	679	181	498	...	...	1	1	3	3	3	11	11	14
V	60	32	28	...	...	...	...	...	1	1	4	1	3
VI	642	161	481	...	...	...	1	...	7	7	20	5	45
VII	377	104	273	...	...	1	...	3	1	2	2	9	6
VIII	1,918	541	1,377	...	...	...	1	32	10	29	84	28	61
IX	1,338	381	957	...	1	...	1	3	24	11	17	27	24
X	670	154	516	...	...	...	...	2	2	4	14	9	18
XI	105	19	86	...	...	...	...	...	1	...	...	1	8
XII	43	35	8	...	...	...	...	...	...	1	...	...	...
XIII	844	200	644	...	...	1	...	1	7	4	22	15	69
XIV	1,518	335	1,183	...	...	...	2	1	4	6	31	10	36
XV	591	109	482	...	...	...	...	...	2	4	4	8	15
XVI	62	21	41	...	...	...	...	...	1	1	2	1	1
XVII	88	50	38	...	...	...	...	...	1	...	3	5	1
XVIII	125	34	91	...	...	1	...	1	2	2	1	4	3
XIX	1,005	249	756	...	...	...	2	...	10	3	28	11	34
XX	1,532	275	1,257	1	...	2	...	4	4	4	30	16	40
XXI	1,275	207	1,068	...	...	..	...	2	6	8	34	8	43
XXII	706	182	524	...	1	...	1	1	2	9	8	12	16
XXIII	322	116	206	...	...	...	...	...	1	7	4	3	1
XXIV	1,041	157	884	...	...	...	1	2	7	1	16	8	33
XXV	851	185	666	...	...	...	...	...	3	3	15	7	39
Total ...	17,065	4,000	13,065	1	3	9	10	59	104	118	366	216	553
Fort William ...	13	9	4	...	...	...	...	1	...	...	...	...	...
Port and Canals ...	233	233	...	...	...	1	...	...	...	13	...	23	...

SEX *and* AGE—PART B.—*Muhammadans.*

WED.

PERIODS.

25—29.		30—34.		35—39.		40—44.		45—49.		50—54.		55—59.		60 and over.		WARD NO.
Males.	Females.	Males.	Females.	Males.	Females.	Males.	Females.	Males.	Females.	Males.	Females.	Males.	Females.	Males.	Females.	
15	16	17	18	19	20	21	22	23	24	25	26	27	28	29	30	
10	34	28	56	6	29	19	57	8	39	10	44	6	19	15	53	I
...	3	...	3	...	2	2	5	2	1	...	8	...	...	2	13	II
13	32	10	68	14	38	21	121	12	17	20	97	5	20	28	177	III
13	27	24	47	10	23	32	86	18	27	18	72	17	55	31	132	IV
4	2	2	6	...	4	7	3	4	1	8	2	...	...	5	2	V
10	45	15	54	15	36	24	58	14	31	19	56	8	30	44	98	VI
11	19	11	26	11	28	11	51	11	28	10	51	3	12	21	49	VII
38	73	60	136	40	108	80	266	39	92	64	170	31	99	100	277	VIII
34	37	39	72	36	61	61	160	24	73	37	180	17	41	92	266	IX
21	42	15	43	20	35	18	84	11	22	10	90	16	38	28	128	X
3	3	3	9	1	6	2	21	...	3	4	15	1	3	4	17	XI
1	1	8	...	4	1	11	...	3	1	4	...	2	4	1	1	XII
16	93	40	86	21	58	29	89	20	24	27	78	3	9	23	109	XIII
12	49	31	94	27	91	62	151	24	77	41	196	21	46	100	406	XIV
16	21	13	54	7	33	12	114	5	30	12	65	2	18	30	126	XV
3	...	2	4	2	3	2	4	1	2	2	8	2	4	5	12	XVI
8	2	9	1	7	3	6	10	7	3	5	8	1	2	2	4	XVII
4	4	4	8	3	3	5	11	2	12	2	13	1	12	5	22	XVIII
27	50	40	63	23	35	34	113	8	60	51	102	10	43	42	216	XIX
18	70	24	102	21	79	32	218	12	136	40	198	12	59	89	321	XX
15	44	17	74	18	63	24	170	15	82	23	168	11	70	66	314	XXI
13	23	15	44	15	31	23	89	16	47	30	71	7	36	41	155	XXII
13	11	17	22	10	13	22	46	6	21	10	28	4	13	24	46	XXIII
7	32	7	60	8	40	20	119	14	68	19	137	11	58	60	313	XXIV
17	56	29	70	19	37	48	98	9	43	18	116	6	43	29	146	XXV
327	773	463	1,202	338	860	607	2,144	285	940	493	1,973	197	734	887	3,403	Total.
1	1	2	...	1	1	1	...	...	...	2	2	...	...	1	...	Fort William
29	...	26	...	34	...	20	...	31	...	21	...	12	...	23	...	Port and Canals.

TABLE VI.—CIVIL CONDITION *by* RELIGION

Ward No.	Total unmarried.			(1) UNMAR Age 0—4.		5—9.		10—14.		15—19.		20—24.	
	Total.	Males.	Females.	Males.	Females.	Males.	Females.	Males.	Females.	Males.	Females.	Males.	Females.
1	2	3	4	5	6	7	8	9	10	11	12	13	14
I	6	3	3	2	1	...	1	...	...	...	...	...	...
II	...	...	...	...	...	...	...	...	...	...	...	...	...
III	107	10	97	1	16	...	6	2	53	1	16	...	4
IV	245	138	107	18	24	10	7	10	7	7	37	13	10
V	21	15	6	6	2	1	3	1	...	2	...	2	...
VI	119	39	80	10	10	4	11	2	30	4	10	4	4
VII	350	291	59	20	14	41	20	112	8	5	3	12	5
VIII	1,164	667	497	198	157	87	140	128	78	82	52	78	42
IX	687	392	295	60	67	87	80	73	39	30	64	34	14
X	2,227	1,327	900	209	235	240	210	269	179	251	148	134	49
XI	828	395	433	80	72	77	135	72	76	52	75	41	30
XII	523	323	200	48	55	17	39	23	22	19	30	57	25
XIII	1,685	949	736	169	126	153	160	228	190	139	105	92	67
XIV	1,464	772	692	153	170	167	140	136	149	128	106	70	45
XV	927	522	405	71	79	82	73	108	66	107	107	49	42
XVI	585	360	225	30	28	43	24	39	37	38	30	68	39
XVII	339	205	134	18	17	20	16	76	31	24	24	19	13
XVIII	206	124	82	27	27	21	11	11	10	16	15	14	7
XIX	1,309	447	862	95	117	107	230	83	292	52	109	38	56
XX	299	170	129	42	41	30	41	21	23	16	4	17	7
XXI	344	256	88	39	20	34	16	61	16	46	10	19	12
XXII	530	308	222	67	41	37	67	37	48	42	22	41	14
XXIII	152	96	56	25	22	4	5	24	8	8	...	4	...
XXIV	265	128	137	27	23	53	10	14	22	15	36	9	17
XXV	146	91	55	17	16	11	10	12	12	16	6	5	2
Total ...	14,528	8,028	6,500	1,432	1,370	1,326	1,455	1,547	1,396	1,100	1,009	820	504
Fort William ...	989	888	101	41	48	29	24	9	17	67	5	82	4
Port and Canals ...	859	850	9	5	2	3	2	4	1	102	2	140	1

and Age—Part C.—*Christians.*

RIED.

PERIODS.

25—29.		30—34.		35—39.		40—44.		45—49.		50—54.		55—59.		60 and over.		Ward No.
Males.	Females.	Males.	Females.	Males.	Females.	Males.	Females.	Males.	Females.	Males.	Females.	Males.	Females.	Males.	Females.	
15	16	17	18	19	20	21	22	23	24	25	26	27	28	29	30	
1	1	...	...	...	...	...	...	...	...	...	...	...	...	...	...	I
...	...	...	...	...	...	...	...	...	...	...	...	...	...	...	...	II
2	1	3	1	1	...	...	...	...	...	...	...	...	...	...	...	III
2	3	30	4	12	11	25	2	5	2	6	...	...	...	...	...	IV
1	1	...	...	1	...	...	...	1	...	...	...	...	...	...	...	V
5	3	6	2	4	10	...	...	...	...	...	...	...	...	...	...	VI
18	9	33	...	37	...	10	...	3	...	...	...	...	...	...	...	VII
40	10	23	3	8	5	6	6	4	3	2	...	7	...	4	1	VIII
84	26	12	6	4	8	1	...	3	1	2	...	1	...	1	...	IX
106	26	47	18	28	11	12	6	13	3	9	6	3	5	6	4	X
33	15	20	9	8	5	3	4	2	2	2	2	1	5	4	3	XI
65	14	38	5	18	8	15	2	9	...	7	...	4	...	3	...	XII
67	23	55	16	10	19	21	10	5	5	2	3	3	5	5	7	XIII
51	19	28	14	11	12	12	19	4	4	6	7	2	1	4	6	XIV
36	18	14	4	18	2	18	3	8	2	2	3	2	...	7	6	XV
55	22	29	12	22	11	21	8	7	5	8	7	...	...	...	2	XVI
15	13	11	5	6	4	6	6	3	1	...	3	1	1	6	...	XVII
10	2	9	3	4	3	4	1	3	2	1	1	4	...	...	...	XVIII
16	21	17	7	16	11	7	4	2	5	1	4	8	3	1	3	XIX
20	5	17	5	2	2	1	1	1	...	1	...	1	...	1	...	XX
18	2	20	3	9	4	4	2	3	...	1	2	1	1	1	...	XXI
35	7	21	5	12	4	5	7	5	2	3	5	1	...	2	...	XXII
3	15	24	...	2	2	1	1	...	2	1	...	...	...	...	1	XXIII
4	10	2	6	1	6	...	2	3	3	...	1	...	1	...	...	XXIV
13	5	7	1	2	...	7	1	...	...	1	2	...	...	...	...	XXV
700	271	466	129	235	138	179	85	84	42	55	46	39	22	45	33	Total.
269	3	86	...	62	...	1	...	2	...	1	...	...	...	...	...	Fort William.
139	1	134	...	127	...	92	...	53	...	21	...	11	...	19	...	Port and Canals.

TABLE VI.—CIVIL CONDITION *by* RELIGION,

WARD No.	TOTAL MARRIED.			(2) MAR AGE									
				0—4.		5—9.		10—14.		15—19.		20—24.	
	Total.	Males.	Females.	Males.	Females.	Males.	Females.	Males.	Females.	Males.	Females.	Males.	Females.
1	2	3	4	5	6	7	8	9	10	11	12	13	14
I	7	3	4	...	...	...	...	...	...	...	...	...	...
II	4	3	1	...	...	...	...	...	...	...	...	...	...
III	15	7	8	...	...	...	...	...	...	...	...	...	1
IV	70	34	36	...	...	...	...	1	1	6	4	2	4
V	30	16	14	...	...	...	...	1	1	1	...	1	1
VI	48	28	20	...	...	...	...	...	1	6	3	2	6
VII	190	124	66	...	...	...	...	...	1	...	4	2	14
VIII	1,187	617	570	...	...	...	1	3	8	59	64	71	94
IX	481	263	218	...	...	...	...	2	5	1	27	27	42
X	1,614	936	678	...	...	...	...	6	8	33	57	88	106
XI	610	313	297	...	...	...	...	3	4	3	47	25	53
XII	379	224	155	...	...	...	...	...	1	1	5	10	20
XIII	970	521	480	...	...	...	...	1	3	17	35	33	78
XIV	1,005	505	500	...	...	...	2	7	6	23	24	41	68
XV	466	240	226	...	...	...	...	...	1	13	19	26	31
XVI	352	204	148	...	...	...	...	...	3	1	21	6	14
XVII	244	152	92	...	...	...	...	...	...	8	8	17	7
XVIII	107	49	58	...	...	...	...	...	...	...	6	3	9
XIX	689	342	347	...	...	...	...	...	5	13	38	34	44
XX	214	118	96	...	...	...	...	...	1	8	19	7	21
XXI	175	96	79	...	...	...	...	...	...	5	1	8	15
XXII	374	186	188	...	...	...	...	...	3	2	26	13	36
XXIII	116	61	55	...	...	...	...	...	3	...	20	2	7
XXIV	92	40	52	...	...	...	...	...	...	...	4	3	12
XXV	114	67	47	...	...	...	...	...	...	...	5	3	9
Total ...	9,584	5,149	4,435	...	...	...	3	24	55	200	437	419	692
Fort William ...	240	158	82	...	...	...	...	1	...	30	6	24	21
Port and Canals ...	462	458	7	...	...	...	...	...	...	36	3	51	2

Sex and Age—Part C.—*Christians.*

RIED. PERIODS.																
25—29.		30—34.		35—39.		40—44.		45—49.		50—54.		55—59.		60 and over.		Ward No.
Males.	Females.	Males.	Females.	Males.	Females.	Males.	Females.	Males.	Females.	Males.	Females.	Males.	Females.	Males.	Females.	
15	16	17	18	19	20	21	22	23	24	25	26	27	28	29	30	
...	...	...	...	1	2	2	2	...	...	...	...	...	...	...	...	I
2	...	...	1	1	...	...	...	...	...	...	...	...	...	...	...	II
3	2	1	1	...	2	1	...	...	2	1	...	1	...	...	...	III
7	4	5	8	2	7	...	2	3	2	3	...	2	2	3	2	IV
1	6	3	1	3	1	1	3	4	1	1	...	...	...	...	...	V
3	1	4	2	2	3	2	1	3	2	2	...	4	1	...	...	VI
29	11	25	11	17	11	11	5	11	3	10	2	5	1	14	3	VII
61	94	91	69	71	75	61	35	42	41	47	30	53	33	58	26	VIII
53	41	44	29	29	20	29	29	21	9	24	8	11	5	22	3	IX
157	125	203	131	106	81	112	72	64	32	67	37	31	14	69	15	X
47	51	63	55	38	23	48	35	26	9	24	8	13	8	23	4	XI
37	41	37	25	41	20	28	18	28	16	25	3	11	3	6	3	XII
72	89	95	85	64	54	77	49	64	36	45	23	20	10	33	18	XIII
58	128	77	87	70	65	87	46	43	19	36	20	19	9	41	26	XIV
21	50	26	31	22	23	30	29	36	15	29	14	9	8	28	5	XV
12	28	35	22	31	18	32	14	33	14	30	6	15	4	9	4	XVI
26	20	19	14	21	13	18	14	21	8	14	3	1	3	7	2	XVII
8	6	9	10	2	10	13	5	1	6	7	1	6	3	...	2	XVIII
62	67	38	57	45	39	51	28	35	25	24	15	15	10	25	19	XIX
19	12	13	10	21	16	11	8	8	2	15	4	8	2	8	1	XX
14	24	15	11	17	8	10	7	12	2	10	5	3	3	7	3	XXI
29	21	39	33	25	17	19	17	9	10	18	10	12	7	20	8	XXII
12	3	7	9	7	3	18	6	7	2	4	...	1	...	3	2	XXIII
9	9	1	10	8	5	10	5	...	2	5	2	2	2	2	1	XXIV
7	12	15	6	18	7	8	2	8	1	2	1	4	2	2	2	XXV
749	845	865	718	662	523	679	432	479	259	443	192	246	130	383	149	Total.
29	26	32	17	26	7	11	3	1	...	4	...	...	1	...	1	Fort William.
76	1	73	...	51	...	74	...	36	1	25	...	17	...	19	...	Port and Canals.

TABLE VI.—RELIGION *by* CIVIL CONDITION,

WARD No.	TOTAL WIDOWED.			WIDO AGE									
				0—4.		5—9.		10—14.		15—19.		20—24.	
	Total.	Males.	Females.	Males.	Females.	Males.	Females.	Males.	Females.	Males.	Females.	Males.	Females.
1	2	3	4	5	6	7	8	9	10	11	12	13	14
I	2	...	2	...	...	...	...	...	...	...	...	...	2
III	5	...	5	...	...	...	...	...	...	...	...	...	...
IV	56	16	40	...	...	...	...	...	...	...	1	1	5
V	4	1	3	...	...	...	...	...	...	...	...	...	...
VI	10	3	7	...	...	...	...	...	...	...	1	...	2
VII	21	4	17	...	...	...	...	...	...	...	...	...	...
VIII	277	54	223	...	...	...	...	...	...	1	10	...	...
IX	112	22	90	...	..	...	1	...	...	...	...	...	5
X	480	98	382	...	...	...	...	...	3	2	29	3	12
XI	121	27	94	...	...	...	...	...	...	...	2	1	5
XII	76	30	46	...	...	...	...	...	...	...	...	...	1
XIII	245	49	196	...	...	2	...	...	...	...	2	1	17
XIV	246	63	183	...	...	...	...	...	2	...	3	1	11
XV	127	29	98	...	...	...	...	...	...	...	2	...	2
XVI	45	15	30	...	...	...	...	1	...	...	1	...	...
XVII	33	8	25	...	...	...	...	...	...	1	...	...	...
XVIII	34	7	27	...	...	...	...	...	...	...	...	...	...
XIX	161	35	126	...	...	...	...	...	1	2	...	1	5
XX	50	11	39	...	...	...	...	...	...	...	...	...	1
XXI	31	4	27	...	...	...	...	...	...	...	...	...	1
XXII	85	15	70	...	...	...	...	...	...	...	...	1	5
XXIII	19	4	15	...	...	...	...	...	...	...	...	...	1
XXIV	23	4	19	...	...	...	...	...	...	...	...	...	...
XXV	31	14	17	...	...	...	...	...	...	...	...	...	...
Total ...	2,294	513	1,781	...	...	2	1	1	6	6	51	9	75
Fort William ...	23	6	17	...	...	...	...	...	...	2	1	...	2
Port and Canals ...	16	16	...	..	...	...	...	...	...	...	...	...	...

Sex *and* Age—Register C.—*Christian.*

WED.																
PERIODS.																
25—29.		30—34.		35—39.		40—44.		45—49.		50—54.		55—59.		60 and over.		Ward No.
Males.	Females.	Males.	Females.	Males.	Females.	Males.	Females.	Males.	Females.	Males.	Females.	Males.	Females.	Males.	Females.	
15	16	17	18	19	20	21	22	23	24	25	26	27	28	29	30	
...	...	...	...	...	...	...	...	...	...	...	...	...	...	...	...	I
...	...	...	1	...	...	...	2	...	...	...	1	...	1	...	...	III
...	6	...	...	...	1	10	11	...	12	5	2	...	...	...	2	IV
...	...	...	2	..	...	1	1	...	...	...	...	...	...	...	...	V
...	1	...	...	...	...	1	2	2	1	...	...	...	...	...	...	VI
1	...	...	...	...	4	1	1	...	...	1	4	1	4	...	4	VII
4	24	4	16	4	14	3	23	3	27	9	25	5	17	21	67	VIII
2	5	...	13	...	6	5	15	3	22	5	9	4	1	3	13	IX
2	19	1	16	10	10	...	100	4	85	13	51	12	22	51	36	X
1	4	1	5	5	5	3	8	4	8	3	19	2	7	7	31	XI
...	4	1	8	5	4	4	5	4	8	4	6	6	4	6	6	XII
1	7	8	27	3	13	6	22	8	8	5	25	7	8	13	67	XIII
4	9	2	16	10	10	8	18	6	17	6	25	6	17	20	55	XIV
1	8	2	6	...	6	9	8	3	8	3	13	4	6	7	39	XV
2	3	2	3	...	2	2	8	2	4	...	1	4	1	2	7	XVI
2	3	...	...	...	1	...	...	5	2	...	4	...	3	...	12	XVII
...	2	2	...	1	3	1	5	1	3	1	4	1	3	..	7	XVIII
1	5	3	7	3	7	4	15	3	13	8	13	3	28	7	32	XIX
1	2	1	3	1	4	1	5	1	9	2	4	1	4	3	7	XX
...	2	...	2	1	3	1	3	1	2	...	3	...	4	1	7	XXI
...	6	1	7	1	7	3	11	2	7	1	12	...	6	6	9	XXII
...	2	...	2	1	...	...	2	1	5	2	1	...	...	...	2	XXIII
...	8	...	2	...	4	1	3	2	1	...	4	1	1	...	1	XXIV
1	1	4	...	1	1	2	3	2	1	2	2	1	2	1	7	XXV
28	116	27	136	46	105	66	271	57	243	70	228	58	139	148	410	Total.
1	1	...	4	2	3	1	1	...	1	...	...	...	3	...	1	Fort William.
1	...	3	...	...	...	8	...	...	...	4	...	...	...	...	...	Port and Canals.

TABLE VI.—RELIGION *by* CIVIL CONDITION,

WARD NO.	TOTAL UNMARRIED.			(1) UNMAR AGE 0—4.		5—9.		10—14.		15—19.		20—24.	
	Total.	Males.	Females.	Males.	Females.	Males.	Females.	Males.	Females.	Males.	Females.	Males.	Females.
1	2	3	4	5	6	7	8	9	10	11	12	13	14
II	4	3	1	...	...	...	1	...	...	...	...	...	...
III	17	12	5	5	5	1	...	1	...	1	...	1	...
IV	55	22	33	12	12	2	...	1	11	...	6	3	4
VI	85	31	54	7	9	8	6	4	26	4	7	1	1
VIII	70	45	25	19	3	6	20	6	1	7	1	1	...
IX	116	77	39	8	16	25	2	9	11	10	2	11	1
X	18	12	6	5	3	...	...	1	1	...	...	...	1
XI	11	7	4	...	...	2	2	3	...	...	...	...	...
XIII	2	2	...	...	...	...	...	...	...	...	...	...	...
XII	1	1	...	...	...	...	...	...	...	...	...	...	...
XX	5	5	...	...	...	...	...	...	...	2	...	1	...
XXI	3	1	2	...	2	...	...	...	...	...	...	...	...
XXII	6	6	...	2	...	1	...	1	...	2	...	...	...
XXIII	5	4	1	3	1	...	...	...	...	...	...	1	...
XXV	6	2	4	2	1	...	1	...	1	...	...	...	...
Total ...	404	230	174	63	52	45	32	26	51	26	16	19	7

TABLE VI.—RELIGION *by* CIVIL CONDITION,

WARD NO.	TOTAL MARRIED.			(2) MAR									
II	2	1	1	...	...	...	...	...	...	...	...	...	1
III	17	8	9	...	...	...	...	...	2	...	2	1	...
IV	32	17	15	...	...	...	...	...	...	...	5	4	...
V	1	1	...	...	...	...	...	...	...	1	...	...	...
VI	46	23	23	...	...	...	...	..	...	2	3	3	3
VIII	75	45	30	...	...	...	...	...	3	18	4	1	6
IX	50	32	18	...	...	...	...	...	...	...	4	2	3
X	14	11	3	...	...	...	...	...	...	2	2	1	...
XI	6	4	2	...	...	...	...	...	...	...	...	1	...
XIII	2	1	1	...	...	...	...	...	...	...	...	...	...
XXI	2	1	1	...	...	...	...	...	...	...	...	...	...
XXII	9	7	2	...	...	...	...	...	...	...	...	2	...
XXIII	1	...	1	...	...	...	1	...	...	...	...	...	...
XXV	4	2	2	...	...	...	...	...	...	...	...	...	1
Total ...	261	153	108	...	...	...	1	...	5	23	20	15	14

Sex and Age.—Part D.—*Brahmos.*

RIED.

Periods.

25—29. Males.	25—29. Females.	30—34. Males.	30—34. Females.	35—39. Males.	35—39. Females.	40—44. Males.	40—44. Females.	45—49. Males.	45—49. Females.	50—54. Males.	50—54. Females.	55—59. Males.	55—59. Females.	60 and over. Males.	60 and over. Females.	Ward No.
15	16	17	18	19	20	21	22	23	24	25	26	27	28	29	30	
...	...	3	...	...	...	...	...	...	...	...	...	...	...	...	...	II
1	...	1	...	...	...	1	...	...	...	...	...	...	...	...	...	III
3	...	...	...	...	...	1	...	...	...	...	...	...	...	...	...	IV
2	...	3	...	2	...	...	3	...	..	...	2	...	...	...	...	VI
6	...	...	...	...	...	...	...	...	...	...	...	...	...	...	...	VIII
1	1	12	4	1	2	...	...	...	...	...	...	...	...	...	...	IX
2	...	2	1	1	...	...	...	1	...	...	...	...	...	...	...	X
...	...	2	2	...	...	...	...	...	...	...	...	...	...	...	...	XI
2	...	...	...	...	...	...	...	...	...	...	...	...	...	...	...	XIII
...	...	1	...	...	...	...	...	...	...	...	...	...	...	...	...	XII
..	...	...	...	...	...	...	...	...	...	...	...	...	...	...	...	XX
...	...	...	...	...	...	1	...	...	...	...	—	...	...	...	...	XXI
...	...	...	...	...	...	...	...	...	...	...	...	...	...	...	...	XXII
...	...	...	...	...	...	...	...	...	...	...	...	...	...	...	...	XXIII
...	1	...	...	...	...	...	...	...	...	...	...	...	...	...	...	XXV
19	2	24	7	4	2	8	3	1	...	...	2	...	...	...	...	Total.

Sex and Age.—Part D.—*Brahmos.*

RIED.

15	16	17	18	19	20	21	22	23	24	25	26	27	28	29	30	Ward No.
...	...	...	...	...	...	1	...	...	...	...	...	...	...	...	...	II
2	4	2	...	2	...	2	1	...	...	...	...	...	...	...	...	III
4	4	2	6	3	...	2	...	1	...	1	...	...	...	...	...	IV
...	...	...	...	...	...	...	...	...	...	...	...	...	...	...	...	V
4	4	5	6	1	5	2	1	1	...	3	1	1	...	1	...	VI
2	12	10	2	...	1	9	1	2	...	2	1	1	...	...	...	VIII
2	3	4	4	10	2	13	2	...	...	...	...	1	...	...	...	IX
...	...	3	...	3	...	1	1	1	...	...	...	...	...	...	...	X
...	...	...	1	1	1	2	...	...	...	...	...	...	...	...	...	XI
...	...	...	1	1	...	...	...	...	...	...	...	...	...	...	...	XIII
...	1	1	...	...	...	...	...	...	...	...	...	...	...	...	...	XXI
1	2	...	...	1	...	1	...	2	...	...	...	...	...	...	...	XXII
...	...	...	...	...	...	...	...	...	...	...	...	...	...	...	...	XXIII
...	1	1	...	...	...	...	...	...	...	...	...	1	...	...	...	XXV
15	31	28	20	22	9	32	6	7	...	6	2	4	...	1	...	Total.

TABLE VI.—RELIGION by CIVIL CONDITION,

WARD No.	TOTAL WIDOWED.			(3) WI									
				AGE									
				0—4.		5—9.		10—14.		15—19.		20—24.	
	Total.	Males.	Females.	Males.	Females.	Males.	Females.	Males.	Females.	Males.	Females.	Males.	Females.
1	2	3	4	5	6	7	8	9	10	11	12	13	14
II	2	...	2	...	...	...	...	...	...	...	...	...	1
III	1	...	1	...	...	...	...	...	...	...	...	...	...
IV	4	...	4	...	...	...	...	...	...	...	1	...	1
VI	7	3	4	...	...	...	...	...	...	1	...	...	...
VIII	9	2	7	...	...	...	...	...	...	...	2	...	1
IX	8	2	6	...	...	...	...	...	...	...	...	...	...
X	11	3	8	...	...	...	...	...	...	...	...	...	1
XXI	1	...	1	...	...	...	...	...	...	...	...	...	1
Total ...	43	10	33	...	...	...	...	...	...	1	3		5

CIVIL CONDITION by RELIGION

	TOTAL UNMARRIED.			(1) UNMAR									
V	1	1	...	...	...	...	...	...	...	...	...	1	...
VII	19	15	4	4	1	1	1	1	2	4	...	3	...
VIII	218	182	36	20	10	11	11	12	2	37	2	12	1
IX	7	4	3	2	...	...	1	1	2	...	...	...	...
X	315	262	53	27	24	25	13	43	10	56	3	32	2
XI	2	1	1	1	1	...	...	...	...	...	...	...	...
XII	37	29	8	4	2	3	4	3	2	5	...	5	...
XIII	10	6	4	...	1	1	1	...	2	...	...	1	...
XIV	44	21	23	5	6	3	7	4	6	1	1	2	1
XVI	17	15	2	...	2	4	...	5	...	3	...	...	...
XVII	19	19	...	...	...	2	...	...	...	4	...	5	...
XIX	1	1	...	...	...	...	...	...	...	...	...	...	...
XXI	20	15	5	1	5	2	...	5	...	4	...	2	...
XXII	3	3	...	...	...	...	...	...	...	1	...	...	...
XXIII	48	48	...	...	...	...	...	1	...	2	...	29	...
Total ...	761	622	139	64	52	52	38	75	26	117	6	92	4
Port and Canals ...	5	5	...	...	...	...	...	...	...	...	...	3	...

Sex *and* **Age.—Part D.—*Brahmos.***

DOWED.																
PERIODS.																
25—29.		30—34.		35—39.		40—44.		45—49.		50—54.		55—59.		60 and over.		Ward No.
Males.	Females.	Males.	Females.	Males.	Females.	Males.	Females.	Males.	Females.	Males.	Females.	Males.	Females.	Males.	Females.	
15	16	17	18	19	20	21	22	23	24	25	26	27	28	29	30	
...	...	...	...	...	...	...	1	...	...	...	...	...	...	...	...	II
...	...	...	...	...	...	...	1	...	...	...	...	...	...	...	...	III
...	...	...	...	...	...	...	...	...	...	...	1	...	1	...	...	IV
...	...	1	...	...	...	1	3	...	1	...	...	...	...	...	...	VI
...	...	...	...	...	...	2	2	...	1	...	1	...	...	...	...	VIII
...	...	...	...	...	3	...	2	...	...	2	1	...	...	...	...	IX
...	1	1	...	...	1	...	...	1	1	...	1	1	1	...	2	X
...	...	...	...	...	...	...	...	...	...	...	...	...	...	...	...	XXI
...	1	2	...	...	4	3	9	1	3	2	4	1	2	...	2	Total.

and Age.—Part E.—*Buddhists.*

RIED.																
...	...	...	...	...	...	...	...	...	...	...	...	...	...	...	...	V
1	...	...	...	...	...	1	...	...	...	...	...	...	...	...	...	VII
19	2	25	...	12	...	7	1	12	3	8	3	3	1	4	...	VIII
...	...	1	...	...	...	...	...	...	...	...	...	...	...	...	...	IX
38	1	23	...	10	...	2	...	3	...	3	...	...	...	...	...	X
...	...	...	...	...	...	...	...	...	...	...	...	...	...	...	...	XI
5	...	1	...	1	...	2	...	...	...	...	...	...	...	...	...	XII
1	...	3	...	...	...	...	...	...	...	...	...	...	...	...	...	XIII
1	...	1	2	3	...	...	...	...	...	1	...	...	...	...	...	XIV
...	...	3	...	...	...	...	...	...	...	...	...	...	...	...	...	XVI
7	...	...	...	...	...	...	...	1	...	...	...	...	...	...	...	XVII
...	...	...	...	...	...	...	...	1	...	...	...	...	...	...	...	XIX
...	...	1	...	...	...	...	...	...	...	...	...	...	...	...	...	XXI
1	...	...	...	1	...	...	...	...	...	...	...	...	...	...	...	XXII
9	...	5	...	2	...	...	...	...	...	...	...	...	...	...	...	XXIII
82	3	63	2	29	...	12	1	17	3	12	3	3	1	4	...	Total.
...	...	2	...	...	...	...	...	...	...	...	...	...	...	...	...	Port and Canals.

TABLE VI.—CIVIL CONDITION *by* RELIGION,

WARD No.	TOTAL MARRIED.			(2) MAR AGE									
				0—4.		5—9.		10—14.		15—19.		20—24.	
	Total.	Males.	Females.	Males.	Females.	Males.	Females.	Males.	Females.	Males.	Females.	Males.	Females.
1	2	3	4	5	6	7	8	9	10	11	12	13	14
VII	60	51	9	...	...	...	...	...	5	4	3	6	...
VIII	361	334	27	...	...	1	1	3	1	21	4	43	5
IX	2	1	1	...	...	...	...	...	...	...	...	1	...
X	479	365	114	...	...	...	...	...	5	18	14	46	19
XI	6	3	3	...	...	...	...	...	...	...	1	...	1
XII	73	66	7	...	...	...	...	1	...	4	1	14	1
XIII	41	37	4	...	...	1	...	1	...	4	...	6	...
XIV	46	19	27	...	...	...	...	...	1	2	4	4	2
XV	1	1	...	...	...	...	...	...	...	...	...	...	...
XVI	3	1	2	...	...	...	...	...	...	...	2	...	...
XVII	53	52	1	...	...	...	...	...	...	1	1	4	...
XIX	1	1	...	...	...	...	...	...	...	...	...	...	...
XXI	16	11	5	...	...	...	...	...	...	...	...	...	...
XXII	6	6	...	...	...	...	...	...	...	1	...	1	...
XXIII	113	113	...	...	...	...	...	...	...	2	...	34	...
XXV	1	1	...	...	...	...	...	...	...	...	...	...	...
Total ...	1,262	1,062	200	...	...	2	1	5	12	57	30	159	28
Port and Canals ...	48	48	8	...	...	...	...	...	...	6	...	10	...

TABLE VI.—CIVIL CONDITION *by* RELIGION,

	TOTAL WIDOWED.			(3) WIDO									
VII	6	3	3	...	...	...	...	...	...	...	...	...	...
VIII	37	28	9	...	...	...	...	3	...	1	1	...	...
IX	1	...	1	...	...	...	...	...	...	...	...	...	...
X	56	12	44	...	...	...	...	...	2	...	1	1	1
XI	1	...	1	...	...	...	...	...	...	...	...	...	...
XII	2	2	...	...	...	...	...	...	...	...	...	...	...
XIII	6	...	6	...	...	...	...	...	...	...	2	...	...
XIV	8	3	5	...	...	...	...	...	...	...	...	...	...
XXI	2		2	...	...	...	...	...	...	...	...	...	1
XXIII	3	3	...	...	...	...	...	...	...	...	...	...	...
Total ...	112	51	71	...	...	...	...	3	2	1	4	1	2
Port and Canals ...	1	1	...	...	...	...	...	...	...	...	...	...	...

Sex *and* **Age.—Part E.**—*Buddhists.*

RIED.

PERIODS.

25—29.		30—34.		35—39.		40—44.		45—49.		50—54.		55—59.		60 and over.		Ward No.
Males.	Females.	Males.	Females.	Males.	Females.	Males.	Females.	Males.	Females.	Males.	Females.	Males.	Females.	Males.	Females.	
15	16	17	18	19	20	21	22	23	24	25	26	27	28	29	30	
8	...	8	...	9	...	2	1	3	...	2	...	2	...	7	...	VII
56	5	43	5	47	2	34	2	21	2	30	...	15	...	20	...	VIII
...	...	...	...	...	...	...	1	...	...	...	...	...	...	...	...	IX
63	27	69	17	44	5	43	11	29	5	27	7	16	3	10	1	X
...	1	1	...	...	...	2	...	...	...	...	...	...	...	...	...	XI
12	2	11	1	7	2	10	...	...	...	4	...	...	...	3	...	XII
4	1	4	...	2	1	3	...	4	1	4	1	2	...	2	...	XIII
2	8	4	2	1	4	4	3	...	1	2	...	...	1	...	1	XIV
...	...	1	...	...	...	...	...	...	...	...	...	...	...	...	...	XV
...	...	1	...	...	...	...	...	...	...	...	...	...	...	...	...	XVI
5	...	11	...	14	...	16	...	...	...	1	...	...	...	...	...	XVII
...	...	...	...	...	...	...	...	1	...	...	...	...	...	...	...	XIX
...	1	5	2	4	2	2	...	...	...	...	...	...	...	...	...	XXI
...	...	...	...	...	...	2	...	1	...	1	...	..	...	..	...	XXII
23	...	34	...	...	...	19	...	...	...	...	...	...	...	1	...	XXIII
...	...	1	...	...	...	...	...	...	...	...	...	...	...	...	...	XXV
173	45	193	27	128	16	137	18	59	9	71	8	35	4	43	2	Total.
5	...	14	...	8	...	5	...	...	...	...	...	...	...	...	...	Port and Canals.

Sex *and* **Age.—Part E.**—*Buddhists.*

WED.

15	16	17	18	19	20	21	22	23	24	25	26	27	28	29	30	Ward No.
...	...	1	...	...	...	1	...	...	1	...	1	...	1	1	...	VII
2	...	2	...	...	...	5	...	1	2	7	1	...	...	7	5	VIII
...	1	...	...	...	...	...	...	...	...	...	...	...	...	...	...	IX
...	3	2	2	2	1	3	8	1	3	2	8	1	7	...	8	X
...	1	...	...	...	...	...	...	...	...	...	...	...	...	...	...	XI
...	1	...	...	1	1	...	...	...	1	...	1	...	...	1	...	XII
...	...	...	...	...	...	...	...	...	...	...	...	...	...	...	...	XIII
1	...	...	...	1	...	1	...	...	...	...	1	...	1	...	3	XIV
...	...	...	...	...	...	...	1	...	...	...	...	...	...	...	...	XXI
1	...	1	...	1	...	...	...	...	...	...	...	...	...	...	...	XXIII
4	6	6	2	5	2	10	9	2	7	9	12	1	9	9	16	Total.
...	...	1	...	...	...	...	...	...	...	...	...	...	...	...		Port and Canals.

TABLE VI.—CIVIL CONDITION BY RELIGION,

WARD No.	TOTAL UNMARRIED.			(f) UNMAR… AGE									
				0—4.		5—9.		10—14.		15—19.		20—24.	
	Total.	Males.	Females.	Males.	Females.	Males.	Females.	Males.	Females.	Males.	Females.	Males.	Females.
1	2	3	4	5	6	7	8	9	10	11	12	13	14
II	1	1	...	...	...	...	...	1	...	...	...	...	...
III	1	1	...	...	...	...	...	...	...	...	...	1	:
V	59	37	22	12	7	5	12	14	3	2	...	...	...
VI	3	2	1	...	...	2	1	...	...	...	...	...	...
VII	11*	9	2	3	2	...	..	2	...	1	...	1	...
VIII	3	3	...	2	...	1	...	...	...	...	...	...	...
IX	3	2	1	...	...	2	1	...	...	...	...	...	...
X	3	2	1	...	1	2	...	...	...	...	...	...	...
XIV	4	2	2	...	...	...	2	...	...	...	...	...	...
XVII	7	6	1	1	...	...	...	3	...	1	1	1	...
XXII	2	...	2	...	1	...	1	...	...	...	...	...	...
XXIII	1	1	...	...	...	...	...	...	...	1	...	...	...
Total ...	98	66	32	18	11	12	17	20	3	5	1	3	...

Sex and Age.—Part F.—*Jains.*

RIED.																
PERIODS.																
25 - 29.		30--34.		35—39.		40 - 44,		45—49.		50—54.		55—59.		60 and over.		WARD No.
Males.	Females.	Males.	Females.	Males.	Females.	Males.	Females.	Males.	Females.	Males.	Females.	Males.	Females.	Males.	Females.	
15	16	17	18	19	20	21	22	23	24	25	26	27	28	29	30	
...	...	...	...	...	...	...	...	...	...	...	...	...	...	...	...	II
...	...	...	...	...	...	...	...	...	...	...	...	...	...	...	...	III
2	...	...	...	1	...	...	...	...	...	1	...	...	...	...	...	V
...	...	...	...	...	...	...	...	...	...	...	...	...	...	..	...	VI
...	...	...	...	...	...	2	...	...	...	...	...	...	..	...	...	VII
...	...	...	...	...	...	...	...	...	...	...	...	...	...	...	...	VIII
...	...	...	...	...	...	...	...	...	...	...	...	...	...	...	...	IX
...	...	...	...	...	...	...	...	...	...	...	...	...	...	...	...	X
...	...	2	...	...	...	...	...	...	...	...	...	...	...	...	...	XIV
...	...	...	...	...	...	...	...	...	...	...	...	...	...	...	...	XVII
...	...	...	...	...	...	...	...	...	...	...	...	...	...	...	...	XXII
...	...	...	...	...	...	...	...	...	...	...	...	...	...	...	...	XXIII
2	...	2	...	1	...	2	...	...	...	1	...	...	...	...	...	Total.

TABLE VI.—CIVIL CONDITION *by*

WARD No.	TOTAL MARRIED.			(2) MAR AGE									
				0—4.		5—9.		10—14.		15—19.		20—24.	
	Total.	Males.	Females.	Males.	Females.	Males.	Females.	Males.	Females.	Males.	Females.	Males.	Females.
1	2	3	4	5	6	7	8	9	10	11	12	13	14
I	1	1	...	...	...	...	...	...	...	...	...	...	...
II	3	1	2	...	...	...	2	...	...	...	...	...	...
III	1	1	...	...	...	...	...	...	...	...	...	...	...
V	220	139	81	...	...	1	1	3	6	30	16	10	16
VI	12	5	7	...	...	...	...	...	...	2	2	2	1
VII	41	38	3	...	...	...	...	...	...	6	...	8	...
VIII	7	3	4	...	...	...	...	..	...	...	2	1	1
IX	10	4	6	...	...	...	...	1	2	...	...	...	...
X	7	3	4	...	...	...	...	1	2	...	1	2	...
XIV	23	17	6	...	...	...	...	...	1	...	...	...	...
XV	2	...	2	...	...	...	...	...	...	...	...	...	...
XVII	26	19	7	...	...	...	...	...	1	6	1	1	1
XXII	5	3	2	...	...	...	...	...	...	...	2	...	...
XXV	1	1	...	...	...	...	...	...	...	1	...	...	...
Total ...	359	235	124	...	...	1	3	5	12	45	24	24	19
Port and Canals ...	1	1	...	...	...	...	...	...	...	1	...	..	...

TABLE VI.—CIVIL CONDITION *by*

	TOTAL WIDOWED.			WIDO									
V	15	3	12	...	...	...	...	...	...	1	2	...	2
VII	8	4	4	...	...	...	...	...	...	...	...	...	...
VIII	3	...	3	...	...	...	...	...	...	...	1	...	...
IX	3	...	3	...	...	...	...	...	...	...	...	...	...
X	3	...	3	...	...	...	...	...	...	...	...	...	...
XVII	4	3	1	...	...	...	...	...	...	...	...	...	...
Total ...	36	10	26	...	...	...	...	...	...	1	3	...	2

RELIGION *and* AGE.— PART F.—*Jains.*

RIED.

PERIODS.

25—29.		30—34.		35—39.		40—44.		45—49.		50—54.		55—59.		60 and over.		WARD No.
Males.	Females.	Males.	Females.	Males.	Females.	Males.	Females.	Males.	Females.	Males.	Females.	Males.	Females.	Males.	Females.	
15	16	17	18	19	20	21	22	23	24	25	26	27	28	29	30	
...	...	1	...	...	...	...	...	...	...	...	...	...	...	...	...	I
...	...	1	...	...	...	...	...	...	...	...	...	...	...	...	...	II
...	...	1	...	...	...	...	...	...	...	...	...	...	...	...	...	III
20	14	23	12	14	8	10	8	11	...	9	...	7	...	1	...	V
...	3	1	1	...	...	...	...	...	...	...	...	...	...	...	...	VI
3	3	3	...	...	...	8	...	10	...	...	...	...	...	...	...	VII
...	1	...	...	...	...	2	...	...	...	...	...	...	...	...	...	VIII
...	...	2	3	1	...	...	1	...	...	...	...	...	...	...	...	IX
...	...	...	...	...	...	...	1	...	...	...	...	...	...	...	...	X
5	...	5	3	...	...	7	2	...	...	...	...	...	...	...	...	XIV
...	...	...	1	...	...	...	1	...	...	...	...	...	...	...	...	XV
1	1	3	1	1	1	4	1	1	...	1	...	1	...	...	...	XVII
...	...	3	...	...	...	...	...	...	...	...	...	...	...	...	...	XXII
...	...	...	...	...	...	...	...	...	...	...	...	...	...	...	...	XXV
29	22	43	21	16	9	31	14	22	...	10	...	8	...	1	...	Total.
...	...	...	...	...	...	...	...	...	...	...	...	...	...	...	...	Port and Canals.

RELIGION, SEX *and* AGE.—PART F.—*Jains.*

WED

...	...	1	2	...	2	1	3	...	1	...	...	...	...	...	...	V
...	...	1	...	1	...	1	2	...	...	1	...	...	1	...	1	VII
...	...	...	...	...	...	...	2	...	...	...	...	...	...	...	...	VIII
...	...	...	2	...	...	...	...	...	...	...	...	...	...	...	1	IX
...	...	...	2	...	...	...	1	...	...	...	...	...	...	...	...	X
...	...	...	1	...	...	...	...	1	...	1	...	1	...	...	...	XVII
...	...	2	7	1	2	2	8	1	1	2	...	1	1	...	2	Total.

TABLE VI.—CIVIL CONDITION *by*

WARD No.	TOTAL UNMARRIED.			(1) UNMAR AGE 0—4.		5—9.		10—14.		15—19.		20—24.	
	Total.	Males.	Females.	Males.	Females.	Males.	Females.	Males.	Females.	Males.	Females.	Males.	Females.
1	2	3	4	5	6	7	8	9	10	11	12	13	14
V	1	1	...	...	...	1	...	...	...	...	...	...	...
VII	335	190	145	40	27	42	54	47	25	13	9	7	10
VIII	246	125	121	30	48	32	30	32	28	5	...	...	...
X	22	12	10	3	4	2	5	1	...	6	1	...	...
XI	5	4	1	1	...	1	...	...	...	2	1	...	...
XII	4	4	...	1	...	1	...	...	...	...	...	...	...
XIII	50	20	30	5	4	...	2	8	4	...	8	2	10
XV	7	3	4	1	1	2	1	...	...	...	2	...	...
XVI	10	6	4	1	2	...	...	...	1	5	...	...	...
XIX	6	2	4	1	...	...	...	1	...	...	...	...	...
XX	5	3	2	...	...	...	...	1	...	...	...	2	...
XXI	5	3	2	1	1	...	1	...	...	...	...	...	...
Total ...	695	373	323	84	87	81	93	90	58	31	21	11	20
Port and Canals ...	4	4	...	1	...	2	...	1	...	...	...	...	...

RELIGION *and* **AGE.—PART G.—*Jews.***

RIED.																
PERIODS.																
25—29		30—34		35—39		40—44		45—49		50—54		55—59		60 and over.		WARD NO.
Males.	Females.	Males.	Females.	Males.	Females.	Males.	Females.	Males.	Females.	Males.	Females.	Males.	Females.	Males.	Females.	
15	16	17	18	19	20	21	22	23	24	25	26	27	28	29	30	
...	...	...	...	...	...	...	...	...	...	...	...	...	...	...	...	V
12	7	11	6	10	6	5	...	2	1	1	...	...	...	...	...	VII
9	8	9	7	7	4	1	...	...	...	...	...	...	...	...	1	VIII
...	...	...	...	...	...	...	...	...	...	...	...	...	...	...	...	X
...	...	...	...	...	...	...	...	...	...	...	...	...	...	...	...	XI
...	...	2	...	...	...	...	...	...	...	...	...	...	...	...	...	XII
...	...	3	...	...	...	...	2	2	...	...	...	...	...	...	...	XIII
...	...	...	...	...	...	...	...	...	...	...	...	...	...	...	...	XV
...	...	...	...	...	1	...	...	...	...	...	...	...	...	...	...	XVI
...	...	...	3	...	1	...	...	...	...	...	...	...	...	...	...	XIX
...	2	...	...	...	...	...	...	...	...	...	...	...	...	...	...	XX
...	...	...	...	1	...	1	...	...	...	...	...	...	...	...	...	XXI
21	12	25	16	18	12	7	2	4	1	1	...	...	...	...	1	Total.
...	...	...	...	...	...	...	...	...	...	...	...	...	...	...	...	Port and Canals.

TABLE VI.—CIVIL CONDITION *by* RELIGION

Ward No.	Total Married.			II.—MAR									
				AGE									
				0—4		5—9		10—14		15—19		20—24	
	Total.	Males.	Females.	Males.	Females.	Males.	Females.	Males.	Females.	Males.	Females.	Males.	Females.
1	2	3	4	5	6	7	8	9	10	11	12	13	14
V	4	2	2	...	...	...	...	...	1	1	1	1	...
VII	250	123	127	...	...	...	...	1	1	9	20	9	25
VIII	230	114	116	...	...	...	...	...	...	10	24	21	6
X	19	12	7	...	...	...	...	...	...	3	6	3	...
XI	2	1	1	...	...	...	...	...	...	...	1	...	...
XII	6	2	4	...	...	...	...	...	...	...	2	...	2
XIII	44	26	18	...	...	...	...	...	2	3	6	6	...
XV	7	4	3	...	...	...	...	...	...	...	1	...	2
XVI	1	...	1	...	...	...	...	...	...	...	...	...	...
XVII	1	1	...	...	...	...	...	...	...	...	...	...	...
XX	4	2	2	...	...	...	...	...	...	...	1	...	...
XXI	2	1	1	...	...	...	...	...	...	...	...	...	...
Total ...	570	288	282	...	...	...	...	1	4	26	62	40	35
Port and Canals ...	7	5	2	...	...	...	...	...	...	...	...	2	...

d Age—Part G.—*Jews.*

ed.																
sions.																
25—29		30—34		35—39		40—44		45—49		50—54		55—59		60 & over.		Ward No.
Males.	Females.	Males.	Females.	Males.	Females.	Males.	Females.	Males.	Females.	Males.	Females.	Males.	Females.	Males.	Females.	
15	16	17	18	19	20	21	22	23	24	25	26	27	28	29	30	
...	...	...	...	...	...	...	...	...	...	...	...	...	...	...	...	V
11	82	12	1	13	7	30	21	6	6	17	6	4	3	11	5	VII
8	16	6	28	6	12	7	5	16	6	12	7	20	9	8	3	VIII
...	...	...	...	...	...	...	1	2	...	4	...	...	...	...	...	X
...	...	...	...	...	...	1	...	...	...	...	...	...	...	...	...	XI
...	...	1	...	...	...	1	...	...	...	...	...	...	...	...	...	XII
2	9	...	...	...	...	10	...	5	...	...	1	...	...	...	...	XIII
...	...	2	...	...	...	...	...	...	...	2	...	...	...	...	...	XV
...	...	...	1	...	...	...	...	...	...	...	...	...	...	...	...	XVI
...	...	1	...	...	...	...	...	...	...	...	...	...	...	...	...	XVII
...	...	...	...	...	...	2	1	...	...	...	...	...	...	...	...	XX
1	1	...	...	...	...	...	...	...	...	...	...	...	...	...	...	XXI
22	58	22	30	19	19	51	28	29	12	35	14	24	12	19	8	Total.
2	1	...	1	...	...	...	...	1	...	...	...	...	...	...	...	Port and Canals.

TABLE VI—CIVIL CONDITION *by* RELIGION

WARD No.	TOTAL WIDOWS.			III.—WI									
				AGE									
				0–4		5–9		10–14		15–19		20–24	
	Total.	Males.	Females.	Males.	Females.	Males.	Females.	Males.	Females.	Males.	Females.	Males.	Females.
1	2	3	4	5	6	7	8	9	10	11	12	13	14
V	1	1	...	...	...	...	...	...	...	...	...	...	...
VII	53	7	46	...	...	...	...	...	...	2	4	...	2
VIII	45	11	34	...	...	...	...	...	...	...	...	...	...
X	7	...	7	...	...	...	...	...	...	...	...	...	...
XII	2	...	2	...	...	...	...	...	...	...	...	...	...
XIII	7	1	6	...	...	...	...	...	...	...	...	...	...
XV	1	...	1	...	...	...	...	...	...	...	...	...	...
XVI	2	...	2	...	...	...	...	...	...	...	...	...	...
XIX	1	1	...	...	...	...	...	...	...	...	...	...	...
XX	2	1	1	...	...	...	...	...	...	...	...	...	...
Total ...	121	22	99	...	...	...	...	...	...	2	4	...	2
Port and Canals ...	1	...	1	...	...	...	...	...	...	...	...	...	...

and Age—Part G.—*Jews.*

DOWED.																
Periods.																
25—29		30—34		35—39		40—44		45—49		50—54		55—59		60 & over.		Ward No.
Males.	Females.	Males.	Females.	Males.	Females.	Males.	Females.	Males.	Females.	Males.	Females.	Males.	Females.	Males.	Females.	
15	16	17	18	19	20	21	22	23	24	25	26	27	28	29	30	
...	...	...	...	...	...	1	...	...	...	...	...	...	...	...	...	V
...	...	...	...	...	...	3	20	2	12	...	8	...	...	...	...	VII
1	2	...	3	...	...	...	9	...	7	...	6	6	4	4	3	VIII
...	...	...	2	...	...	...	5	...	...	...	...	...	...	...	...	X
...	...	...	...	...	...	...	2	...	...	...	...	...	...	...	...	XII
...	3	...	...	...	...	...	...	...	...	...	...	1	3	...	...	XIII
...	...	...	...	...	...	...	...	...	...	...	...	...	...	...	1	XV
...	...	...	...	...	1	...	...	...	...	...	...	...	1	...	...	XVI
...	...	...	...	...	...	...	...	...	...	...	...	...	...	1	...	XIX
...	...	...	...	...	...	...	1	1	...	...	...	...	...	...	...	XX
1	5	...	5	...	1	4	37	3	19	...	14	7	8	5	4	Total.
...	...	...	...	...	...	...	...	...	...	...	...	...	1	...	...	Port and Canals.

TABLE VI.—CIVIL CONDITION *by* RELIGION,

WARD No.	TOTAL UNMARRIED.			(1) UNMAR AGE-									
				0—4		5—9		10—14		15—19		20—24	
	Total.	Males.	Females.	Males.	Females.	Males.	Females.	Males.	Females.	Males.	Females.	Males.	Females.
1	2	3	4	5	6	7	8	9	10	11	12	13	14
III	1	1	...	...	...	...	...	1	...	...	...	...	...
VII	15	9	6	4	2	4	2	1	2	...	...	...	...
X	3	3	...	1	...	...	...	1	...	...	...	...	...
XII	4	4	...	...	...	...	...	1	...	2	...	1	...
XIII	1	1	...	...	...	...	...	1	...	...	...	...	...
XXI	3	3	...	1	...	1	...	...	...	1	...	...	...
XXV	5	5	...	1	...	1	...	3	...	...	...	...	...
Total ...	32	26	6	7	2	6	2	8	2	3	...	1	...

	TOTAL MARRIED.			(2) MAR									
III	5	4	1	...	...	...	...	...	...	2	1	1	...
IV	22	12	10	...	...	2	1	1	1	5	3	...	...
VII	66	55	11	...	...	...	...	1	...	3	...	3	4
X	3	1	2	...	...	...	...	...	...	...	...	...	1
XII	8	5	3	...	...	...	...	...	1	...	...	...	...
XIII	10	7	3	...	...	...	...	...	...	...	...	...	1
XXI	5	3	2	...	...	...	...	...	...	...	...	...	...
XXV	10	6	4	...	...	...	...	...	...	...	...	...	1
Total ...	129	93	36	...	...	2	1	2	2	10	4	4	7

	TOTAL WIDOWED.			(3) WID									
III	2	2	...	...	...	...	...	...	...	...	...	...	...
VII	2	1	1	...	...	...	...	...	...	...	...	...	...
X	1	1	...	...	...	...	...	...	...	...	...	...	...
Total ...	5	4	1	...	...	...	...	1	...	...	...	...	...

Sex and Age.—Part H.—*Parsis.*

RIED.

PERIODS.

25—29		30—34		35—39		40—44		45—49		50—54		55—59		60 and over.		Ward No.
Males.	Females.	Males.	Females.	Males.	Females.	Males.	Females.	Males.	Females.	Males.	Females.	Males.	Females.	Males.	Females.	
15	16	17	18	19	20	21	22	23	24	25	26	27	28	29	30	
...	...	...	...	...	...	...	...	...	...	...	...	...	...	...	...	III
...	...	...	...	...	...	...	...	...	...	...	...	...	...	...	...	VII
1	...	...	...	...	...	...	...	...	...	...	...	...	...	...	...	X
...	...	...	...	...	...	...	...	...	...	...	...	...	...	...	...	XII
...	...	...	...	...	...	...	...	...	...	...	...	...	...	...	...	XIII
...	...	...	...	...	...	...	...	...	...	...	...	...	...	...	...	XXI
...	...	...	...	...	...	...	...	...	...	...	...	...	...	...	...	XXV
1	...	...	...	...	...	...	...	...	...	...	...	...	...	...	...	Total.

RIED.

25—29 Males	25—29 Females	30—34 Males	30—34 Females	35—39 Males	35—39 Females	40—44 Males	40—44 Females	45—49 Males	45—49 Females	50—54 Males	50—54 Females	55—59 Males	55—59 Females	60 and over Males	60 and over Females	Ward No.
1	...	...	...	...	...	...	...	...	...	...	...	...	...	...	...	III
...	1	...	1	2	...	2	3	...	...	...	...	...	...	...	...	IV
4	4	15	...	8	...	8	3	6	...	3	...	...	...	4	...	VII
...	...	...	...	1	...	...	...	...	1	...	...	...	...	...	...	X
...	1	3	...	...	...	...	1	...	...	...	...	1	...	1	...	XII
2	2	2	...	...	...	3	...	...	...	...	...	...	...	...	...	XIII
1	...	2	...	...	...	...	2	...	...	...	...	...	...	...	...	XXI
2	1	2	1	...	...	2	1	...	...	...	...	...	...	...	...	XXV
10	9	24	2	11	...	15	10	6	1	3	...	1	...	5	...	Total.

OWED.

25—29 Males	25—29 Females	30—34 Males	30—34 Females	35—39 Males	35—39 Females	40—44 Males	40—44 Females	45—49 Males	45—49 Females	50—54 Males	50—54 Females	55—59 Males	55—59 Females	60 and over Males	60 and over Females	Ward No.
...	...	1	...	...	...	1	...	...	...	...	...	...	...	...	...	III
...	...	1	1	...	...	...	...	...	...	...	...	...	...	...	...	VII
...	...	...	...	...	...	...	...	1	...	...	...	...	...	...	...	X
...	...	2	1	...	...	1	...	1	...	...	...	...	...	...	...	Total.

TABLE VI.—CIVIL CONDITION *by* RELIGION,

WARD No.	TOTAL UNMARRIED.			(1) UNMAR — AGE									
				0—4.		5—9.		10—14.		15—19.		20—24.	
	Total.	Males.	Females.	Males.	Females.	Males.	Females.	Males.	Females.	Males.	Females.	Males.	Females.
1	2	3	4	5	6	7	8	9	10	11	12	13	14
XIV	21	13	8	5	5	3	2	3	...	2	...	...	...
XXV	15	15	...	1	...	2	...	...	...	5	...	7	...
Total ...	36	28	8	6	5	5	2	3	...	7	...	7	...
Fort William ...	63	63	...	...	...	1	1	1	...	25	...	15	...
(2) MAR													
XIV	26	15	11	...	...	...	...	2	1	...	4	2	4
XXV	40	38	2	...	1	...	...	...	...	...	1	...	...
Total ...	66	53	13	...	1	...	...	2	1	...	5	2	4
Fort William ...	107	107	...	...	...	...	...	...	...	15	...	20	...
(3) WID													
XIV	2	...	2	...	...	...	...	...	...	...	...	...	...
XXV	4	...	4	...	...	...	1	...	...	...	...	...	...
Total ...	6	...	6	...	...	...	1	...	...	...	...	...	...
Fort William ...	9	9	...	...	...	...	...	...	...	2	...	3	...

Sex and Age.—Part I.—*Sikhs.*

25—29.		30—34.		35—39.		40—44.		45—49.		50—54.		55—59.		60 and over.		Ward No.
Males.	Females.	Males.	Females.	Males.	Females.	Males.	Females.	Males.	Females.	Males.	Females.	Males.	Females.	Males.	Females.	
15	16	17	18	19	20	21	22	23	24	25	26	27	28	29	30	
RIED. — **PERIODS.**																
...	1	...	...	...	...	...	...	...	...	...	...	...	...	...	...	XIV
...	...	...	...	...	...	...	...	...	...	...	...	...	...	...	...	XXV
...	1	...	...	...	...	...	...	...	...	...	...	...	...	...	...	Total.
9	...	4	...	8	...	...	...	...	...	...	...	...	...	...	...	Fort William.
RIED.																
2	...	1	...	1	1	1	1	1	...	1	...	2	...	2	...	XIV
10	...	11	...	6	...	1	...	2	...	3	...	2	...	3	...	XXV
12	...	12	...	7	1	2	1	3	...	4	...	4	...	5	...	Total.
29	...	30	...	6	...	3	...	2	...	2	...	...	...	...	...	Fort William.
OWED.																
...	...	...	...	...	...	...	2	...	...	...	...	...	...	...	...	XIV
...	...	...	3	...	...	...	...	...	...	...	...	...	...	...	...	XXV
..	...	...	3	...	...	...	2	...	...	...	...	...	...	...	...	Total.
2	...	...	...	1	...	...	...	...	...	...	...	1	...	...	...	Fort William.

TABLE VII.—EDUCATION *by*

CASTES.	TOTAL.			TOTAL BY EDUCATION.					
				Learning.		Literate.		Illiterate.	
	Total.	Males.	Females.	Males.	Females.	Males.	Females.	Males.	Females.
Hindus	428,762	272,432	156,330	15,697	1,914	91,046	8,248	165,689	146,168
Muhammadans ...	189,226	125,591	63,635	2,614	194	18 343	1,028	104,634	62,418
Christians	26,406	13,690	12,716	2,037	2,052	8,213	6,908	3,440	3,756
Brahmos	708	393	315	94	75	205	136	94	104
Buddhists	2,145	1,735	410	70	16	892	88	773	306
Jains	493	311	182	28	6	196	10	87	166
Jews	1,387	683	704	56	47	372	217	255	440
Parsis	166	123	43	7	4	84	20	32	19
Sikhs	108	81	27	11	2	26	3	44	22
Total ...	649,401	415,039	234,362	20,614	4,310	119,377	16,653	275,048	213,399

TABLE VII.—EDUCATION *by*

CASTES.	AGE-							
	15—24.							
	Total.		Learning.		Literate.		Illiterate.	
	Males.	Females.	Males.	Females.	Males.	Females.	Males.	Females.
Hindus ...	55,668	26,950	1,057	878	32,796	4,008	21,815	22,064
Muhammadans.	23,500	11,560	616	35	4,455	308	18,429	11,217
Christians ...	2,554	2,768	401	407	1,881	2,065	272	296
Brahmos ...	84	65	22	19	54	43	8	3
Buddhists ...	427	74	24	3	246	29	157	42
Jains ...	78	49	6	...	60	2	12	47
Jews ...	110	144	6	2	74	82	30	60
Parsis ...	18	11	2	1	16	4	...	6
Sikhs ...	16	9	3	...	8	2	5	7
Total ...	82,455	41,630	2,137	1,345	39,590	6,543	40,728	33,742

RELIGION *and* AGE.

AGE-PERIODS.								CASTES.
0—14.								
Total.		Learning.		Literate.		Illiterate.		
Males.	Females.	Males.	Females.	Males.	Females.	Males.	Females.	
51,431	40,483	13,918	671	19,023	2,213	18,490	37,599	Hindus.
25,124	18,822	1,786	138	1,132	188	22,206	18,496	Muhammedans.
4,332	4,286	1,600	1,609	757	737	1,975	1,910	Christians.
134	141	69	52	8	23	57	66	Brahmos.
201	131	39	13	26	14	136	104	Buddhists.
56	46	22	5	12	1	22	40	Jains.
256	242	50	44	40	39	166	159	Jews.
25	9	4	2	2	2	19	5	Parsis.
16	10	8	2	6	1	2	7	Sikhs.
81,575	64,170	17,496	2,536	21,006	3,218	43,073	58,416	Total.

RELIGION *and* AGE—continued.

PERIODS.—*concluded.*								CASTES.
25 and over.								
Total.		Learning.		Literate.		Illiterate.		
Males.	Females.	Males.	Females.	Males.	Females.	Males.	Females.	
165,333	88,897	722	365	39,227	2,027	125,384	86,505	Hindus.
76,967	33,253	212	21	12,756	527	63,939	32,705	Muhammedans.
6,804	5,662	36	36	5,575	4,106	1,193	1,520	Christians.
175	109	3	4	143	70	29	35	Brahmos.
1,107	205	7	...	620	45	480	160	Buddhists.
177	87	...	1	124	7	53	79	Jains.
317	318	...	1	258	96	59	221	Jews.
80	23	1	1	66	14	13	8	Parsis.
49	8	...	...	12	...	37	8	Sikhs.
251,009	128,562	981	429	58,781	6,892	191,247	121,241	Total.

TABLE VII.—EDUCATION *by*

RELIGIONS.	TOTAL.									0—14.							
				Learning.		Literate.		Illiterate.		Total.		Learning.		Literate.		Illiterate.	
	Total.	Males.	Females.	Males.	Females.	Males.	Females.	Males.	Females.	Males.	Females.	Males.	Females.	Males.	Females.	Males.	Females.
																	FORT
Hindus ...	1,441	1,333	108	9	...	610	1	714	107	84	31	2	...	1	...	81	31
Mussulmans ...	597	555	42	14	...	210	5	331	37	31	11	4	...	1	1	26	10
Christians ...	1,251	1,052	199	43	42	964	111	45	46	80	89	39	40	15	13	26	36
Sikhs ...	179	179	...	12	...	100	...	67	...	2	...	2	...	...	...	...	...
Total ...	3,468	3,119	349	78	42	1,884	117	1,157	190	197	131	47	40	17	14	133	77
																	PORT AND
Hindus ...	13,934	13,858	76	73	...	1,005	...	12,780	76	601	12	28	...	73	...	500	12
Mussulmans...	13,350	13,342	8	29	...	716	1	12,597	7	476	1	13	...	36	...	427	1
Christians ...	1,340	1,324	16	70	9	1,004	6	250	1	12	5	12	5	...	...	...	...
Budhists ...	54	54	...	2	...	9	...	43	...	...	...	...	...	...	...	...	...
Jains ...	1	1	...	...	...	1	...	...	...	...	...	...	...	...	...	...	...
Jews ...	12	9	3	...	...	3	...	6	3	4	...	...	...	...	...	4	...
Total ...	28,691	28,588	103	174	9	2,738	7	25,676	87	1,093	18	53	5	109	...	931	13

Religion *and* **Age—continued.**

15—24.								25 and over.							
Total.		Learning.		Literate.		Illiterate.		Total.		Learning.		Literate.		Illiterate.	
Males.	Females.	Males.	Females.	Males.	Females.	Males.	Females.	Males.	Females.	Males.	Females.	Males.	Females.	Males.	Females.
WILLIAM.															
341	20	1	...	220	...	120	20	908	67	6	...	389	1	513	56
149	9	1	...	92	3	56	6	375	22	9	...	117	1	249	21
444	39	4	1	421	32	19	6	528	71	...	1	528	66	...	4
80	...	10	...	30	...	40	...	97	...	...	...	70	...	27	...
1,014	68	16	1	763	35	235	32	1,908	150	15	1	1,104	68	789	81
CANALS.															
3,690	21	22	...	239	...	3,429	21	9,567	43	23	...	693	...	8,851	43
3,816	1	4	...	239	...	3,573	1	9,050	6	12	...	441	1	8,597	5
329	8	25	4	225	4	79	...	983	3	33	...	779	2	171	1
19	...	2	...	1	...	16	...	35	...	...	...	8	...	27	...
1	...	...	...	1	...	...	...	...	...	...	...	...	...	...	...
2	...	...	...	...	...	2	...	3	3	...	...	3	...	...	3
7,857	30	63	4	705	4	7,099	22	19,638	55	68	...	1,924	3	17,646	52

TABLE VIII.—*Languages spoken by the inhabitants of Calcutta as their mother-tongue.*

I.—ASIATIC.

LANGUAGE.	TOWN.			FORT WILLIAM.			PORT AND CANALS.		
	Males.	Females.	Total.	Males.	Females.	Total.	Males.	Females.	Total.
(*A*)—WITHIN THE INDIAN EMPIRE.									
Assamese	38	11	49	...	...	...	...	...	...
Bengali	208,377	152,948	361,325	59	34	93	14,049	61	14,110
Bhutia	3	4	7	...	...	...	...	...	...
Burmese	454	60	514	...	...	...	...	...	...
Canarese	1	...	1	...	...	...	...	...	...
Cancanese	5	...	5	...	...	...	23	...	23
Cutchi	8	1	9	...	...	...	...	...	...
Gujarati	547	168	715	2	...	2	85	...	85
Gurkha	11	...	11	9	...	9	...	...	...
Hindi	149,256	57,819	207,075	1,741	134	1,875	10,950	3	10,953
Khasia	2	...	2	...	...	...	...	...	...
Madrasi	270	276	546	...	...	...	19	...	19
Manipuri	1	...	1	...	...	...	...	...	...
Marathi	11	5	16	...	...	...	36	...	36
Marwari	9	3	12	...	...	...	...	...	...
Panjabi	164	4	168	174	...	181	19	...	19
Pahariya	2	...	2	...	...	...	...	...	...
Peshawari	12	...	12	...	7	...	...	...	...
Pusthu	1	...	1	1	...	1	...	...	...
Tamil	538	251	789	...	...	...	20	...	20
Telugu	227	152	379	...	...	...	40	...	40
Urdu	17,523	8,064	25,587	40	...	40	2,101	14	2,115
Uriya	21,701	1,919	23,620	20	...	20	259	...	259
Total ...	399,161	221,685	620,846	2,046	175	2,221	7,601	78	27,679

II.—ASIATIC.

LANGUAGE.	TOWN. Males.	TOWN. Females.	TOWN. Total.	FORT WILLIAM. Males.	FORT WILLIAM. Females.	FORT WILLIAM. Total.	PORT AND CANALS. Males.	PORT AND CANALS. Females.	PORT AND CANALS. Total.
(*B*)—OUTSIDE OF THE INDIAN EMPIRE.									
Arabic	919	435	1,354	10	...	10	...	...	...
Armenian	176	126	302	...	...	..	8	...	8
Chinese	586	100	686	..	...	...	13	...	13
Cochin	6	10	16	...	...	...	...	...	...
Hebrew	229	224	453	...	...	...	...	...	...
Japanese	1	13	14	...	...	...	1	...	1

II.—Asiatic—*continued.*

Language.	Town.			Fort William.			Port and Canals.		
	Males	Females.	Total.	Males.	Females.	Total.	Males.	Females.	Total.
(*B*)—Outside of the Indian Empire.—*concluded.*									
Kashmiri	36	3	39	...	...	...	...	...	...
Malayalam	2	3	5	..	...	...	...	...	...
Malabari	2	5	7	...	...	...	...	...	...
Nepalese	51	1	52	...	...	...	...	...	...
Persian	2,010	843	2,853	7	...	7	228	1	229
Russian	9	14	23	...	...	...	...	...	...
Siamese	15	4	19	...	...	...	...	...	...
Turk	2	1	3	...	...	...	...	...	...
Total ...	4,044	1,782	5,826	17	...	17	250	1	251

III. —Non-Asiatic.

Language.	Town. Males	Town. Females.	Town. Total.	Fort William. Males.	Fort William. Females.	Fort William. Total.	Port and Canals. Males.	Port and Canals. Females.	Port and Canals. Total.
Abyssinian	1	...	1	...	...	...	...	...	...
Austrian	...	1	1	...	...	...	2	...	2
Danish	4	3	7	...	...	...	7	...	7
Dutch	1	1	2	...	...	...	1	...	1
English	10,918	10,474	21,392	1,052	166	1,218	585	20	605
French	343	129	472	...	...	...	53	...	53
Fin	2	...	2	...	...	...	2	...	2
Gaelic	4	...	4	...	...	...	...	...	...
German	327	195	522	...	...	...	22	2	24
Greek	79	18	97	...	...	...	1	...	1
Hungarian	1	...	1	...	...	...	5	1	6
Italian	16	18	34	...	...	...	5	...	5
Irish	17	10	27	4	8	12	3	...	3
Maltese	2	...	2	...	...	...	2	...	2
Norwegian	3	...	3	...	...	...	9	...	9
Polish	2	5	7	...	...	...	...	...	...
Portuguese	59	14	73	...	...	...	36	...	36
Roumanian	6	1	7	...	...	...	2	1	3
Scotch	37	19	56	...	...	...	2	...	2
Spanish	9	7	16	...	...	...	4	...	4
Swedish	1	...	1	...	...	...	11	...	11
Welsh	2	...	2	...	...	...	7	...	7
Total ...	11,834	10,895	22,729	1,056	174	1,230	759	24	783

TABLE IX.—BIRTH-PLACES.

DISTRICTS.	TOWN.			FORT WILLIAM.			PORT AND CANALS.		
	Males.	Females.	Total.	Males.	Females.	Total.	Males.	Females.	Total.
(*A*)—DISTRICTS WITHIN THE PROVINCE OF BENGAL.									
Bakarganj	4,745	674	5,419	...	...	...	67	13	80
Balasore	4,524	480	5,004	1	...	1	22	...	22
Bankura	2,139	1,080	3,219	...	...	...	...	...	...
Birbhum	647	367	1,014	16	...	16	...	...	...
Bhagalpur	1,196	570	1,766	...	...	...	472	...	472
Bogra	245	13	258	...	...	...	...	...	...
Burdwan	16,206	10,065	26,271	1	2	3	235	...	235
Calcutta	104,137	103,028	207,165	56	24	80	439	4	443
Champarun	323	30	353	...	...	...	5	...	5
Chandernagore ...	137	105	242	...	...	...	...	...	...
Chittagong	1,683	337	2,020	...	...	...	346	...	346
Cuttack	18,057	2,119	20,176	17	1	18	137	...	137
Dacca	9,633	2,928	12,561	2	...	2	735	22	757
Darjeeling	134	52	186	...	...	...	13	...	13
Dinajpur	246	134	380	...	...	...	...	...	...
Darbhanga	1,681	164	1,845	4	2	6	218	...	218
Faridpur	3,360	1,103	4,463	...	...	...	822	6	827
Gaya	24,838	7,574	32,412	49	...	49	718	...	718
Hazaribagh	2,285	504	2,789	43	...	43	36	...	36
Hughli	34,198	18,498	52,696	35	1	36	2,848	4	2,852
Howrah	3,103	1,801	4,904	...	...	...	...	...	...
Jessore	6,157	1,695	7,852	17	...	17	972	...	972
Jalpaiguri	27	7	34	...	...	...	...	...	...
Khulna	883	400	1,283	...	...	...	187	...	187
Lohardaga	133	68	201	...	...	...	5	...	5
Maldah	858	63	921	...	...	...	...	...	...
Manbhum	271	104	375	36	3	39	...	...	...
Midnapur	15,254	9,731	24,985	...	...	...	1,921	15	1,936
Monghyr	6,640	1,122	7,762	121	...	121	2,542	15	2,557
Murshidabad ...	1,722	934	2,656	4	...	4	158	...	158
Muzaffarpur ...	10,314	1,315	11,629	11	3	14	925	...	925
Mymensingh ...	1,491	286	1,777	...	...	...	978	...	978
Noakhali	383	72	455	...	...	...	1,250	...	1,250
Nadiya	11,827	5,131	16,958	...	...	...	562	...	562
Orissa	...	...	...	...	...	...	39	...	39
Patna	13,333	7,534	20,867	44	16	60	3,820	5	3,825

TABLE IX.—BIRTH-PLACES—*continued.*

DISTRICTS.	TOWN.			FORT WILLIAM.			PORT AND CANALS.		
	Males.	Females.	Total.	Males.	Females.	Total.	Males.	Females.	Total.
(*A*)—DISTRICTS WITHIN THE PROVINCE OF BENGAL—*conluded.*									
Puri	98	23	121	...	...	...	...	...	...
Pabna	1,015	406	1,421	...	...	...	171	...	171
Parniya	1,470	234	1,704	...	...	...	39	...	39
Rajshahi	508	208	716	...	...	...	...	...	...
Rangpur	167	98	265	...	...	...	27	...	27
Saran	10,932	1,951	12,883	35	...	35	1,106	...	1,106
Shahabad	12,502	4,229	16,731	113	18	131	899	...	899
Singhbhum ...	14	3	17	...	...	...	...	...	...
Santal Parganas ...	225	151	376	...	...	...	4	...	4
Tippera	612	176	788	...	...	...	49	1	50
24-Pergunnahs ...	29,342	26,133	55,475	56	7	63	2,932	...	2,932
Unspecified Bengal ...	264	259	523	52	20	72	12	...	12
Total of Bengal ...	359,959	213,959	573,918	712	97	809	25,706	85	25,811
(*B*)—PROVINCES AND STATES OUTSIDE BENGAL BUT WITHIN THE INDIAN EMPIRE.									
Andaman Islands ...	30	4	34	...	...	...	...	...	...
Assam	568	305	873	12	8	20	205	...	205
Bengal Feudatory States	52	58	110	...	...	...	...	...	...
Berar	16	5	21	...	...	...	...	...	...
Bombay and Sind ...	956	489	1,445	9	2	11	91	...	91
Burma	454	220	674	...	...	...	7	...	7
Central Provinces, Central India, and Rajputana ...	6,388	2,239	8,627	247	3	250	14	...	14
The Deccan	1,079	315	1,394	1	...	1	3	...	3
Madras (including Diu and Pondichery).	666	500	1,166	14	7	21	...	...	...
Malacca	...	...	...	...	...	...	5	...	5
Mysore	17	17	34	...	...	...	...	...	...
North-Western Provinces and Oudh ...	38,048	13,467	51,515	708	106	814	1,781	8	1,781
Panjab	2,475	766	3,241	300	19	319	31	...	31
India unspecified ...	...	...	...	21	35	56	45	...	45
Total of India outside Bengal ...	50,749	18,385	69,134	1,312	180	1,492	2,182	8	2,190

TABLE IX.—BIRTH-PLACES—*continued.*

DISTRICTS.	TOWN.			FORT WILLIAM.			PORT AND CANALS.		
	Males.	Females.	Total.	Males.	Females.	Total.	Males.	Females.	Total.
(*C*)—COUNTRIES IN ASIA BEYOND THE INDIAN EMPIRE.									
Afghanistan	203	73	276	...	...	...	...	...	...
Arabia	84	28	112	...	...	...	3	...	3
Armenia	9	13	22	...	...	...	...	...	...
Beluchistan	3	2	5	...	...	...	...	...	...
Cashmere	56	25	81	...	...	...	...	...	...
Ceylon	44	18	62	1	...	1	...	...	...
China	688	70	758	3	1	4	4	...	4
Cochin	5	2	7	...	...	...	62	...	62
Japan	8	8	16	...	...	...	...	...	...
Mongolia	7	7	14	...	...	...	...	...	...
Nepal	369	194	563	12	...	12	...	...	...
Palestine and Syria ...	3	1	4	...	...	...	4	...	4
Persia	78	26	104	...	...	...	7	...	7
Straits Settlements ..	41	39	80	2	1	3	...	...	...
Tibet	36	20	56	...	...	...	...	...	...
Total ...	1,634	526	2,160	18	2	20	80	...	80
(*D*)—COUNTRIES IN EUROPE.									
Austria	49	33	82	...	...	...	1	...	1
Belgium	7	2	9	...	...	...	...	...	...
Denmark	3	10	13	...	...	...	7	...	7
England	1,424	701	2,125	915	43	958	371	10	381
Finland	...	...	...	...	...	...	3	...	3
France	125	36	161	1	...	1	62	...	62
Germany	110	54	164	...	...	...	9	...	9
Greece	15	5	20	...	...	...	1	...	1
Holland	...	...	...	...	...	...	1	...	1
Hungary	...	...	...	...	...	...	4	...	4
Ireland	146	97	243	56	13	69	...	...	...
Italy	57	41	98	...	...	...	4	...	4
Malta	...	...	...	4	...	4	...	...	...
Norway	9	8	17	...	...	...	5	...	5
Portugal	12	2	14	...	...	...	...	...	...
Roumania	25	2	27	...	...	...	...	...	...
Russia	21	21	42	...	...	...	2	...	2

TABLE IX.—BIRTH-PLACES—*concluded.*

DISTRICTS.	TOWN.			FORT WILLIAM.			PORT AND CANALS.		
	Males.	Females.	Total.	Males.	Females.	Total.	Males.	Females.	Total.
(*D*)—COUNTRIES IN EUROPE—*concld.*									
Scotland	239	134	373	58	1	59	97	...	97
Spain	14	9	23	...	...	...	2	...	2
Sweden	7	...	7	...	...	...	14	...	14
Switzerland	9	6	15	...	...	...	...	...	...
Turkey	41	122	163	...	...	...	...	...	...
Wales	5	1	6	9	5	14	...	...	...
Europe (unspecified)	13	10	23	...	...	...	...	...	...
Total of persons born in Europe ...	2,331	1,294	3,625	1,043	72	1,105	583	10	593
(*E*)—COUNTRIES IN AFRICA.									
Aden	1	...	1	...	...	...	...	...	...
Cape Town ...	7	4	11	...	...	...	...	...	...
Egypt	1	...	1	...	...	...	...	...	...
Mauritius	4	3	7	...	...	...	...	...	...
Timbuctoo	2	1	3	...	...	...	...	...	...
Africa (unspecified) ...	22	4	26	...	...	...	...	...	...
Total ...	37	12	49	...	...	...	...	...	...
(*F*)—COUNTRIES IN AMERICA.									
Brazil	7	4	11	...	...	...	7	...	7
Canada	8	3	11	...	...	...	...	...	...
Newfoundland ...	6	...	6	...	...	...	...	...	...
United States ...	48	12	60	...	...	...	2	...	2
America (unspecified)	45	17	62	...	3	3	4	...	4
West Indies ...	9	3	12	5	...	5	3	...	3
Total ...	123	39	162	5	3	8	16	...	16
(*G*)—AUSTRALIA (9 countries) ...	30	10	40	15	1	16	21	...	21
(*H*)—AT SEA ...	9	9	18	...	...	...	...	...	...
(*I*)—UNSPECIFIED ...	167	128	295	12	4	16	...	...	...
GRAND TOTAL ...	415,041	234,362	649,401	3,119	349	3,468	28,588	103	28,691

TABLE X.—

TOTAL.			AGE 0—4.		5—9.		10—14.		15—19.		20—24.		25—29.	
Total.	Males.	Females.	Males.	Females.	Males.	Females.	Males.	Females.	Males.	Females.	Males.	Females.	Males.	Females.
433	318	115	4	3	4	2	4	5	12	6	33	4	48	9

TABLE XI.—

Total.	Males.	Females.	Males.	Females.	Males.	Females.	Males.	Females.	Males.	Females.	Males.	Females.	Males.	Females.
312	171	141	6	3	4	3	10	5	10	1	8	4	6	2

TABLE XII.—DEAF-

Total.	Males.	Females.	Males.	Females.	Males.	Females.	Males.	Females.	Males.	Females.	Males.	Females.	Males.	Females.
206	107	99	6	5	9	7	6	9	10	2	10	4	9	4

TABLE XIII.—

Total.	Males.	Females.	Males.	Females.	Males.	Females.	Males.	Females.	Males.	Females.	Males.	Females.	Males.	Females.
173	115	58	2	2	2	2	4	5	5	3	9	5	10	...

Insane by Age.

PERIODS.

30—34.		35—39.		40—44.		45—49.		50—54.		55—59.		60 and over.	
Males.	Females.	Males.	Females.	Males.	Females.	Males.	Females.	Males.	Females.	Males.	Females.	Males.	Females.
46	6	52	29	37	14	32	14	16	11	18	7	12	5

Blind by Age.

30—34. Males.	30—34. Females.	35—39. Males.	35—39. Females.	40—44. Males.	40—44. Females.	45—49. Males.	45—49. Females.	50—54. Males.	50—54. Females.	55—59. Males.	55—59. Females.	60 and over. Males.	60 and over. Females.
8	8	10	2	14	14	12	12	22	21	47	32	14	34

Mutes by Age.

30—34. Males.	30—34. Females.	35—39. Males.	35—39. Females.	40—44. Males.	40—44. Females.	45—49. Males.	45—49. Females.	50—54. Males.	50—54. Females.	55—59. Males.	55—59. Females.	60 and over. Males.	60 and over. Females.
18	10	10	5	7	11	7	6	7	8	5	14	8	14

Lepers by Age.

30—34. Males.	30—34. Females.	35—39. Males.	35—39. Females.	40—44. Males.	40—44. Females.	45—49. Males.	45—49. Females.	50—54. Males.	50—54. Females.	55—59. Males.	55—59. Females.	60 and over. Males.	60 and over. Females.
13	5	21	3	17	5	6	6	8	4	5	10	13	8

TABLE XIV.—*Castes of Hindus, Tribes of Muhammadans and Races of Christians.*

A.—HINDUS.

RELIGION.	Caste.	Males.	Females.	Total.
Hindu ...	Agarwala ...	1,296	74	1,370
Do. ...	Aguri ...	820	549	1,369
Do. ...	Ahir ...	88	26	114
Do. ...	Assamese ...	...	2	2
Do. ...	Bagdi ...	2,581	3,107	5,688
Do. ...	Bahelia ...	127	55	182
Do. ...	Baidya ...	2,679	1,796	4,475
Do. ...	Baishya ...	131	68	199
Do. ...	Baisnab ...	6,940	9,821	16,761
Do. ...	Baiti ...	29	15	44
Do. ...	Barai ...	6	4	10
Do. ...	Baratri ...	3	...	3
Do. ...	Barhi ...	39	16	55
Do. ...	Barui ...	993	282	1,275
Do. ...	Baruni ...	58	13	71
Do. ...	Basauriya ...	6	...	6
Do. ...	Bauri ...	11	31	42
Do. ...	Bedia ...	29	24	53
Do. ...	Behara ...	158	56	214
Do. ...	Bhunawala ...	707	395	1,102
Do. ...	Bhurmuga ...	4	3	7
Do. ...	Bhutia ...	37	15	52
Do. ...	Bhuyan ...	328	87	415
Do. ...	Brahman ...	41,546	20,162	61,708
Do. ...	Chamar ...	18,060	6,428	24,488
Do. ...	Chandal ...	511	429	940
Do. ...	Chasadhopa ...	330	273	603
Do. ...	Chatri ...	4,558	868	5,426
Do. ...	Chitrakar ...	52	56	108
Do. ...	Chunari ...	9	78	87
Do. ...	Chutar ...	2,975	2,237	5,212

A.—HINDUS—*continued.*

RELIGION.	Caste.	Males.	Females.	Total.
Hindu ...	Daigar ...	2	2	4
Do. ...	Dhangur ...	615	110	725
Do. ...	Dhanuk ...	77	15	92
Do. ...	Dhuriya ...	58	8	66
Do. ...	Doga ...	5	2	7
Do. ...	Dom ...	1,848	1,505	3,353
Do. ...	Dosadh ...	4,479	1,980	6,459
Do. ...	Dulia ...	78	48	126
Do. ...	Gandhabania ...	9,057	5,025	14,082
Do. ...	Gareriya ...	195	116	311
Do. ...	Gazali ...	2	2	4
Do. ...	Ghariyal ...	18	5	23
Do. ...	Gharuk ...	16	2	18
Do. ...	Ghattak ...	1	...	1
Do. ...	Ghatwal ...	104	26	130
Do. ...	Ghasi ...	2	...	2
Do. ...	Gonriya ...	156	49	205
Do. ...	Gurkha ...	1	3	4
Do. ...	Gwala ...	14,043	5,888	19,931
Do. ...	Hari ...	514	377	891
Do. ...	Jahar ...	5	1	6
Do. ...	Jalia ...	1,661	1,181	2,842
Do. ...	Jaswara ...	907	217	1,124
Do. ...	Jugi ...	1,414	1,277	2,691
Do. ...	Kahar ...	11,244	2,852	14,096
Do. ...	Kaibarta .	12,967	10,397	23,364
Do. ...	Kairi ...	1,583	404	1,987
Do. ...	Kaistha ...	37,474	21,213	58,687
Do. ...	Kalu ...	2,272	1,791	4,063
Do. ...	Kalwar ...	1,055	242	1,297
Do. ...	Kamar ..	778	610	1,388
Do. ...	Kamati ...	2	2	4
Do. ..	Kansari ...	1,832	1,599	3,431

A.—Hindus—*continued.*

Religion.	Caste.	Males.	Females.	Total.
Hindu ...	Kanu ...	645	68	713
Do. ...	Kapali ...	143	127	270
Do. ...	Karan ...	23	3	26
Do. ...	Karat ...	3	1	4
Do. ...	Kashbi ...	6	...	6
Do. ...	Kathary ...	3	2	5
Do. ...	Kaura ...	2,259	2,000	4,259
Do. ...	Keaut ...	43	15	58
Do. ...	Khandait ...	1,588	89	1,677
Do. ...	Khandu ...	207	64	271
Do. ...	Khasiya ...	3	3	6
Do. ...	Khettri ...	612	1,085	3,697
Do. ...	Kumhar ...	4,110	2,526	6,636
Do. ...	Kunjra ...	65	11	76
Do. ...	Kurmi ...	3,793	1,047	4,840
Do. ...	Kusi ...	20	...	20
Do. ..	Madak ...	3,738	1,633	5,371
Do. ...	Madrasi ...	166	169	335
Do. ...	Maheswari ...	73	25	98
Do. ...	Malakar ...	707	364	1,071
Do. ...	Malo ...	...	1	1
Do. ...	Marhatta ...	11	2	13
Do. ...	Marwari ...	80	29	109
Do. ...	Methar ...	5,531	4,243	9,774
Do. ...	Mudra ...	14	1	15
Do. ...	Muhari ...	24	35	59
Do. ...	Musahar ...	4	...	4
Do. ...	Naga ...	46	6	52
Do. ...	Napit ...	5,720	3,256	8,976
Do. ...	Nuniya ...	491	108	599
Do. ...	Panika ...	1	...	1
Do. ...	Pasban ...	29	1	30
Do. ...	Pasi ...	456	263	719

A.—HINDUS—*concluded.*

RELIGION.	Caste.	Males.	Females.	Total.
Hindu ...	Patni ...	66	32	98
Do. ...	Pod ...	890	723	1,613
Do. ...	Rajak ...	4,879	2,902	7,781
Do. ...	Rajput ...	818	248	1,066
Do. ...	Rajwar ...	448	53	501
Do. ...	Rastogi ...	5	1	6
Do. ...	Rakor ...	76	30	106
Do. ...	Sadgop ...	5,153	4,843	9,996
Do. ...	Samodhiya ...	8	3	11
Do. ...	Sankhari ...	153	154	307
Do. ...	Sarnakar ...	1,820	1,107	2,927
Do. ...	Sazawal ...	1	...	1
Do. ...	Siunri ...	3,806	1,619	5,425
Do. ...	Subarnabarnik ...	10,660	8,960	10,626
Do. ...	Sukli ...	15	17	32
Do. ...	Sukuja ...	1	...	1
Do. ...	Tailangi ...	74	66	140
Do. ...	Tamli ...	1,919	1,026	2,945
Do. ...	Tanti ...	8,225	7,911	16,136
Do. ...	Teor ...	357	198	555
Do. ...	Teli ...	7,054	3,643	10,697
Do. ...	Thakaiyal ...	...	1	1
Do. ...	Tilli ...	1,255	867	2,122
Do. ...	Tuniya ...	8	5	13
Do. ...	Turiya ...	168	10	178
Do. ...	Uria ...	1,352	208	1,560
Do. ...	Unspecified ...	1,025	607	1,632
	Total Hindus ...	272,482	156,330	428,732

B.—Mahomedans.

Religion.	Caste.	Males.	Females	Total.
Mahomedans	Dhunia ...	30	6	36
Do. ...	Mogul ...	437	260	697
Do. ...	Momin ...	224	33	257
Do. ...	Pathan ...	8,176	2,925	11,101
Do. ...	Saydi ...	2,607	1,196	3,803
Do. ...	Shaik ...	114,117	59,215	173,332
	Total ...	125,591	63,635	189,226

C.—Christians.

Religion.	Caste.	Males.	Females	Total.
Non-Asiatic	European ...	5,089	4,234	9,323
Do. ...	African ...	3	3	6
Do. ...	American ...	39	50	89
	Total of Non-Asiatic Christians ...	5,131	4,287	9,418
Mixed races	Eurasian ...	4,771	5,032	9,803
Asiatic ...	Armenian ...	296	261	557
Do. ...	Arabian ...	1	...	1
Do. ...	Native Christian ...	3,487	3,133	6,620
Do. ...	Syrian ...	4	3	7
	Total of Asiatic Christians ...	3,788	3,397	7,185
	Grand Total ...	13,690	12,716	26,406

TABLE XIV.—*Castes of Hindus, Tribes of Mohamadans and Races of Christians.*

FORT WILLIAM.

HINDUS.

RELIGION.	Castes.	Males.	Females.	Total.
Hindus ...	Agarwala ...	1	...	1
Do. ...	Ahir	21	...	21
Do. ...	Baishnab ...	8	...	8
Do. ...	Beldar ...	1	...	1
Do. ...	Brahman ...	278	...	278
Do. ...	Chamar ...	296	32	328
Do. ...	Chandal ...	1	...	1
Do. ...	Chatri ...	20	1	21
Do. ...	Dhangar ...	3	...	3
Do. ...	Dom	6	...	6
Do. ...	Dosadh ...	25	3	28
Do. ...	Gandabania ...	32	2	34
Do. ...	Gareriya ...	1	...	1
Do. ...	Ghatwal ...	1	2	3
Do. ...	Gwala ...	33	...	33
Do. ...	Jaswara ...	23	4	27
Do. ...	Kahar ...	74	5	79
Do. ...	Kairi ...	68	3	71
Do. ...	Kaistha ...	109	23	132
Do. ...	Kamar ...	7	...	7
Do. ...	Kaura ...	1	...	1
Do. ...	Kurmi ...	6	1	7
Do. ...	Madak ...	1	...	1
Do. ...	Madrassi ...	4	1	5
Do. ...	Mehtar ...	47	14	61
Do. ...	Napit ...	1	...	1
Do. ...	Nuniya ...	3	...	3
Do. ...	Rajak ...	62	14	76
Do. ...	Rajput ...	192	3	195

HINDUS—*concld.*

RELIGION.	Castes.	Males.	Females.	Total.
Hindus ...	Tanti ...	1	...	1
Do. ...	Teli	5	...	5
Do. ...	Uria	1	...	1
Do. ..	Unspecified ...	1	...	1
	Total Hindus ...	1,333	108	1,441

MAHOMEDANS.

Mussalman ..	Dhunia ...	7	...	7
Ditto ...	Mogul ...	4	...	4
Ditto ...	Momin ...	2	..	2
Ditto ...	Pathan ...	181	12	193
Ditto ...	Sayid ...	13	...	13
Ditto ...	Shaikh ...	348	30	378
	Total ...	555	42	597

CHRISTIANS.

Non-Asiatic	European ...	1,041	192	1,233
Mixed Races	Eurasian ...	1	...	1
Asiatics ...	Native Christians ...	10	7	17
	Total ...	1,052	199	1,251

TABLE XIV.—*Castes of Hindus, Tribes of Mohammadans and Races of Christians.*

PORT AND CANALS.

A.—HINDUS—*continued.*

RELIGION.	Castes.	Males.	Females.	Total.
Hindu ..	Ahir ..	2	...	2
Do. ...	Bagdi ...	1,173	1	1,174
Do. ...	Baidya ...	20	...	20
Do. ...	Baishnab ...	284	..	284
Do. ...	Baiti ...	14	...	14
Do. ...	Banpar ...	7	...	7
Do. ..	Bansphul ...	48	...	48
Do. ...	Barai ...	30	...	30
Do. ...	Barui ...	21	...	21
Do. ...	Bind ...	159	...	159
Do. ...	Bedia ...	41	...	41
Do. ...	Brahman ...	386	2	388
Do. ...	Chamar ...	5	...	5
Do. ...	Chandal ...	381	1	382
Do. ...	Chasadhopa ...	21	...	21
Do. ...	Chatri ...	62	...	62
Do. ...	Chimut ...	5	...	5
Do. ...	Dhanuk ..	2	...	2
Do. ...	Dhunia ...	1	...	1
Do. ...	Dom ...	18	...	18
Do. ...	Dosadh ...	45	...	45
Do. ...	Dulia ...	19	...	19
Do. ...	Gandhabania ...	107	...	107
Do. ...	Gareriya ...	40	...	40
Do. ...	Garcha ...	58	4	62
Do. ...	Gumi ...	2	...	2
Do. ..	Gwala ...	157	...	157
Do. ...	Hari ...	4	...	4
Do. ...	Jalaha ...	6	...	6
Do. ...	Jalia ...	972	10	982
Do. ...	Jugi ...	19	...	19

A.—Hindus—*continued.*

Religion.	Castes.	Males.	Females.	Total.
Hindu ...	Kahar ...	52	...	52
Do. ..	Kaibarta ...	4,931	30	4,961
Do. ...	Kaistha ...	194	10	204
Do. ...	Kairi ...	65	...	35
Do. ...	Kalu ...	1	...	1
Do. ...	Kamar ...	20	4	24
Do. ...	Kanu ...	11	...	11
Do. ...	Kapali ...	35	...	35
Do. ...	Karan ...	1	1	2
Do. ...	Kaura ...	269	...	269
Do. ...	Keut ...	7	...	7
Do. ...	Khandait ...	8	...	8
Do. ...	Khetri ...	16	...	16
Do. ...	Kumhar ...	14	...	14
Do. ...	Kurmi ...	18	...	18
Do. ...	Madak ...	14	...	14
Do. ...	Malakar ...	79	...	79
Do. ...	Marhatta ...	5	...	5
Do. ...	Marwari ...	271	...	271
Do. ...	Methar ...	6	...	6
Do. ...	Naga ...	5	...	5
Do. ...	Napit ...	41	...	41
Do. ...	Nuniya ...	6	...	6
Do. ...	Pasban ...	7	...	7
Do. ...	Pari ...	5	...	5
Do. ...	Patni ...	1,640	3	1,643
Do. ...	Pod ...	160	...	160
Do. ...	Rajak ...	22	...	22
Do. ...	Rajput ...	85	...	85
Do. ...	Rajwar ...	1	...	1
Do. ...	Sadgop ...	43	...	43
Do ...	Sarnakar ...	96	7	103
Do. ...	Satun ...	1	...	1

A.—HINDUS—*concluded.*

RELIGION.	Castes.	Males.	Females.	Total.
Hindu ...	Siunri ...	31	...	31
Do. ...	Subarnabanik ...	9	...	9
Do. ...	Sukli ...	11	...	11
Do. ...	Sulaiya ...	8	...	8
Do. ...	Suru ...	382	...	382
Do. ...	Sustikaran ...	5	...	5
Do. ...	Tamli ...	2	...	2
Do. ...	Tanti ...	152	...	152
Do. ...	Tapas ...	3	...	3
Do. ...	Tiar ...	551	...	551
Do. ...	Teli ...	50	3	53
Do. ...	Uria ...	14	...	14
Do. ...	Unspecified ...	432	...	432
	Total Hindus ...	13,858	76	13,934

B.—MOHAMMADANS.

RELIGION.	Castes.	Males.	Females.	Total.
Musulmans ..	Mogal ...	32	...	32
Ditto ...	Momin ...	29	...	29
Ditto ...	Pathan ...	1,159	...	1,159
Ditto ...	Sayid ...	206	...	206
Ditto ...	Shaikh ...	11,916	8	11,924
	Total Mohammadans	13,342	8	13,350

C.—CHRISTIANS.

RELIGION.	Castes.	Males.	Females.	Total.
Non-Asiatic	European ...	1,120	16	1,136
Ditto ...	American ...	121	...	121
Ditto ...	Australian ...	2	...	2
Mixed Races	Eurasian ...	14	...	14
Asiatic ...	Armenian ...	37	...	37
Do. ...	Native Christians ...	30	...	30
	Total ...	1,324	16	1,340

TABLE XV.—*Christians*

	TOTAL.			A.—NON-ASIATICS.								
				All ages.			0—14.		15—34.		35—49.	
	Total.	Males.	Females.	Total.	Males.	Females.	Males.	Females.	Males.	Females.	Males.	Females.
Town ...	26,406	13,690	12,716	9,418	5,131	4,287	1,280	1,273	2,258	1,672	1,041	889
Fort William ...	1,251	1,052	199	1,233	1,041	192	77	88	854	86	105	13
Port and Canals	1,340	1,324	16	1,263	1,247	16	10	5	711	10	418	1
Total ...	28,997	16,066	12,931	11,914	7,419	4,495	1,367	1,366	3,823	1,767	1,664	903

	C.—ARMENIANS.											D.—NATIVES.						
	All ages.			0—14.		15—34.		35—49.		50 and over.		All ages.			0—14.		15—34.	
	Total.	Males.	Females.	Males.	Females.	Males.	Females.	Males.	Females.	Males.	Females.	Total.	Males.	Females.	Males.	Females.	Males.	Females.
Town	557	296	261	85	76	109	108	68	55	34	22	6,620	3,487	3,133	1,095	1,127	1,358	1,328
Fort William ...	...	...	...	...	...	..	...	...	...	...	...	17	10	7	3	1	6	4
Port and Canals	37	37	...	...	...	20	...	11	..	6	...	26	26	...	...	...	16	...
Total ...	594	333	261	85	76	129	108	79	55	40	22	6,663	3,523	3,140	1,098	1,128	1,380	1,332

by RACE *and* AGE.

50 and over.		B.—EURASIANS.													
		All ages.			0—14.		15—34.		35—49.		50 and over.		
Males.	Females.	Total.	Males.	Females.	Males.	Females.	Males.	Females.	Males.	Females.	Males.	Females.	
562	453	9,803	4,771	5,032	1,872	1,810	1,656	1,876	768	705	475	641	Town.
5	6	1	1	...	...	...	1	...	...	...	...	...	Fort Willam.
108	...	14	14	...	2	...	8	...	4	...	...	...	Port and Can als.
665	459	9,818	4,786	5,032	1,874	1,810	1,665	1,876	772	705	475	641	Total.

35—49.		50 and over.		E.—ASIATICS.												
				All ages.			0—14.		15—34.		35—49.		50 and over.		
Males.	Females.	Males.	Females.	Total.	Males.	Females.	Males.	Females.	Males.	Females.	Males.	Females.	Males.	Females.	
610	449	424	229	8	5	3	...	...		2	...	...	2	1	Town.
1	2	...	...	...	...	...	...	...	...	...	...	...	...	...	Fort William.
8	...	2	...	...	...	...	...	...	...	...	...	...	...	...	Port and Canals.
619	451	426	229	8	5	3	...	...	3	2	...	...	2	1	Total.

TABLE XVI.—*Christians and others*

Name of Sect.	Total.			Town.							
				Total.		Foreign.		Eurasian.		Native.	
	Total.	Males.	Females.	Males.	Females.	Males.	Females.	Males.	Females.	Males.	Females.
Churches of England and Ireland.	8,765	4,902	3,624	4,104	3,548	1,837	1,268	1,511	1,369	756	911
Church of Scotland ...	2,686	1,623	1,063	1,553	1,063	567	282	575	444	411	337
Presbyterian	172	140	32	29	32	24	24	5	4	...	4
Non-conformist ...	386	200	186	200	186	102	80	34	98	64	8
Baptist	1,605	943	662	943	662	280	234	384	296	279	132
Quaker	5	3	2	3	2	3	2	...	...	...	...
Protestant	5,733	3,025	2,642	2,425	2,593	1,084	1,244	628	680	713	669
Salvation Army ...	2	2	...	2	...	2	...	...	...	...	...
Roman Catholic ...	9,498	4,905	4,479	4,108	4,389	1,240	1,212	1,614	2,119	1,254	1,058
Greek Church	150	74	76	74	76	74	76	...	...	...	...
Armenian Church ...	230	142	88	142	88	142	88	...	...	...	...
Unsectarian	149	88	61	88	61	68	39	20	22	...	...
Unitarian	7	5	2	5	2	5	2	...	...	...	...
Agnostic	2	2	...	2	...	1	...	...	...	1	...
Positivist	1	1	...	1	...	1	...	...	...	...	...
Free-thinker	1	1	...	1	...	1	...	...	...	...	...
Specialist	1	1	...	1	...	1	...	...	...	...	...
No religion	23	9	14	9	14	...	...	...	...	9	14
Total ...	28,997	16,066	12,931	13,690	12,716	5,432	4,551	4,771	5,032	3,487	3,133

by SECT *and* RACE.

Fort William.								Port and Canals.							
Total.		Foreign.		Eurasian.		Native.		Total.		Foreign.		Eurasian.		Native.	
Males.	Females.	Males.	Females.	Males.	Females.	Males.	Females.	Males.	Females.	Males.	Females.	Males.	Females.	Males.	Females.
470	67	464	67	...	...	6	...	328	9	318	9	...	...	10	...
...	...	...	...	...	...	...	...	70	...	70	...	...	...	...	...
111	...	111	...	...	...	...	...	...	...	...	...	...	...	...	...
...	...	...	...	...	...	...	...	...	...	...	...	...	...	...	...
...	...	...	...	...	...	...	...	...	...	...	...	...	...	...	...
...	...	...	...	...	...	...	...	...	...	...	...	...	...	...	...
131	49	127	49	...	...	4	...	469	...	455	...	6	...	8	...
...	...	...	...	...	...	...	...	...	...	...	...	...	...	...	...
340	83	339	76	1	...	...	7	457	7	441	7	8	...	8	...
...	...	...	...	...	...	...	...	...	...	...	...	...	...	...	...
...	...	...	...	...	...	...	...	...	...	...	...	...	...	...	...
...	...	...	...	...	...	...	...	...	...	...	...	...	...	...	...
...	...	...	...	...	...	...	...	...	...	...	...	...	...	...	...
...	...	...	...	...	...	...	...	...	...	...	...	...	...	...	...
...	...	...	...	...	...	...	...	...	...	...	...	...	...	...	...
...	...	...	...	...	...	...	...	...	...	...	...	...	...	...	...
...	...	...	...	...	...	...	...	...	...	...	...	...	...	...	...
...	...	...	...	...	...	...	...	...	...	...	...	...	...	...	...
1,052	199	1,041	192	1	...	10	7	1,324	16	1,284	16	14	...	26	...

TABLE XVII.—*Occupations*

Class.	Order.	Sub-order.	Group.	Occupation.
A ...	I.—Administration...	1. Service of the Imperial and Provincial Governments.	1. The Viceroy and Governors and Lieutenant-Governors.	Viceroy ... ...
				Lieutenant-Governor ...
			2. Officers in superior service.	Administrative and Executive
				Judicial and Legal ...
				Accounts officers ... ...
			3. Officers in subordinate service.	High Court Interpreter ...
				Jail Superintendent ...
				Police and Excise Inspectors ...
				Mint clerks ... ...
				Port Superintendents and clerks
				Peshkars ... ...
				Government clerks ...
				Government servants unspecified
			4. Officers in inferior service.	Government darwans ...
				Peons, chaprasis and burkandazes.
				Income-tax peon ... ...
				Police jamadars and constables
				Bailiffs ... ...
		2. Service of Local and Municipal bodies.	5. Inspecting and supervising officials	Municipal Chairman and inspecting agency.
				Municipal commissioners ...
			6. Clerical establishment.	Municipal clerks ... ...
				Census enumerators ...
				Municipal tax-collectors ...
				Municipal inspectors ...
				Municipal sircars ... ...
				Road-cess clerk ... ...
				Registrar of births and deaths...
			7. Menials ...	Municipal coolies ... ...
				" durwans and guards
				" gas lighters ...
				" jamadars and scavengers.
				" bullock shoers and pound-keepers, &c.

by Ages.

MALES.							FEMALES.						
WORKERS.			DEPENDENTS.			Total males.	WORKERS.			DEPENDENTS.			Total females.
0—4.	5—14.	15.	0—4	5—14.	15.		0—4.	5—14.	15.	0—4.	5—14.	15.	
...	...	1	...	...	...	1	...	...	...	...	...	1	1
...	...	1	1	...	...	2	...	...	...	...	...	2	2
...	...	70	42	99	88	299	...	...	2	73	83	144	302
...	...	56	23	37	47	163	...	...	...	35	58	56	149
...	...	24	4	11	3	42	...	...	...	6	6	18	30
...	...	1	...	...	...	1	...	...	...	...	...	...	...
...	...	7	2	2	...	11	...	...	1	1	3	...	5
...	...	164	14	25	81	284	...	...	1	24	27	109	161
...	1	38	3	1	...	43	...	...	...	2	26	36	64
...	...	30	4	7	1	42	...	...	...	6	10	9	25
...	...	17	1	...	3	21	...	...	...	10	20	22	52
...	26	6,353	883	1,530	1,810	10,602	...	...	1	601	1,112	2,811	4,525
...	...	230	19	26	73	348	...	...	...	38	66	79	183
...	...	21	1	7	7	36	...	...	...	3	14	23	40
...	10	508	22	20	56	616	...	...	...	38	45	74	157
...	...	1	...	...	...	1	...	...	...	2	3	1	6
...	2	3,180	43	96	242	3,563	...	...	2	34	61	161	258
...	...	5	4	5	7	21	...	...	...	9	3	7	19
...	...	150	34	69	115	368	...	...	...	44	73	146	263
...	...	1	1	2	...	4	...	...	...	1	3	4	8
...	1	187	11	24	22	244	...	...	...	9	56	44	109
...	...	122	2	15	7	146	...	...	...	2	5	12	19
...	...	220	7	11	17	255	...	...	...	16	21	28	65
...	...	13	6	10	3	32	...	...	...	1	1	3	5
...	9	713	3	6	14	745	...	...	...	11	23	55	89
...	...	...	...	1	2	3	...	...	...	...	...	...	...
...	...	4	2	...	...	6	...	...	...	...	...	...	...
...	24	834	25	53	112	1,048	...	2	1	29	17	48	97
...	1	82	...	1	1	85	...	...	...	...	...	...	...
...	1	49	5	4	4	63	...	...	...	...	2	2	4
...	11	283	19	27	33	373	...	...	8	22	20	88	138
...	9	9	10	11	9	48	...	2	12	8	16	20	58

TABLE XVII—*Occupations*

Class.	Order.	Sub-order.	Group.	Occupation.
	II.—Defence ...	4.—Army	12 & 13	Assistant Military Accountant, Military Officers and soldiers.
			14	Body-guards and band-players
				Military office clerks ... ...
	III.—Foreign and Feudatory State service.	6.—Administrative service ...	19	Prime Minister, Ambassador of other Foreign Feudatory State service.
B ...	IV.—Livestock ...	8.—Stock breeding and dealing ...	24	Horse breeders and dealers ...
			25	Cattle breeders and dealers ...
			27	Buffalo breeders and dealers ...
			31	Sheep and goat breeders and dealers.
			32	Pig breeders and sellers ...
		9.—Subsidiary services to stock...	a)34	Farriers and gelders ...
			35	Elephant breakers and trainers
		10.—Interest in land ...	37	Land occupants not cultivating
			37A	Estate managers and zamindars' clerks.
			38	Land occupants cultivating ...
			39	Lessees of villages ...
			39A	Zamindars' clerks ...
		11.—Agricultural labourer ...	42	Farm servants ... ...
			44	Tea planters ... ...
			49	Indigo planters ... ...
			52	Gardeners ... ...
			55	Forest rangers ... ...
C VI.—Personal or household services.		14.—Personal domestic services ...	59	Barbers ... ...
			63	Washermen ... ...
			65	Cooks ... ...
			66	House servants (unspecified) ...
			......	House bearers ... ...
			......	Table servants ... ...
			......	Farashes ... ...
			......	Scullions ... ...
			......	Ayahs and maid servants ...
			......	Nurses ... ...
			......	Coachmen ... ...
			......	Grooms ... ...
			68	Door-keepers ... ...

by Ages—continued.

MALES.							FEMALES.						
WORKERS.			DEPENDENTS.			Total males.	WORKERS.			DEPENDENTS.			Total females.
0–4.	5–14.	15.	0–4.	5–14.	15.		0–4.	5–14.	15.	0–4.	5–14	15.	
...	1	2,604	50	37	33	2,725	...	...	...	64	75	144	283
...	2	142	9	3	8	164	4	7	5	6	...	1	23
...	...	5	...	...	...	5	...	...	...	...	...	...	...
...	...	2	...	1	8	11	...	...	...	...	1	3	4
...	1	52	7	6	5	71	...	...	..	43	31	36	110
...	1	35	2	2	3	43	...	...	...	4	3	19	26
1	3	17	...	8	...	29	2	...	4	...	7	9	22
...	11	348	10	23	17	409	...	...	2	17		50	96
...	4	30	...	...	...	34	...	...	...	...	...	...	...
...	2	175	11	20	9	217	...	...	...	25	28	41	94
...	...	1	15	23	5	44	...	...	...	...	...	...	...
26	132	3,967	613	1,370	1,785	7,893	3	13	407	628	1,000	2,957	5,003
...	...	968	135	273	398	1.774	...	2	31	22	62	112	229
1	34	1,168	50	104	160	1,517	...	2	72	49	94	327	544
...	...	4	1	2	...	7	...	...	2	...	...	1	3
...	...	2	3	9	9	23	...	...	..	...	3	15	18
...	...	3	...	...	...	3	...	...	...	...	...	...	...
...	...	75	4	8	9	96	...	...	4	9	16	45	74
...	...	10	...	...	...	10	...	...	...	...	...	3	3
...	27	1,472	34	45	49	1,627	...	...	2	26	61	125	214
...	...	2	1	1	2	6	...	...	...	...	...	...	...
1	82	2,574	81	128	82	2.898	...	3	156	110	204	519	992
8	120	3,530	287	496	401	4,812	3	26	438	261	393	955	2,076
5	129	6,248	252	464	401	7,498	2	12	1,198	312	529	1,214	326
...	524	18,879	212	486	763	20,864	...	...	...	199	337	1,103	1,639
6	91	3,011	45	102	72	3,327	...	7	179	109	128	295	718
7	116	3,806	615	1,068	584	6,191	...	1	18	531	905	2,818	4,273
...	2	258	4	8	6	278	...	...	1	5	3	13	22
...	4	360	...	2	5	371	...	1	54	11	17	21	104
...	...	...	84	197	74	355	17	151	13,997	112	234	1,205	15,716
...	...	...	18	52	23	93	...	8	1,072	25	53	69	1,227
...	107	6,336	192	326	207	7,168	...	...	...	171	354	741	1,266
...	34	6,029	39	53	67	6.222	...	...	1	54	71	258	384
...	86	7,183	89	149	989	8,395	...	...	9	130	195	410	744

TABLE XVII.—*Occupations*

Class.	Order.	Sub-order.	Group.	Occupation.
			......	Private peons, &c. ...
			69	Hotel-keepers ... ...
			71	Club Secretaries, Stewards, &c.
		16.—Sanitation	72	Chemical Examiner to Government.
			73	Sanitary Inspectors ...
			74	Sweepers and scavengers ...
D— ... Preparation and supply of material substances.	VII.—Food and drink.	17.—Animal food	76	Cow and buffalo keepers, and milk and butter sellers.
			77	Ghee sellers ... ...
			78	Cheese sellers ... ...
			79	Butchers and meat sellers ...
			80	Fowl and egg dealers ...
			81	Fishermen ...
		18.—Vegetable food	83	Grain dealers ...
			84	Grain parchers ...
			85	Pulse and flour preparers and sellers.
			87	Bakers ... ...
			88	Bran sellers ... ...
			89 & 90	Vegetable and fruit sellers ...
			92	Confectioners and sweetmeat makers and sellers.
		19.—Drink, condiments and narcotics.	94	Ice manufacturers and sellers...
			95	Aërated water manufacturers and sellers.
			98	Toddy drawers and sellers ...
			99	Foreign wine and spirit dealers
			101	Tea sellers and tasters ...
			102	Coffee preparers and sellers ...
			103	Sugar sellers ... ...
			104	Molasses sellers ... ...
			109	Grocers and general condiment dealers.
			111	Betel-leaf and areca nut sellers
			112	Tobacco sellers ... ...
			113	Opium sellers ... ...
			115	Bhang, ganja, &c., sellers ...

by Ages—continued.

MALES.							FEMALES.						
WORKERS.			DEPENDENTS.			Total males.	WORKERS.			DEPENDENTS.			Total females.
0—4.	5—14.	15.	0—4.	5—14.	15.		0 - 4.	5—14.	15.	0—4.	5—14.	15.	
6	24	945	60	96	45	1,176	...	...	...	25	60	226	311
...	2	291	18	30	37	378	...	...	18	28	69	70	185
...	...	4	...	...	...	4	...	...	...	...	...	...	...
...	...	1	...	...	...	1	...	...	...	...	...	...	...
...	...	5	3	2	...	10	...	...	...	1	3	3	7
7	148	5,247	620	548	315	6,885	17	58	1,257	477	679	1,001	3,439
1	43	2,467	214	297	335	3,357	...	12	514	152	287	1,094	2,059
...	...	199	3	11	11	224	...	...	14	20	26	39	99
...	...	21	...	...	...	21	...	...	...	...	...	...	...
...	31	1,415	152	245	141	1,984	...	...	38	124	250	472	884
...	10	91	6	24	22	153	...	...	3	9	17	40	69
1	32	1,388	153	301	168	2,043	...	6	538	165	232	684	1,625
2	48	1,293	120	295	234	1,992	...	23	847	89	166	483	1,608
1	11	394	19	38	32	495	2	4	8	81	61	91	197
3	18	1,736	47	91	119	2,014	5	17	465	80	137	396	1,100
...	9	817	129	124	124	1,203	...	4	19	44	100	269	436
...	...	32	14	21	11	78	...	...	...	2	4	7	13
3	11	922	108	157	61	1,262	...	...	111	103	202	236	652
5	66	3,346	99	220	230	3,936	3	6	120	100	186	543	958
...	3	100	9	23	16	151	...	1		4	5	25	40
...	...	87	1	3	...	91	...	1	...	2	6	17	21
...	7	587	29	46	74	743	...	...	18	34	74	119	245
..	4	428	58	100	179	769	...	...	20	87	144	241	492
...	2	97	10	21	18	148	...	3	30	27	29	52	141
...	...	1	...	1	1	3	...	...	...	...	...	2	2
...	...	203	2	6	12	223	...	...	...	1	7	20	31
...	...	6	...	2	...	8	...	...	1	...	1	10	12
2	127	6,535	465	1,112	1,770	10,011	7	13	346	501	795	2,761	4,423
1	30	1,189	77	154	175	1,626	...	1	201	125	168	369	864
...	20	1,101	90	162	232	1,605	...	...	35	89	123	377	624
...	2	128	7	14	37	188	...	...	...	27	33	36	96
...	...	20	2	2	4	28	...	...	...	18	27	32	77

Class.	Order.	Sub-order.	Group.	Occupation.
D—*contd.*	VIII.—Light, firing and forage.	20.—Lighting	116	Oil pressers and sellers ...
			117	Salt sellers ... ...
			118	Oilcake dealers ... ...
			119	Candle makers and sellers ...
			121	Kerosine oil dealers ...
			124	Gas workers ... ...
		21.—Fuel and forage ...	125	Firewood and grass gatherers and sellers.
			127	Coal miners ... ...
			128	Coal dealers and brokers, &c. ...
			128A	Pitch sellers ... ...
			130	Cowdung fuel sellers ...
			131	Hay contractors and dealers ...
	IX.—Buildings ...	22.—Building materials ...	133	Lime sellers ... ...
			135	Thatch dealers ... ...
		23.—Artificers in building ...	136	Building contractors ...
			137	Stone and marble workers ...
			138	Masons ... ...
			140	Painters and plasterers ...
			141	Mud wall and roof builders ...
			142	Plumbers ... ...
	X.—Vehicles and Vessels.	24.—Railway plant	144	Railway mechanics ...
			145	Plate-layers ... ...
		25.—Carts and carriages ...	146	Carriage makers ... ...
		26.—Ships and boats ...	148	Boat builders, &c. ... ...
	XI.—Supplementary requirements.	27.—Paper, &c.	153	Paper sellers ... ...
			154	Stationers ... ...
D ...	......	28.—Books and prints ...	157	Press proprietors, printers and lithographers.
			157A	Clerks in printing presses ...
			158	Book-binders ... ...
			159	Book-sellers and publishers ...
			161	Newspaper sellers ...
			162	Picture sellers ... ...
		29.—Watches, clocks and scientific instruments.	163	Watch and clock makers, sellers and repairers.
			164	Opticians ... ...
		30.—Carving, engraving, &c. ...	173	Die sinkers, engravers, &c. ...
			174	Type-founders ... ...

by Ages—continued.

MALES.							FEMALES.						
WORKERS.			DEPENDENTS.			Total males.	WORKERS.			DEPENDENTS.			Total females.
0—4.	5—14.	15.	0—4.	5—14	15.		0—4.	5—14.	15.	0—4.	5—14.	15.	
6	35	833	78	149	122	1,222	...	1	91	57	118	271	538
...	...	20	...	4	7	31	...	...	...	...	...	9	9
...	6	302	44	79	80	511	...	...	17	46	83	152	298
...	...	102	13	39	74	228	...	...	...	6	15	83	104
...	4	146	1	...	1	152	...	...	...	33	38	76	147
...	...	70	1	4	13	88	...	...	...	4	5	10	19
9	16	1,268	96	102	91	1,582	2	1	118	34	31	162	348
...	...	5	...	...	...	5	...	...	...	...	...	1	1
...	2	244	8	23	16	293	9	1	16	43	65	132	266
...	...	20	...	...	...	20	...	...	...	...	...	...	...
...	5	281	11	17	10	324	...	1	79	8	11	47	146
2	3	247	73	72	114	511	...	...	2	32	46	192	272
...	1	202	8	16	24	251	17	...	62	10	24	75	188
...	1	42	2	1	29	75	...	...	...	...	...	...	...
...	1	57	2	2	...	62	...	...	...	4	6	17	27
...	7	285	6	20	27	345	...	...	2	15	29	66	112
21	189	5,326	397	617	440	6,990	...	11	130	415	568	1,647	2,771
...	12	881	20	33	34	980	...	...	3	70	114	223	410
...	18	1,239	48	143	136	1,584	1	2	19	63	108	297	490
...	1	54	9	9	10	83	...	...	...	18	23	36	77
...	15	23	10	6	13	67	3	6	4	7	9	29	58
...	...	11	...	3	1	15	...	...	1	...	...	6	7
...	10	262	9	21	12	314	...	...	...	38	68	129	235
...	...	14	47	85	39	185	...	...	41	41	69	151	302
...	3	223	17	43	54	340	...	...	...	13	21	54	88
...	34	1,111	111	183	276	1,715	1	4	20	138	233	589	985
...	98	5,986	460	672	820	8,027	...	...	5	428	768	1,730	2,931
...	...	45	5	6	4	60	...	...	...	2	8	4	14
3	104	1,972	81	139	88	2,387	...	...	1	90	254	485	830
...	4	295	45	74	80	498	...	...	1	37	75	154	267
...	...	12	...	2	...	14	...	...	1	...	...	...	1
...	2	60	6	12	14	84	...	...	4	11	16	35	66
...	7	525	56	94	128	810	...	...	...	85	151	421	657
...	...	1	...	...	...	1	...	...	...	...	...	...	...
...	...	85	...	...	5	90	...	...	14	3	5	19	41
...	6	14	7	5	4	36	...	...	...	2	12	26	40

TABLE XVII.—*Occupations*

Class.	Order.	Sub-order.	Group.	Occupation.
		31.—Toys, curiosities ...	177	Toy, kite, &c., makers and sellers
			178	Hukka-stem sellers ...
		32.—Music and musical instruments.	183	Dealers in musical instruments
			184	Drum makers ... ...
		33.—Necklaces, bracelets, beads, sacred threads, &c.	185	Lac Bangle sellers ...
			188	Clay Ditto ...
			191	Imitation and pewter jewellery makers and sellers.
			194	Flower garland makers and sellers.
			195	Artificial flower makers and sellers.
		34.—Furniture	198	Furniture makers ... ...
			199	Frame makers ... ...
		35.—Harness	201	Saddle and harness makers and sellers.
			203	Whip makers ... ...
		36.—Tools and machinery ...	207	Mechanics (not Railway) ...
			208	Machinery dealers, &c. ...
		37.—Arms and ammunition ...	209	Gun makers, menders and sellers.
			212	Firework makers and sellers ...
			213	Sword seller ... ...
D ...	XII.—Textile fabrics and dress.	38.—Wool and fur	221	Dealers in woollen cloth ...
		39.—Silk	228	Silk weavers and dealers ...
			230	Ribbon sellers ... ...
		40.—Cotton	231	Cotton cleaners ... ...
			232	Do. sellers ... ...
			233	Do. spinners ... ...
			234	Do. weavers, &c. ...
			236	Do. printers ... ...
			237	Do. dyers ... ...
			238	Tape sellers ... ...
		41.—Jute, flax, coir, &c. ...	241	Rope sellers ... ...
			242	Jute manufacturers, managers and agents and mill hands.
			243	Tarpaulin and gunny sellers ...
			244	Net makers and sellers ...
			246	Coir manufacturers and sellers

by Ages—continued.

MALES.							FEMALES.						
WORKERS.			DEPENDENTS.			Total males.	WORKERS.			DEPENDENTS.			Total females.
0—4.	5—14.	15.	0—4.	5—14.	15.		0—4.	5—14.	15.	0—4.	5—14.	15.	
1	5	129	17	31	12	195	...	...	16	22	43	116	198
...	...	138	4	13	11	166	...	...	1	5	13	43	62
...	11	95	13	20	10	149	...	...	1	19	32	31	83
...	5	4	10	20	13	52	...	...	...	10	19	39	68
...	...	19	1	5	.	25	...	...	...	2	5	5	12
...	2	16	...	...	...	18	...	...	4	13	22	29	68
...	...	23	...	...	...	23	...	...	...	...	...	...	...
...	...	...	2	2	1	5	...	...	...	5	3	13	21
...	1	333	22	47	26	429	...	1	14	5	16	46	81
...	8	679	25	67	31	810	...	...	34	42	95	108	270
...	...	1	1	4	6	12	...	...	...	1	2	3	6
...	4	142	11	13	18	188	...	...	6	29	37	47	119
...	...	1	...	...	...	1	...	...	...	...	...	...	...
...	...	32	3	6	1	42	...	...	1	2	3	6	12
...	...	5	...	...	...	5	...	...	...	...	...	4	4
...	5	297	4	20	25	351	...	...	...	29	60	107	196
...	...	6	...	...	2	8	...	...	...	1	2	7	10
...	...	1	...	...	...	1	...	...	...	...	...	...	...
49	163	4,015	241	418	620	5,506	...	20	92	320	516	1,289	2,237
...	...	31	3	14	21	69	...	...	1	...	...	...	1
...	3	1	...	...	...	4	...	...	...	...	...	...	...
...	4	91	1	...	90	186	...	...	3	21	46	55	125
...	...	57	...	...	...	57	...	...	...	...	...	...	...
...	...	98	8	20	15	141	...	...	16	16	40	82	154
4	16	375	30	61	58	544	...	...	52	45	94	139	330
...	...	80	...	...	7	87	...	...	...	...	...	2	2
...	...	173	3	15	50	241	...	...	14	2	8	28	52
...	...	146	24	23	26	219	...	...	11	38	43	69	161
...	7	201	25	19	27	279	...	...	19	10	16	46	91
4	48	2,346	65	141	277	2,881	1	...	92	77	117	283	570
20	22	627	19	39	107	834	...	1	8	52	68	103	232
...	...	5	...	2	1	8	...	...	...	8	37	12	57
...	...	3	...	...	...	3	...	2	4	...	...	...	6

TABLE XVII.—*Occupations*

Class.	Order.	Sub-order.	Group.	Occupation.
		42.—Dress	247	Tailors and darners ...
			249	Dealers in old clothes ...
			251	Hat makers and sellers ...
			253	Umbrella makers and sellers ...
			254	Embroiderers ... ...
			256	False plait makers and sellers...
	XIII ...	43.—Gold, silver, &c. ...	260	Gold and silver workers ...
			265	Electro-platers ... ...
			268	Diamond dealers ... ...
			276	Brass-workers ... ...
			279	Copper-smiths ... ...
			280	Brass-ware sellers ... ...
			283	Brass-dealers ... ...
		45.—Tin, zinc, &c.	284	Tin-workers ... ...
			287	Lead &c. dealers ... ...
			288	General workers in tin, lead and zinc.
D ...	XIII ...	46.—Iron and steel	289	Iron and steel founders ...
			290	Blacksmiths ... ...
			291	Iron dealers ... ...
			293	Lock-makers and sellers ...
	XIV ...	47.—Glass and chinaware ...	295	Lantern sellers ... ...
			296	Bottle dealers ... ...
			297	Glass and chinaware-dealers ...
		48.—Earthen and stoneware ...	298	Potters ... ...
			300	Mortar sellers ... ...
	XV ...	49.—Timber and wood ...	302	Timber and bamboo-dealers ...
			303	Wood-cutters ... ...
			304	Carpenters ... ...
			305	Box-makers ... ...
		50.—Cane work, matting and leaves.	306	Cane dealers ... ...
			307	Basket-makers ... ...
			308	Mat-makers ... ...
			312	Leaf fan-makers ... ...
			314	Broom-makers ... ...
	XVI ...	51.—Gums, wax and similar forest produce.	321	Sealing wax-makers ...
			323	Wax-collector ... ...

by Ages—continued.

MALES.							FEMALES.						
WORKERS.			DEPENDENTS.			Total males.	WORKERS.			DEPENDENTS.			Total females.
0—4.	5—14.	15.	0—4.	5—14.	15.		0—4	5—14.	15.	0—4.	5-14.	15.	
13	244	5,763	831	1,221	649	8,721	1	2	177	575	1,442	2,632	4,829
...	...	114	...	...	...	114	...	...	2	...	...	...	2
1	21	638	63	71	73	857	6	...	8	54	68	201	337
...	1	233	17	22	24	297	...	...	...	15	29	63	107
...	...	47	3	5	4	59	...	...	19	3	8	23	53
...	...	4	...	...	...	4	...	...	...	...	...	...	...
22	260	4,319	475	711	756	6,543	...	1	27	278	524	1,496	2,326
...	4	116	8	17	9	154	...	...	...	16	26	51	93
...	...	12	1	4	1	18	...	...	...	1	...	2	3
1	1	167	67	149	127	512	...	...	1	50	61	163	275
...	...	22	...	4	3	29	...	...	...	...	1	...	1
1	15	333	30	42	49	470	...	...	14	40	66	124	244
...	20	274	6	4	10	314	...	...	2	17	21	58	98
1	79	1,518	161	277	172	2,208	...	...	23	177	417	928	1,545
...	...	4	30	46	40	120	...	...	...	3	12	33	48
...	5	454	4	8	7	478	...	1	13	14	19	43	90
...	1	79	13	24	45	162	...	...	...	19	38	75	132
1	41	1,558	99	179	212	2,090	...	78	112	160	191	636	1,177
1	14	960	91	125	155	1,346	...	...	13	120	150	220	503
...	...	17	4	...	5	26	...	...	4	...	3	6	13
...	...	9	3	6	10	28	...	...	...	18	21	33	72
8	9	190	4	29	17	257	5	1	17	12	14	80	129
...	44	417	22	45	49	577	...	...	6	55	88	191	340
5	33	615	72	142	127	994	...	14	108	68	112	225	527
...	...	8	2	1	2	13	...	...	...	2	2	4	8
5	25	957	94	164	191	1,436	...	...	244	108	140	473	965
1	8	276	4	11	11	311	...	...	...	14	18	38	70
19	83	5,671	356	580	638	7,347	...	...	4	329	603	1,724	2,660
...	...	471	11	25	84	591	...	1	1	24	31	72	129
...	15	113	6	10	9	153	...	...	11	7	6	15	39
3	14	240	42	32	13	344	8	6	30	16	29	34	123
...	9	51	13	30	23	126	...	3	13	9	33	49	107
...	...	35	...	1	...	36	...	...	...	...	...	8	8
...	...	2	...	3	4	9	...	...	...	...	...	...	...
...	...	56	3	19	218	296	...	...	...	2	12	45	59
...	...	1		...	...	1	...	...	...	...	...	...	...

TABLE XVII.—*Occupations*

Class.	Order.	Sub-order.	Group.	Occupation.
		52.—Drugs, dyes, pigments, &c....	324	Chemists and druggists ...
			326	Saltpetre sellers ... ...
			328	Soap-makers and sellers ...
			330	Indigo sellers ... ...
			332	Ink sellers ... ...
	XVI ...	52.—Drugs, dyes, &c. ...	337	Musk shop ... ...
	XVII ...	53.—Leather, &c.	338	Tanners, &c. ... ...
			339	Boot and shoe-makers and sellers.
			342	Hide, horn and bone-dealers ...
			342A	Feather-sellers ... ...
E.—Commerce, transport, storage.	XVIII.—Commerce	54.—Dealers in money and securities.	346	Bankers, and bank managers ...
			347	Money-lenders ... ...
			348	Bill-discounters ... ...
			350	Money-changers ... ...
			351	Bank-clerks, accountants, &c....
		55.—General merchants ...	352	General merchants ...
			353	Merchants' clerks ... ...
		56.—Dealing unspecified ...	354	Shopkeepers' clerks ...
			355	Shopkeepers' servants ...
			356	Shopkeepers otherwise unspecified.
			357	General hawkers ... ...
		57A.—Middlemen, &c. ...	358	Brokers, agents, &c. ...
			359	Auctioneers, appraisers, &c. ...
		57B	362	Public Works contractors ...
		57B	363	Contractors of municipality ...
			364	Contractors for emigration, &c.
	XIX.—Transport and storage.	58A	365	Railway Registrars ...
			366	Railway Superintendents, &c. ...
			368	Store-keepers ... ...
			369	Engineers ... ...
			370	Goods clerks ... ...
		58B	371	Station-masters, and assistants and inspectors, overseers, &c.
			372	Railway drivers, guards, firemen and servants.
		59A	374	Tramway servants... ...
			375	Cart-owners ... ...

by Ages—continued.

MALES.							FEMALES.						
WORKERS.			DEPENDENTS.			Total males.	WORKERS.			DEPENDENTS.			Total females.
0—4	5—14.	15.	0—4.	5—14.	15.		0—4	5—14.	15.	0—4.	5—14.	15.	
2	1	155	33	64	164	419	3	9	233	33	72	134	484
...	...	3	...	...	...	3	...	...	...	1	...	1	2
1	5	76	7	12	20	121	...	...	2	18	29	34	83
...	6	137	1	6	14	164	...	...	...	13	10	17	40
...	9	114	9	13	12	157	...	...	...	23	30	30	83
...	...	63	...	1	63	117	...	...	...	1	3	5	9
...	17	1,183	115	219	204	1,738	...	...	8	142	207	509	866
1	332	10,128	248	334	217	11,260	4	1	45	255	389	1,159	1,853
...	1	39	1	5	2	48	...	...	1	3	4	12	20
...	...	...	...	...	...	...	...	...	...		8	21	35
...	6	405	65	30	35	541	...	1	10	26	25	81	143
...	15	1,312	81	170	337	1,915	...	5	180	75	137	381	778
...	...	...	...	1	...	1	...	...	...	1	1	...	2
...	...	19	...	...	4	23	...	...	1	44	32	34	111
...	3	268	25	39	113	448	...	...	...	15	26	101	142
...	16	4,417	312	613	1,078	6,436	...	2	112	259	351	1,543	2,267
...	33	7,824	969	2,075	2,730	13,631	...	...	...	1,220	2,098	4,455	7,773
...	1	459	56	112	215	843	...	...	...	46	82	177	305
...	3	444	17	19	48	531	...	...	...	98	193	383	674
8	91	5,248	379	701	874	7,301	...	2	203	357	875	1,678	3,115
...	42	1,892	102	185	127	2,348	...	5	77	69	113	408	672
...	35	4,163	300	708	900	6,106	...	...	15	296	534	1,681	2,526
...	...	21	5	16	8	50	...	...	...	11	13	11	35
...	...	8	4	4	3	19	...	...	...	2	4	6	12
...	...	31	5	2	6	44	...	...	...	5	6	16	27
...	...		...	...	...	3	...	...	...	...	...	...	...
...	1	13	3	2	5	24	...	1	1	...	...	3	5
...	...	8	...	...	...	8	...	...	...	5	1	4	10
...	...	325	8	16	27	376	...	...	...	16	32	58	106
...	...	...	2	1	...	3	...	...	...	11	27	7	45
...	6	697	63	128	232	1,126	...	...	...	100	213	535	848
...	...	38	4	11	5	58	...	...	...	3	4	13	20
..	15	1,177	45	65	69	1,371	...	...	1	48	97	195	340
...	6	163	10	33	16	228	...	...	...	5	9	30	44
2	85	4,878	240	359	213	5,777	...	...	2	206	359	1,004	1,571

TABLE XVII.—*Occupations*

Class.	Order.	Sub-order.	Group.	Occupation.
E.—Commerce, transport, storage—*concld.*			376	Livery stable-keepers ...
			377	Drivers and stable-boys, &c. ...
			378	Palki-bearers ... ...
		60A	381	Ship-owners ... ...
			382	Shipping clerks and stevedores
		60B	384	Captains of ships and boats ...
				Sailors ... ...
	XIX.—Transport and storage.	60B	385	Native sailors and Boat-men ...
			387	Superintendent of Canal ...
			388	Dock, and shipping khalasies ...
			389	Drivers ... ...
		61A	390	Postal directors, postmasters and clerks.
			391	Postal messengers, runners, &c.
			393	Telegraphers ... ...
			394	Signallers and messengers ...
		62.—Storage and weighing ...	398	Porters (general) ... ...
			399	Weigh and measure men ...
F.—Profession.	XX.—Learned and Artistic Profession.	63.—Religion	401	Priests and missionaries ...
			402	Catechists ... ...
			404	Inmates of monasteries ...
			405	Pilgrim conductors ...
			......	Undertakers ... ...
		64.—Education	406	Administrative and inspecting officials.
			407	Principals, professors and teachers, &c.
		65.—Literature	409	Authors, Editors, &c. ...
			409	Journalists ... ...
			410	Reporters ... ...
			411	Private Secretaries and clerks
			412	Copyists and public scribes ...
			413	Librarians ... ...
		66.—Law	414	Barristers, advocates and pleaders.
			415	Solicitors and attorneys ...
			416	Law agents and mukhtars ...
			417	Articled and other Lawyers' clerks.
			418	Stamp vendors ... ...

by Ages—continued.

MALES.							FEMALES.						
WORKERS.			DEPENDENTS.			Total males.	WORKERS.			DEPENDENTS.			Total females.
0—4.	5—14.	15.	0—4.	5—14.	15.		0—4.	5—14.	15.	0—4.	5—14.	15.	
...	...	8	6	11	18	43	...	...	...	1	8	12	21
3	11	3,819	548	436	521	5,338	...	...	...	166	326	1,042	1,534
...	2	740	7	15	25	789	...	...	...	...	...	1	1
...	...	5	3	7	4	19	...	...	...	1	7	2	10
...	2	532	267	114	114	1,029	...	...	...	29	57	156	242
...	...	217	180	164	28	589	...	...	...	10	23	125	158
...	...	1,355	180	201	98	1,834	...	...	...	205	302	840	1,347
2	397	21,685	22	17	36	22,159	...	...	1	28	37	126	192
...	...	1	...	...	...	1	...	...	...	2	...	1	3
6	87	3,653	207	415	993	5,311	...	...	...	399	416	1,443	2,258
...	...	34	2	3	1	40	...	...	...	3	15	23	41
...	...	815	14	63	81	473	...	...	...	22	147	138	307
...	11	699	26	33	18	787	...	...	1	34	57	11	103
...	1	55	19	44	59	178	...	...	...	21	32	94	147
...	...	49	8	6	2	65	...	...	...	6	16	26	48
...	...	81	10	11	9	111	...	...	...	3	4	6	13
1	7	646	16	25	61	756	...	...	8	19	40	77	144
10	79	3,840	355	355	396	5,035	2	2	119	183	415	1,366	2,087
...	1	45	1	10	3	60	...	...	4	7	23	39	73
...	...	25	2	2	...	29	...	...	2	...	...	...	2
...	...	35	1	2	1	39	...	...	2	...	3	2	7
...	...	17	1	4	6	28	...	...	...	6	6	20	32
...	...	4	...	...	...	4	...	...	...	...	1	1	2
...	5	2,137	237	613	560	3,552	...	...	214	258	485	1,0 6	2,033
...	...	75	13	30	29	147	...	...	5	14	19	59	97
...	...	16	2	4	...	22	...	...	...	3	...	2	5
...	...	18	3	20	18	59	...	...	2	1	8	26	37
...	...	3,874	104	219	436	4,654	...	...	29	252	361	1,092	1,734
...	52	3,390	760	1,487	1,711	7,400	...	...	29	434	822	2,130	3,415
...	...	1	...	...	3	4	...	...	2	...	...	2	4
...	...	74	9	9	19	111	...	...	...	46	41	63	150
...	...	61	14	24	28	127	...	...	...	9	18	33	60
...	9	1,030	161	356	437	1,998	...	...	...	205	432	993	1,630
...	4	308	25	60	128	525	...	...	...	32	47	155	234
...	...	41	2	3	6	52	...	...	...	9	9	28	46

TABLE XVII.—*Occupations*

Class.	Order.	Sub-order.	Group.	Occupation.
F. Profession —*concld.*	XX.—Learned and artistic profession —*concld.*	67.—Medicine	420	Administrative and inspecting staff.
			421	Practitioners by diploma ...
			422	Kabirajes ... ...
			423	Dentists ... ...
			426	Midwifes ... ...
			427	Hospital assistants and apothecaries.
			428	Compounders, nurses, &c. ...
		68.—Engineering and surveying...	429	Administrative and inspecting staff.
			430	Civil Engineers and architects
			431	Surveyors, draughtsmen ...
			432	Overseers, &c. ... ...
		69.—Other sciences	434	Meteorologists ... ...
			......	Astronomers ... ...
			435	Botanists ... ...
			437	Astrologers ... ...
		70.—Pictorial, art and sculpture...	440	Painters ... ...
			441	Sculptors ... ...
			442	Photographers ... ...
		71.—Music, acting, dancing ...	443	Music composers ... ...
			444	Bandmasters and players ..
			446	Actors, singers, dancers, &c. ...
	XXI.—Sports and amusements.	72.—Sport	447	Jockeys, bookmakers, &c. ...
			448	Shikaris ... ...
		73.—Exhibition and games ...	452	Pigeon and cock fanciers ...
			453	Buffoons .. ..
			456	Fortune-tellers ... ...
			457	Acrobats ... ...
			460	Theatre managers and owners...
G. Indefinite and independent.	XXIII.—Indefinite	74.—Unskilled labour	463	Road, canal and railway labourers.
			466	Ricepounders and huskers ...
			467	General labourers ... ...
		75.—Undefined	468	Unspecified ... ...
			468	Prostitutes ... ...

by Ages—continued.

MALES.							FEMALES.						
WORKERS.			DEPENDENTS.			Total males.	WORKERS.			DEPENDENTS.			Total females.
0—4.	5—14.	15.	0—4.	5—14.	15.		0—4.	5—14.	15.	0—4.	5—14	15.	
...	...	1	...	...	...	1	...	...	...	...	...	...	...
...	...	1,081	226	474	536	2,317	...	...	...	324	540	1,092	1,956
...	...	163	20	36	64	283	...	...	14	32	43	98	187
...	...	4	...	...	...	4	...	1	2	...	1	3	7
...	...	2	15	21	22	60	...	...	310	18	50	115	523
...	14	81	4	13	6	118	...	...	...	4	6	15	25
...	14	652	66	76	88	896	...	1	28	27	51	133	240
...	...	372	59	110	80	621	...	...	2	71	108	272	453
...	...	128	30	58	63	279	...	...	...	43	89	179	311
...	...	73	10	9	16	108	...	...	...	14	35	65	114
...	10	325	63	100	96	594	...	...	1	54	115	199	369
...	...	1	...	...	...	1	...	...	...	...	...	...	...
...	1	15	...	2	5	23	...	...	...	1	1	5	7
...	...	...	2	2	1	5	...	...	...	...	1	2	3
...	...	18	...	3	1	22	...	...	...	1	1	4	6
...	35	194	6	19	45	299	...	...	6	41	33	56	136
3	6	86	...	...	3	98	...	...	18	1	2	3	24
...	...	80	7	13	5	105	...	...	...	51	64	75	190
...	10	280	14	24	19	347	...	6	22	31	33	83	175
...	1	40	4	11	8	64	...	...	...	...	2	17	19
...	39	444	17	95	70	665	...	6	86	26	46	129	293
...	2	31	5	3	...	41	...	...	...	...	2	2	4
...	...	5	1	2	...	8	...	...	...	21	15	6	42
...	3	60	15	13	10	101	...	...	...	2	5	10	17
...	...	1	...	1	2	4	...	...	...	1	2	2	5
...	1	73	6	7	2	88	...	...	4	3	11	21	39
...	...	1	...	...	...	1	...	...	...	...	...	...	...
...	...	8	1	1	1	11	...	...	...	...	4	8	12
4	18	745	26	59	89	936	...	...	2	46	94	158	300
...	...	29	...	...	...	29	...	...	15	...	...	...	15
18	551	32,517	1,368	2,120	3,437	40,006	...	96	2,220	978	1,648	4,868	9,810
...	1,840	7,036	5,419	13,076	1,978	29,349	...	549	14,235	3,401	5,148	17,564	40,897
...	...	...	132	251	155	538	...	182	19,944	238	416	1,116	21,895

TABLE XVII.—*Occupations*

Class.	Order.	Sub-order.	Group.	Occupation.
G.	XXIV.—Independent of work.	76.—Property and alms	469	Supported by house-rent, shares, &c.
Indefinite and independent—*concld.*			470	By allowances from relatives ...
			471	Scholarship-holders, educational
			472	Mendicancy ... ...
		77.—Supported at the public charge	473	Pensioners ... ...
			475	Inmates of asylums ... ...
			476	Under-trial prisoners ... ...
			477	Civil prisoners ... ...
			478	Prisoners convicted ... ...
			479	Students ... ...
			480	Markmen ... ...
				Total ...

by Ages—concluded.

MALES.							FEMALES.						
WORKERS.			DEPENDANTS.			Total males.	WORKERS.			DEPENDANTS.			Total females.
0—4.	5—14.	15.	0—4.	5—14.	15.		0—4.	5—14.	15.	0—4.	5—14.	15.	
...	40	1,289	328	679	684	3,020	...	18	1,597	296	716	1,921	4,548
...	4	539	47	86	50	726	...	9	129	55	98	349	640
...	...	3	...	135	30	168	...	...	...	...	...	...	...
15	235	3,487	242	348	232	4,559	7	67	2,840	364	523	821	4,622
...	1	971	183	386	374	1,915	...	...	95	186	345	852	1,478
4	8	316	...	...	...	328	3	7	105	...	...	...	115
...	...	37	...	...	...	37	...	...	1	...	...	...	1
...	...	10	...	...	...	10	...	...	...	...	...	...	...
...	...	2,860	...	...	...	2,860	...	...	53	...	...	...	53
...	5	19	...	76	55	155	2	1	1	12	13	22	51
...	1	186	5	7	41	240	...	...	1	13	29	50	93
362	8,160	320,781	25,931	48,412	43,100	446,746	140	1,515	67,227	23,223	39,441	103,268	234,814

TABLE XVIII.—*Population of the town, block by block.*

Ward.	Block.	Males.	Females.	Total.
Ward No. I.	1	212	57	269
	2	385	168	553
	3	678	595	1,273
	4	624	554	1,178
	5	584	405	989
	6	490	319	809
	7	1,259	859	2,118
	8	739	587	1,326
	9	619	571	1,190
	10, 11	510	162	672
	12	181	116	297
	13	119	103	222
	14	198	113	311
	15	273	215	488
	16	616	485	1,101
	17	904	590	1,494
	18	679	568	1,247
	19	816	620	1,436
	20	661	537	1,198
	21	625	611	1,236
	22	518	450	968
	23	814	661	1,475
	24	140	125	265
	25	169	180	349
	26	118	90	208
	27	182	201	383
	28	224	128	352
	29	438	189	627
	30	103	99	202
	31	496	219	715
	32	590	421	1,011
	31	639	363	1,002
Ward No. I—*concluded.*	33-2	1,173	545	1,718
	34	716	669	1,385
	35	785	615	1,400
	36	507	427	934
	37	334	250	584
	38	403	409	812
	39	1,360	706	2,066
	40	610	412	1,022
Total ...	...	21,491	15,394	36,885
Ward No. II.	1	435	102	537
	2	340	270	610
	3	718	518	1,236
	4	1,360	511	1,871
	5	643	473	1,116
	6	498	351	849
	7	586	466	1,052
	8	253	91	344
	9	594	218	812
	10	781	474	1,255
	11	779	674	1,453
	12	539	282	821
	13	584	376	960
	14	593	393	986
	15	761	651	1,412
	16	627	200	827
	17	419	173	592
	18	161	18	179
	19	555	390	945
	20	444	444	888
	21	624	540	1,164

Table XVIII.—*Population of the town, block by block*—continued.

Ward.	Block.	Males.	Females.	Total.
Ward No. II—*concluded.*	22	572	368	940
	23	742	472	1,214
	24	350	263	613
	25	1,154	993	2,147
	26	430	275	705
	27	636	450	1,086
Total ...	...	16,178	10,436	26,614
Ward No. III.	1	230	162	392
	2	164	117	281
	3	213	113	326
	4	264	195	459
	5	243	134	377
	6	710	429	1,139
	7	600	401	1,001
	8	613	284	897
	9	406	390	796
	10	469	349	818
	11	664	654	1,318
	12	630	497	1,127
	13	590	377	967
	14	603	511	1,114
	15	451	227	678
	16	333	142	475
	17	241	219	460
	18	107	105	212
	19	144	80	224
	20	58	36	94
	21	223	106	329
	22	205	137	342
	23	109	45	154

Ward.	Block.	Males.	Females.	Total.
Ward No. III—*continued.*	24	132	94	226
	25	284	191	475
	26	455	366	821
	27	606	525	1,131
	28	284	191	475
	29	381	274	655
	30	395	291	686
	31	140	122	262
	32	152	145	297
	33	103	104	207
	34	128	67	195
	35	319	273	592
	36	364	253	617
	37	811	632	1,443
	38	664	545	1,209
	39	686	490	1,176
	40	640	505	1,145
	41	603	483	1,086
	42	835	672	1,507
	43	508	397	905
	44	955	490	1,445
	45	976	503	1,479
	46	1,293	1,142	2,435
	47	1,036	946	1,982
Total ...	...	21,020	15,411	36,431
Ward No. IV.	1	211	111	322
	2	170	201	371
	3	180	157	337
	4	218	146	364
	5	489	372	861

TABLE XVIII.—*Population of the town, block by block*—continued.

Ward.	Block.	Males.	Females.	Total.	Ward.	Block.	Males.	Females.	Total.
Ward No. IV—*concluded.*	6	544	467	1,011	Ward No V.	1	179	3	182
	7	615	425	1,040		2	498	45	543
	8	574	464	1,038		3	468	8	476
	9	851	541	1,392		4	257	29	286
	10	562	415	977		5	292	50	342
	11	982	810	1,792		6	1,043	123	1,166
	12	496	405	901		7	857	357	1,214
	13	508	330	838		8	826	594	1,420
	14	831	510	1,341		9	1,110	693	1,803
	15	279	244	523		10	708	330	1,038
	16	126	107	233		11	1,124	559	1,683
	17	236	201	437		12	611	285	896
	18	388	330	718		13	1,006	387	1,393
	19	693	437	1,130		14	888	497	1,385
	20	836	612	1,448		15	737	588	1,325
	21	912	671	1,583		16	694	546	1,240
	22	939	589	1,528		17	610	280	890
	23	1,615	1,041	2,656		18	981	672	1,653
	24	687	428	1,115		19	688	591	1,279
	25	997	673	1,670		20	747	341	1,088
	26	901	598	1,499		21	1,224	219	1,443
	27	1,236	694	1,930		22	1,382	511	1,893
	28	300	247	547		23	1,421	513	1,934
	29	285	252	537		24	1,481	479	1,960
	30	254	149	403		25	932	430	1,362
	31	552	326	878		26	1,071	751	1,822
	32	198	168	366		27	968	606	1,574
	33	615	328	943		28	1,618	957	2,575
	34	418	167	585		29	1,005	716	1,721
	35	629	425	1,054		30	985	609	1,594
	36	306	154	460					
Total ...	...	20,633	14,195	34,828	Total ...	...	26,411	12,769	39,180

TABLE XVIII.—*Population of the town, block by block*—continued.

Ward.	Block.	Males.	Females.	Total.
Ward No. VI.	1	972	673	1,645
	2	780	528	1,308
	3	766	642	1,408
	4	681	430	1,111
	5	466	452	918
	6	546	425	971
	7	793	566	1,359
	8	647	516	1,163
	9	1,309	1,024	2,333
	10	1,018	849	1,867
	11	1,059	798	1,857
	12	767	694	1,461
	13	911	576	1,487
	14	872	689	1,561
	15	1,465	522	1,987
	16	411	291	702
	17	743	542	1,285
	18	1,079	854	1,933
	19	1,134	710	1,844
	20	701	455	1,156
	21	236	108	344
	22	1,252	568	1,820
	23	1,904	572	2,476
	24	524	319	843
	25	1,362	787	2,149
	26	709	423	1,132
	27	717	383	1,100
	28	1,546	891	2,437
Total ...	...	25,370	16,287	41,657
Ward No. VII.	1	378	67	445
	2	990	90	1,080

Ward.	Block.	Males	Females.	Total.
Ward No. VII—*concluded.*	3	529	34	563
	4	723	101	824
	5	656	38	694
	6	490	75	565
	7	480	40	520
	8	376	112	488
	9	531	98	629
	10	562	20	582
	11	521	17	538
	12	582	70	652
	13	670	150	820
	14	679	153	832
	15	368	60	428
	16	583	113	696
	17	860	189	1,049
	18	646	164	810
	19	987	582	1,569
	20	486	234	720
	21	1,284	711	1,995
	22	1,240	625	1,865
	23	841	456	1,297
	24	764	221	985
Total ...	..	16,226	4,420	20,646
Ward No. VIII.	1	900	447	1,446
	2	1,878	934	2,812
	3	1,113	522	1,635
	4	815	289	1,104
	5	1,226	460	1,686
	6	1,578	505	2,083
	7	1,325	567	1,892
	8	409	176	585

TABLE XVIII—*Population of the town, block by block*—continued.

Ward.	Block.	Males.	Females.	Total.	Ward.	Block.	Males.	Females.	Total.
Ward No. VIII—*concluded.*	9	502	144	646	Ward No. IX—*concluded.*	8	773	433	1,206
	10	1,947	339	2,286		9	1,047	550	1,597
	11	886	381	1,267		10	392	210	602
	12	449	303	752		11	1,043	691	1,734
	13	709	279	988		12	167	73	240
	14	418	18	436		13	231	131	362
	15	296	86	382		14	264	213	477
	16	2,241	896	3,137		15	257	153	410
	17	1,278	523	1,801		16	296	192	488
	18	1,229	421	1,650		17	646	251	897
	19	1,486	852	2,338		18	977	544	1,521
	20	345	230	575		19	776	382	1,158
	21	1,444	505	1,949		20	398	235	633
	22	1,251	604	1,855		21	695	259	954
	23	1,311	765	2,076		22	333	210	543
	24	1,003	465	1,468		23	46	34	80
	25	890	471	1,361		24	292	107	399
	26	1,072	401	1,473		25	181	82	263
	27	1,448	830	2,278		26	205	148	353
	28	1,194	503	1,697		27	313	181	494
	29	1,316	957	2,273		28	50	51	101
	30	2,195	1,125	3,320		29	2,728	425	3,153
	31	1,062	468	1,530		30	760	392	1,152
						31	263	135	398
Total ...	...	35,315	15,466	50,781		32	721	437	1,158
						33	812	385	1,197
Ward No. IX.	1, 2	386	183	569		34	886	687	1,573
						35	672	295	967
	3	1,526	810	2,336		36	937	370	1,307
	4	898	404	1,302		37	812	402	1,214
	5	929	628	1,557		38	978	435	1,413
	6	855	564	1,419		39	714	574	1,288
	7	1,143	873	2,016		40	827	604	1,431

TABLE XVIII—*Population of the town, block by block*—continued.

Ward.	Block.	Males.	Females.	Total.
Ward No. IX—*concld.*	41	1,176	709	1,885
	42	538	428	966
	43	931	805	1,736
	44	688	473	1,161
	45	648	233	881
	46	819	505	1,324
	47	189	123	312
	48	158	103	261
	49	167	87	254
	50	243	134	377
	51	190	163	353
Total ...	...	31,976	17,496	49,472
Ward No. X.	1	773	374	1,147
	2	1,174	484	1,658
	3	991	411	1,402
	4	1,184	589	1,773
	5	966	567	1,533
	6	866	569	1,435
	7	1,093	626	1,719
	8	1,118	726	1,844
	9	1,238	524	1,762
	10	938	352	1,290
	11	1,126	319	1,445
	12	747	184	931
	13	1,535	332	1,867
	14	1,026	405	1,431
	15	1,105	326	1,431
Total ...	...	15,880	6,788	22,668

Ward.	Block.	Males.	Females.	Total.
Ward No. XI.	1	1,008	576	1,584
	2	1,321	851	2,172
	3	1,034	637	1,671
	4	688	515	1,203
	5	747	486	1,233
	6	705	440	1,145
	7	939	444	1,383
	8	751	562	1,313
	9	782	572	1,354
	10	839	492	1,331
	11	653	378	1,031
	12	556	442	998
	13	933	611	1,544
	14	593	340	933
	15	799	499	1,298
	16	367	201	568
Total ...	...	12,715	8,046	20,761
Ward No. XII.	1	1,367	51	1,418
	2	1,021	58	1,079
	3	1,272	212	1,484
	4	972	122	1,094
	5	9	3	12
	6	796	49	845
	7	146	5	151
Total ..	...	5,583	500	6,083
Ward No. XIII.	1	1,068	101	1,169
	2	3,528	546	4,074
	3	2,068	518	2,586
	4	783	172	955

TABLE XVIII.—*Population of the town, block by block*—continued.

Ward.	Block.	Males.	Females.	Total.
Ward No. XIII—*concluded.*	5	2,710	533	3,243
	6	1,082	383	1,465
	7	1,436	584	2,020
	8	1,285	548	1,833
	9	2,033	609	2,642
	10	388	173	561
	11	353	70	423
	12	679	354	1,033
	13	1,348	707	2,055
	14	1,372	406	1,778
	15	624	241	865
	16	1,072	592	1,664
Total ...	...	21,829	6,537	28,366
Ward No. XIV.	1	1,350	635	1,685
	2	1,054	504	1,658
	3	411	126	537
	4	985	677	1,762
	5	551	398	949
	6	937	568	1,505
	7	1,106	506	1,212
	8	637	376	1,013
	9	867	644	1,511
	10	801	603	1,404
	11	699	332	1,031
	12	734	482	1,216
	13	882	353	1,235
	14	1,025	446	1,571
	15	1,059	640	1,799
	16	822	420	1,242
	17	980	694	1,774
Ward No XIV—*concluded.*	18	866	601	1,467
	19	1,308	695	2,103
	20	1,029	633	1,762
	21	476	295	771
Total ...	...	18,579	10,628	29,207
Ward No. XV.	1	851	504	1,355
	2	515	355	870
	3	808	577	1,385
	4	744	380	1,124
	5	1,150	471	1,621
	6	1,148	797	1,945
	7	1,033	404	1,437
	8	2,021	759	2,780
	9	627	74	701
Total ...	..	8,897	4,321	13,218
Ward No. XVI.	1	1,031	197	1,228
	2	1,278	202	1,480
	3	1,416	496	1,912
Total ...	...	3,725	895	4,620
Ward No. XVII.	1	942	468	1,410
	2	625	295	920
	3	692	258	950
	4	1,293	25	1,318
Total ...	...	3,552	1,046	4,598

TABLE XVIII.—*Population of the town, block by block*—continued.

Ward.	Block.	Males.	Females.	Total.
Ward No. XVIII.	1	110	27	137
	2	422	183	605
	3	1,403	723	2,126
	4	383	215	598
	5	673	306	979
	6	247	128	375
Total ...	...	3,238	1,582	4,820
Ward No. XIX.	1	372	107	479
	2	102	46	148
	3	198	132	330
	4	344	180	524
	5	276	130	406
	6	281	170	451
	7	236	108	344
	8	315	155	470
	9	958	328	1,286
	10	899	388	1,287
	11	1,560	642	2,202
	12	325	133	458
	13	Included in Ward IX, block 29.		
	14	474	150	624
	15	285	182	467
	16	225	189	414
	17	175	167	342
	18	283	124	407
	19	200	158	358
	20	121	85	206
	21	213	165	378
	22	262	270	532
	23	209	106	315

Ward.	Block.	Males.	Females.	Total.
Ward No. XIX—*continued.*	24	204	162	366
	25	187	124	311
	26	120	96	216
	27	79	60	139
	28	76	92	168
	29	212	125	337
	30	98	72	170
	31	155	90	245
	32	107	99	206
	33	58	48	106
	34	110	97	207
	35	114	114	228
	36	181	130	311
	37	274	163	437
	38	252	125	377
	39	157	143	300
	40	114	111	225
	41	187	172	359
	42	252	196	448
	43	367	254	621
	44	260	145	405
	45	270	200	470
	46	312	205	517
	47	233	146	379
	48	247	163	410
	49	573	285	858
	50	403	339	742
	51	244	177	421
	52	342	318	660
	53	559	418	977
	54	699	390	1,089
	55	687	344	1,031
	56	867	540	1,407

TABLE XVIII.—*Population of the town, block by block*—continued.

Ward.	Block.	Males.	Females.	Total.
Ward No. XIX—*concluded*.	57	304	283	587
	58	321	252	573
	59	282	220	502
	60	174	141	315
	61	238	174	412
	62	110	186	296
	63	238	220	458
	64	291	251	542
	65	152	211	363
	66	151	199	350
	67	125	461	586
	68	175	87	262
	69	76	74	150
	70	93	87	180
Total ...	...	20,043	13,104	33,147
Ward No. XX.	1	238	145	383
	2	376	161	537
	3	227	117	344
	4	295	212	507
	5	500	400	900
	6	558	323	881
	7	628	521	1,149
	8	360	187	547
	9	706	255	961
	10	457	279	736
	11	276	162	438
	12	193	144	337
	13	211	223	434
	14	165	139	304
	15	324	304	628
Ward XX—*continued*.	16	293	239	532
	17	109	176	285
	18	221	210	431
	19	136	95	231
	20	99	80	179
	21	160	121	281
	22	85	92	177
	23	167	109	276
	24	30	30	60
	25	150	128	278
	26	130	104	234
	27	784	272	1,056
	28	198	133	331
	29	210	167	377
	30	267	220	487
	31	210	129	339
	32	454	299	753
	33	336	211	547
	34	206	158	364
	35	131	127	258
	36	179	117	296
	37	507	272	779
	38	439	258	697
	39	206	158	364
	40	342	190	532
	41	237	172	409
	42	136	133	269
	43	256	250	506
	44	357	199	556
	45	178	154	332
	46	183	162	345
	47	56	56	112
	48	103	113	216

TABLE XVIII.—*Population of the town, block by block*—continued.

Ward.	Block.	Males.	Females.	Total.	Ward.	Block	Males.	Females.	Total.
Ward No. XX—*concld.*	49	167	169	336	Ward No. XXI—*continued.*	26	245	85	330
	50	190	192	382		27	581	234	825
	51	195	132	327		28	506	274	782
						29	339	228	567
						30	172	116	288
Total ...	...	13,621	9,399	23,020		31	108	61	169
						32	157	121	278
						33	100	99	199
Ward No. XXI.	1	236	145	381		34	348	115	463
	2	292	144	436		35	323	77	400
	3	210	204	414		36	189	122	311
	4	378	255	633		37	127	132	259
	5	162	160	322		38	92	170	262
	6	187	210	397		39	67	60	127
	7	223	105	328		40	95	102	197
	8	235	179	414		41	178	84	262
	9	155	108	263		42	127	58	185
	10	169	190	359		43	88	80	168
	11	158	139	297		44	194	82	276
	12	123	115	238		45	125	129	254
	13	144	94	238		46	60	56	116
	14	105	127	232		47	125	101	226
	15	99	120	219		48	175	74	249
	16	105	119	224		49	115	110	225
	17	112	104	216		50	68	53	121
	18	71	70	141		51	83	94	177
	19	84	72	156		52	89	70	159
	20	90	87	177		53	100	101	201
	21	34	41	75		54	181	21	202
	22	115	49	164		55	79	83	162
	23	69	46	115		56	138	129	267
	24	174	165	339		57	102	82	184
	25	144	86	230		58	79	54	133

TABLE XVIII.—*Population of the town, block by block*—continued.

Ward.	Block.	Males.	Females	Total.
Ward No. XXI—*concluded.*	59	169	74	243
	60	106	96	202
	61	125	128	253
	62	181	111	292
	63	143	102	245
	64	102	117	219
	65	109	95	204
	66	149	183	332
	67	166	159	325
	68	91	104	195
	69	115	130	245
	70	217	228	445
	71	121	136	257
	72	143	148	291
	73	218	214	432
	74	131	93	224
	75	70	66	136
	76	83	42	125
	77	58	53	111
	78	115	63	178
	79	94	88	182
	80	70	79	149
	81	45	59	104
	82	95	96	191
	83	67	62	129
	84	134	118	252
	85	79	81	160
	86	92	80	172
	87	99	84	183
	88	202	133	335
Total ...	...	13,018	9,813	22,831

Ward.	Block.	Males.	Females.	Total.
Ward No. XXII.	1	444	330	774
	2	384	280	664
	6	505	320	825
	4	528	571	1,099
	5	352	200	552
	6	485	382	867
	7	207	134	341
	8	1,503	525	2,028
	9	914	610	1,524
	10	1,193	525	1,718
	11	602	440	1,042
	12	197	174	371
	13	83	84	167
	14	243	136	379
	15	337	212	549
	16	419	258	677
	17	217	195	412
	18	679	416	1,095
	19	367	320	687
	20	291	210	501
	21	416	350	766
	22	254	199	453
	23	169	125	294
	24	234	139	373
	25	199	143	342
	26	231	178	409
	27	211	202	413
	28	141	100	241
	29	141	128	269
	30	188	143	331
	31	111	115	226
	32	152	125	277
	33	147	153	300

TABLE XVIII.—*Population of the town, block by block*—continued.

Ward.	Block.	Males.	Females.	Total.	Ward.	Block.	Males	Females.	Total.
Ward No. XXII—*continued.*	34	322	194	516	Ward No. XXII—*continued.*	67	162	129	291
	35	428	290	718		68	138	172	310
	36	207	175	382		69	204	172	376
	37	165	110	275		70	162	172	334
	38	214	160	374		71	221	204	425
	39	223	184	407		72	127	65	192
	40	206	156	362		73	179	186	365
	41	113	102	215		74	126	138	264
	42	128	66	194		75	163	125	288
	43	172	152	324		76	149	154	303
	44	191	150	341		77	151	137	288
	45	183	162	345		78	128	115	243
	46	169	133	302		79	136	147	283
	47	143	133	276		80	88	98	186
	48	195	152	347		81	141	122	263
	49	231	108	339		82	123	106	229
	50	183	165	348		83	112	100	212
	51	179	113	292		84	128	142	270
	52	189	184	373		85	159	165	324
	53	98	77	175		86	84	53	137
	54	88	101	189		87	157	109	266
	55	123	91	214		88	85	64	149
	56	156	160	316		89	166	142	308
	57	122	120	242		90	73	86	159
	58	148	129	277		91	115	114	229
	59	135	155	290		92	94	108	202
	60	223	193	416		93	53	49	102
	61	224	172	396		94	84	85	169
	62	120	108	228		95	143	164	307
	63	216	178	394		96	129	138	267
	64	126	123	249		97	186	160	346
	65	151	118	269		98	157	53	210
	66	187	177	364		99	183	73	256

TABLE XVIII.—*Population of the town, block by block*—continued.

Ward.	Block.	Males.	Females.	Total.	Ward.	Block.	Males.	Females.	Total.
Ward No. XXII—*concluded.*	100	109	60	169	Ward No. XXIII—*continued.*	20	118	117	235
	101	75	84	159		21	191	158	349
	102	209	200	409		22	107	68	175
	103	156	125	281		23	89	73	162
	104	126	102	228		24	54	49	103
	105	98	120	218		25	444	129	573
	106	82	84	166		26	82	90	172
	107	125	100	225		27	100	86	186
	108	96	95	191		28	102	63	165
	109	148	129	277		29	71	51	122
						30	102	50	152
Total ...	...	24,232	18,359	42,591		31	123	97	220
						32	70	87	157
						33	132	89	221
Ward No. XXIII.	1	370	38	408		34	102	63	165
	2	1,942	59	2,001		35	80	114	194
	3	290	36	326		36	170	123	293
	4	926	76	1,002		37	92	70	162
	5	301	244	545		38	80	64	144
	6	131	28	159		39	105	102	207
	7	168	112	280		40	90	90	180
	8	192	86	278		41	145	163	308
	9	80	85	165		42	Taken with 36 above.		
	10	90	34	124		43	64	59	123
	11	112	112	224		44	89	65	154
	12	90	79	169		45	139	102	241
	13	134	144	278		46	136	60	196
	14	115	131	246		47	119	118	237
	15	148	115	263		48	180	120	300
	16	109	116	225		49	80	79	159
	17	243	150	393		50	70	54	124
	18	72	62	134		51	122	99	221
	19	90	76	166		52	121	60	181

TABLE XVIII.—*Population of the town, block by block*—continued.

Ward.	Block.	Males.	Females.	Total.
Ward No. XXIII —*concluded.*	53	89	69	158
	54	111	67	178
	55	148	136	284
	56	134	83	217
Total ...	...	9,854	4,950	14,804
Ward No. XXIV.	1	227	272	499
	2	100	139	239
	3	249	257	506
	4	178	187	365
	5	144	118	262
	6	215	193	408
	7	200	136	336
	8	203	183	386
	9	100	173	273
	10	209	213	422
	11	293	163	456
	12	206	119	325
	13	319	253	572
	14	140	101	241
	15	145	173	318
	16	87	89	176
	17	204	160	364
	18	92	115	207
	19	210	196	406
	20	121	117	238
	21	159	161	320
	22	192	199	391
	23	96	105	201
	24	53	44	97
	25	204	194	398
	26	305	161	466
Ward No. XXIV—*concluded.*	27	416	141	557
	28	347	184	531
	29	188	180	368
	30	160	138	298
	31	155	128	283
	32	157	139	296
	33	203	164	367
	34	78	92	170
	35	312	247	559
	36	248	200	448
	37	255	158	413
	38	125	77	202
	39	112	138	250
	40	85	111	196
	41	103	114	217
	42	139	163	302
	43	147	108	255
	44	122	142	264
	45	189	123	312
	46	105	75	180
Total ..	...	8,297	7,043	15,340
Ward No. XXV.	1	416	187	603
	2	388	111	499
	3	126	28	154
	3A	15	4	19
	4	67	5	72
	5	127	42	169
	6	133	23	156
	7	598	223	821
	8	451	123	574
	9	279	100	379

TABLE XVIII.—*Population of the town, block by block*— concluded.

Ward.	Block.	Males.	Females.	Total.	Ward.	Block.	Males.	Females.	Total.
Ward No. XXV—*continued.*	10, 11	371	144	515	Ward No. XXV—*concluded.*	39	110	98	208
	12	200	171	371		40	211	128	339
	13	725	212	937		41	114	58	172
	14	317	65	382		42	193	59	252
	15	572	355	927		43	160	115	275
	16	504	310	814		44	260	106	366
	17	606	318	924		45	321	181	502
	18	433	259	692		46	124	76	200
	19	517	189	706		47	219	205	424
	20	434	255	689		48	221	170	391
	21	230	131	361		49	830	469	1,299
	22	162	117	279		50	381	222	603
	23	264	199	463		51	326	63	389
	24	268	188	456		52	331	187	518
	25	271	236	507		53	229	114	343
	26	238	177	415		54	166	133	299
	27	461	141	602		55	176	150	326
	28	417	159	576		56	143	98	241
	29	213	67	280		57	313	271	584
	30	323	187	510		58	222	202	424
	31	158	151	309		59	303	164	467
	32	126	106	232		60, 61	239	174	413
	33	155	140	295					
	34	106	80	186		62	74	89	163
	35	253	146	399		63	88	114	202
	36	209	123	332		64	160	158	318
	37	34	20	54					
	38	275	181	456	Total ...	...	17,356	9,477	26,833

TABLE X[illegible].—*Conservancy Statistics of [illegible]e houses in Calcutta Ward by Ward.*

Ward.	Houses, masonry.		Houses not masonry.		Having privies.	Having privies connected with		Houses connected with		Number of cattle.	Number of buffaloes.	Horses.		Population of masonry houses.	Population of other houses.
	Inhabited.	Uninhabited.	Inhabited.	Uninhabited.		Filtered water-supply.	Unfiltered water-supply.	Filtered water-supply.	Unfiltered water-supply.			Ticca.	Private.		
I	1,599	184	2,528	232	4,407	247	88	1,026	411	2,449	193	62	77	12,802	24,083
II	1,220	93	1,444	41	2,792	78	...	692	1	971	20	33	125	10,372	16,242
III	1,786	162	2,546	124	4,666	209	60	697	7	2,530	53	83	99	13,559	22,872
IV	1,256	64	2,361	92	3,413	80	220	524	66	1,821	87	62	116	13,003	22,825
V	1,375	72	1,356	62	2,853	31	33	777	31	838	7	12	235	17,337	21,843
VI	1,816	152	1,685	145	3,394	171	45	784	25	1,689	36	59	132	16,146	25,511
VII	1,708	384	365	175	2,632	225	22	374	101	178	...	46	336	11,863	8,783
VIII	1,343	107	1,721	432	3,603	378	135	1,043	304	347	155	267	24	28,700	22,081
IX	1,945	86	2,373	348	4,769	304	384	1,786	165	896	50	450	169	18,620	30,852
X	825	19	725	5	1,674	233	18	434	3	400	17	269	272	11,733	10,935
XI	1,175	99	1,192	217	2,680	179	655	831	177	627	3	38	155	10,867	9,894
XII	438	8	49	5	475	113	21	283	29	21	...	64	177	4,736	1,347
XIII	805	76	988	19	1,888	310	37	649	20	537	75	134	198	11,307	17,059
XIV	1,065	36	1,358	46	2,271	308	17	738	49	612	35	135	154	15,837	17,370
XV	372	113	898	130	1,513	173	246	307	221	156	7	79	242	3,503	9,715
XVI	194	2	46	1	243	109	2	...	...	66	61	...	438	4,466	154
XVII	89	1	310	3	403	2	61	87	368	108	...	105	179	2,755	1,843
XVIII	90	6	166	3	265	31	16	60	4	176	5	36	46	2,183	2,637
XIX	634	139	3,676	198	4,365	214	490	131	596	2,805	76	235	323	5,643	27,504
XX	680	42	3,386	110	2,900	85	375	67	337	1,014	31	120	79	3,356	19,664
XXI	591	153	3,323	326	3,928	69	3	95	31	1,778	118	141	723	4,917	17,914
XXII	1,610	134	4,408	468	5,450	225	437	103	196	2,857	284	537	177	13,769	28,822
XXIII	337	52	1,087	139	2,340	43	86	1	110	1,317	47	40	67	2,730	12,074
XXIV	134	17	2,296	96	2,559	44	169	54	265	787	35	29	38	1,235	14,105
XXV	553	81	2,602	145	2,632	163	368	...	363	1,584	126	120	98	3,629	23,204
GRAND TOTAL ...	23,739	2,531	43,789	3,562	6,896	4,024	3,978	11,493	3,970	26,664	1,520	3,156	4,669	244,068	405,333

APPENDIX A.

PROCLAMATION FIXING THE LIMITS OF THE TOWN OF CALCUTTA.

Issued by the Governor-General in Council on the 10th September 1794.

WHEREAS in and by the 159th section, Chapter 52 of an Act passed in the 33rd year of His Majesty's reign, entitled "an Act for continuing in the East India Company, for a limited time, the possession of the British territories in India, together with their exclusive trade, under certain limitations; for establishing further regulations for the government of the said territories, and the better administration of justice within the same; for appropriating to certain uses the revenues and profits of the said Company; and for making provision for the good order and government of the towns of Calcutta, Madras and Bombay," it is enacted that if any question shall arise touching or concerning the true limits and extent of the said towns and factories, or any of them, the same shall be inquired into by the Governor-General in Council at Fort William in respect to the limits and extent of Calcutta, and by the Governor in Council of Fort St. George in respect to the limits and extent of Madras, and the Governor in Council at Bombay in respect to the town of Bombay, and that such limits as the said respective Governments, by order in Council, shall declare and prescribe to be the limits of the said towns and factories, respectively, shall be held, deemed and taken in law as the true limits of the same, any custom or usage to the contrary notwithstanding. And whereas such question, as in and by the said clause of the said Act is meant and referred to, has arisen and been made with respect to the limits of the said town of Calcutta, and the Governor-General in Council, in pursuance of the authority vested in him by the said Act, has inquired into the same, and by an order duly made in Council has declared and prescribed the limits of the said town, and has directed and commanded the same to be publicly notified, in order that the said limits, so declared and prescribed, may be known to the inhabitants of the said town, and to all persons whom the same may in anywise concern,—

It is hereby publicly notified that the town of Calcutta, in respect to all legal intents and purposes, extends to, and is bounded by, the several lines, limits, and boundaries hereinafter mentioned and described, that is to say—

The Northern boundary is declared to commence, and does accordingly commence, on the west side of the river Hooghly at the post or mete No. 22, situated at the north point of Colonel Robertson's garden called Jackapore, immediately opposite to the mouth of the brook called Chitpore Nullah or Baug Bazar Nullah; and the said Northern boundary is from thence declared to continue, and is continued accordingly, by a line drawn across the river from the aforesaid point to the south corner of the mouth of the said Nullah unto the post or mete No. 1 near the foot of the Chitpore Bridge; and from thence by a line drawn eastward and passing the south end of the said Bridge to No. 2, and from thence along the south side of the said Nullah or brook to the post or mete No. 3, and thence on to the post or mete No. 4, passing the old Powder Mill Bazar until it reaches the foot of the bridge leading to Dum-Dum, where the post or mete No. 5 is.

The Eastern boundary is declared to commence, and does accordingly commence, at the said post or mete No. 5, and is declared to continue, and does accordingly continue, by a line traced along the west or inner side of the Mahratta ditch or entrenchment and the east side of the road adjoining thereunto until it reaches the post or mete No. 6, at the northern angle next to the road of an enclosure called Halsee Bagan, which said Halsee Bagan is included within the said town of Calcutta; and from the said northern angle by a line drawn eastward along the southern side of the ditch or trench which encloses the said Halsee Bagan to the post or mete marked No. 6; and from thence southward along the western side of the said ditch or trench to the post or mete also marked No. 6; and from the said last-mentioned post or mete westward along the northern side of the said ditch or trench until the said line reaches mark No. 7, where there is a thana; and from the said last-mentioned post or mete by a line drawn southward and on the western side of the Mahratta entrenchment and the eastern side of the Boitaconnah Road as far as the remains of the said Mahratta entrenchment are visible to the post or mete No. 8, at the corner of Raja Ramlochun's Bazar, and of the road leading to Ballea Ghaut immediately opposite to Narain Chattoorjee's road; and from the said last-mentioned post or mete No. 8 by a line continued in a southern direction passing through Mirzapore and drawn along the eastern side of the Boitaconnah Road, and leaving the Portuguese burying ground to the east, until it reaches the Boitaconnah tree, where the two posts or metes marked, respectively, No. 9 and No. 10 are fixed on each side of the road opposite to the Bowbazar Road and Boitaconnah Bazar; and from the last-mentioned post or mete marked No. 10 by a line drawn along the eastern side of the said Boitaconnah Road to the post or mete No. 11 opposite to Gopee Baboo's Bazar, which bazar is situated between the Jaun Bazar and Dhurrumtollah Roads; and from thence in the same direction until the said line reaches the post or mete No. 12, at the point of turning of the said road towards the west, leaving Dhee Seerampore on the east, and thereby including within the limits of Calcutta the Protestant burying ground, Chowringhee, and the lands thereunto belonging, called Dhee Birjee.

The Southern boundary is declared to commence, and does accordingly commence, from the last-mentioned post or mete No. 12, and is declared to continue, and does accordingly continue, by a line drawn from thence to the westward with a little inclination to the southward along the southern side of the public road excluding Dhee Chukerbeer, and including Bunneapokah, otherwise called Arreapokah in Dhee Birjee, until the said line reaches the beginning of the Russapuglah Road immediately opposite to Chowringhee High Road, where the post or mete No. 13 is fixed; and from the said post or mete No. 13 by a line running to the westward along the southern side of the public road to the post or mete No. 14, fixed between the thana and the General Hospital, and passing on westerly to the post or mete No. 15 at the foot of the Alipore Bridge, and excluding the General Hospital aforesaid, the Hospital for Insanes, and the Hospital burying ground, situated in Dhee Bowanipore; and from thence and from the south side of the said Alipore Bridge by a line drawn and continued along the south side of the Nullah, commonly called Tolly's Nullah, at high-water mark to the post or mete marked No. 16; and from thence passing the foot or south end of Surmon's Bridge, commonly called Kidderpore Bridge, and extending to the mouth of the said nullah, where it enters the River Hooghly excluding Watson's Dock, and to the post or mete marked No. 17, and then proceeding from east to west across the said River Hooghly to the south-east point of Major Kyd's garden, and excluding the said garden and village of Sheebpore, at which point a post or mete marked No. 18 is directed to be fixed; and

The Western boundary is declared to commence, and does accordingly commence, at the said point where the said post or mete marked No. 18 is fixed, and is declared to continue and does accordingly continue, from thence by a line drawn at low-water mark along the western side of the said River Hooghly, but excluding the ghauts of Ramkissenpore, Howrah, and Sulkea, where posts or metes are fixed, marked respectively Nos. 19, 20, and 21, until the said line reaches the northern point of Colonel Robertson's garden or Jackapore aforesaid, where a post or mete is fixed, marked No. 22, and immediately opposite to the post or mete No. 1, at Chitpore Bridge.

Declared and proclaimed by order of the Governor-General in Council of Fort William in Bengal this 10th day of September 1794.

E. Hay,
Secretary to the Government.

N.B.—It does not appear that the local Government have since the passing of the 55 Geo. 3, c. 84, availed themselves of the power conferred on them by that statute of extending the limits of Calcutta.

R. H. Mytton,
Magistrate.

APPENDIX B.

NOTIFICATION.

DEFINING THE POLICE AND MUNICIPAL JURISDICTION OF THE SUBURBS OF CALCUTTA.

Dated 10th September 1877—In modification of the boundaries declared in the Government notifications dated 17th October 1867, 5th June 1869, 30th March 1868, and 22nd September 1870, and published respectively in the *Calcutta Gazette* of the 23rd October 1867, 16th June 1869, 1st April 1868, and 28th September 1870, the following are declared to be the revised boundaries, with effect from the 1st October 1877:—

NORTHERN BOUNDARY.

Commencing from the north-west angle at Paramanick Ghât on the River Hooghly, the boundary follows the northern side of Paramanick Ghât Road eastwards to its junction with the Cossipore Road; thence northwards along the western side of the Cossipore Road till its junction with Dhareabagan Road; thence eastwards along the northern side of the Dhareabagan Road till it meets the Barrackpore Trunk Road, which it crosses; and thence continues along the northern side of the North Sinthee Road eastwards till it meets the Eastern Bengal Railway line, crossing to the eastern side of the said line at No. 2 Bridge, north of the Dum-Dum station.

EASTERN BOUNDARY.

The boundary on the east follows the eastern side of the Eastern Bengal Railway line southwards till it meets the bridge over the new canal at Ooltadangah; from thence it follows the eastern bank of the new canal till it joins the Balliaghatta Canal at the Dhappa toll-house; thence crosses the Balliaghatta Canal to its southern bank; thence westwards along the southern bank of the Balliaghatta Canal till it meets Pugladanga Canal Road; thence along the eastern side of the Pugladanga Canal Road to its junction with the Pugladanga Road; thence along the eastern side of the Pugladanga Road till it meets the Chingreeghatta Road; thence southwards to the Punchannogram iron boundary pillar; thence southwards along the eastern side of an unmetalled road till it meets the municipal tramway; thence it turns westwards along the southern boundary of the municipal tramway till it meets the South Tangrah Road; thence it follows the eastern side of the Tangrah Road till it meets Christopher's Lane and Topseeah Road; thence along the eastern side and afterwards along the southern side of the Topseeah Road till it joins the Tiljullah Road, thence along the southern side of the Tiljullah Road to No. 4 Bridge of the Calcutta and South-Eastern State Railway line; thence along the eastern side of the line of railway till it meets the Kankilay Road; thence westwards, crossing the railway, it follows the southern side of the Kankilay Road till it meets the Gurreahat Road; thence southwards along the eastern side of the Gurreahat Road till it meets the Mollahatty Road.

SOUTHERN BOUNDARY.

Leaving the Gurreahat Road, the boundary runs westwards along the southern side of the Mollahatty Road till it meets the Russapugla Road; thence northwards along the western side of the Russapugla Road till it meets the Tollygunge Bridge Road; thence along the southern side of the Tollygunge Bridge Road westwards to Tollygunge Suspension Bridge, where it crosses Tolly's Nullah; from thence it runs along the southern side of the Tollygunge, Shahpore, Goragachee, and the Taratolla Roads, which latter passes through the villages of Dowlutpore No. 441, Indree No. 446, and Durreepin No. 383; thence westwards along the southern side of the Circular Garden Reach or Moocheekhola Road to the point where the Durreepin boundary crosses it; and thence along the southern side of the Paharpore Road, which diverges from that point through the villages of Singerathee No. 444, Futtehpore No. 430, and Ramasathee No. 432; and thence northwards along the west side of the above road through the villages of Futtehpore No. 430 and Ramessurpore No. 300, till it joins the western boundary line at the junction of the boundary villages Ramessurpore and Garden Reach; the boundary then proceeds northwards for a short distance up to Garden Reach Road, following the boundary common to Moodially, Dhobapara, and Dum-Dum on the one side and Garden Reach on the other, up to the Dum-Duma drain; thence along the eastern cut of the Dum-Duma drain in a straight line to the river Hooghly.

WESTERN BOUNDARY.

Starting from the trijunction of the village of Dum-Duma, Garden Reach, and River Hooghly, it proceeds along the southern bank of the River Hooghly as far as Hastings Bridge; it thence follows the northern bank of Tolly's Nullah up to Jerut Bridge; thence along the northern approach to the bridge to the Lower Circular Road; thence along the southern and eastern side of the Circular Road up to Manicktollah Road; thence eastwards along the northern side of the road to a point where the Mahratta ditch touches the Manicktollah Road; thence along the Mahratta ditch northwards till it meets the Upper Circular Road; thence northwards along the Circular Road to the point where it meets the Halsee Bagan Road; thence along the northern side of the Halsee Bagan Road eastwards till it meets the Mahratta ditch (which is the boundary between Halsee Bagan and Goureeber), which it follows till it meets the Ooltadangah Road, following the southern side of the said road till it joins the Upper Circular Road, and follows the eastern side of the same road and the eastern and northern banks of the Mahratta ditch till it joins the River Hooghly at Permit Ghât; thence it proceeds along the eastern bank of the Hooghly River up to the Paramanick Ghât.

1. NOTE.—All railways, canals, tramways, drains, lanes, &c. (with the exception of the Calcutta Circular Road and Mahratta ditch), situated on the above boundaries, are included in the Suburbs of Calcutta, together with the drains on both sides of all such roads and lanes.

2. NOTE.—The villages of Nyenan, Neej-Nyenan, Nyenan (east) and Neej-Sinthee, situated north of the northern boundary line of the Suburbs as above defined, are attached to thana Burranagor of district 24-Pergunnahs.

3. NOTE.—The portion of village Neemuckpooktan, situated east of the Pugladanga Road, is attached to thana Tollygunge, of district 24-Pergunnahs.

4. NOTE.—The village of Govindpore and parts of villages Aurukpore, Silimpore, and Dhacoorea, situated west of the Gurreahhât Road and north of the Mollahatty Road, are included in the police and municipal jurisdiction of the Suburbs of Calcutta.

HORACE A. COCKERELL,

Offg Secretary to the Government of Bengal.

APPENDIX C.

Boundaries of Wards.

(*See Section* 15.)

Ward No. 1.—Bounded on the north and east by the Circular Canal; south by Grey Street and Ooltadanga Road; west by Upper Chitpore Road.

Ward No. 2—Bounded on the north by the Mahratta Ditch; west by river Hooghly; south by Nimtollah Ghât Street; east by Upper Chitpore Road.

Ward No. 3.—Bounded on the north by Ooltadanga Main Road, the Mahratta Ditch, and Grey Street; south by Beadon Street and Manicktollah Road; west by Upper Chitpore Road; east by the Circular Canal.

Ward No. 4.—Bounded on the north by Beadon Street and Manicktollah Road; south by Machooa Bazar Road; east by the Circular Canal Narikhaldanga Road; and west by Cornwallis Street.

Ward No. 5.—Bounded on the north by Nimtollah Ghât Street; south by Cotton Street and Meerboher Ghât Street; east by Upper Chitpore Road; west by river Hooghly.

Ward No. 6.—Bounded on the north by Beadon Street; south by Machooa Bazar Road; east by Cornwallis Street; west by Upper Chitpore Road.

Ward No. 7.—Bounded on the north by Cotton Street and Meerboher Ghut Street; south by Loll Bazar Street, Dalhousie Square, North, and Fairlie Place; east by Lower Chitpore Road; west by river Hooghly.

Ward No. 8.—Bounded on the north by Machooa Bazar Road; south by Bow Bazar Street; east by College Street; west by Lower Chitpore Road.

Ward No. 9.—Bounded on the north by Machooa Bazar Road and Narikhaldanga Road; south by Bow Bazar Street and the Balliaghatta Road; east by the Circular Canal; west by College Street.

Ward No. 10.—Bounded on the north by Bow Bazar Street; south by Dhurrumtollah Street; east by Wellington Street; west by Bentinck Street.

Ward No. 11.—Bounded on the north by Bow Bazar Street; south by Dhurrumtollah Street; east by Lower Circular Road; west by Wellington Street.

Ward No. 12.—Bounded on the north by Loll Bazar Street, Dalhousie Square, and Fairlie Place; south by Esplanade Row; east by Bentinck Street; west by river Hooghly.

Ward No. 13.—Bounded on the north by Dhurrumtollah Street; south by Kyd Street, Free School Street, and South Culinga Street; east by Wellesley Street; west by Chowringhee Road.

Ward No. 14.—Bounded on the north by Dhurrumtollah Street; south by South Culinga Street; east by Lower Circular Road; west by Wellesley Street.

Ward No. 15.—Bounded on the north by South Culinga Street; south by Theatre Road; east by Lower Circular Road; west by Wellesley Street and Wood Street.

Ward No. 16.—Bounded on the north by Kyd Street and South Culinga Street; south by Theatre Road; east by Wellesley Street and Wood Street; west by Chowringhee Road.

Ward No. 17.—Bounded on the north by Theatre Road; south by Lower Circular Road; east by Lower Circular Road; west by Chowringhee Road.

Ward No. 18.—Bounded on the north by Clyde Road; south by Tolly's Nullah Road; east by Kidderpore Bridge Road; and west by Strand Road.

Ward No. 19.—Bounded on the north by the Baliaghatta and the New Canal; south by Gobrah Road, Christopher's Lane, Puddopookur Road, Phulbagan Road, Nawab Bagan Road, and Police Hospital Road; east by the Pagladanga Road, Chingrahatta Road, Tangra Road, and Topsea Road; west by Circular Road.

Ward No. 20.—Bounded on the north by Ward No. 19; south by Kumal Road, Sapir Jemadar's Lane, Mohir Mohsin's Lane, Karriah Bagan, Tiljullah Road, and Topsea Road; east by Topsea Road; west by Lower Circular Road.

Ward No. 21.—Bounded on the north by Ward No. 20; south by the new embankment from the Eastern Bengal Railway to Tolly's Nullah; east by the South-Eastern Bengal Railway; west by Lower Circular Road, Chuckerbarree Road, Moley Bustee Road, Gurreah Road, Russapuglah Road, Tollygunge Bridge and Road, and Tolly's Nullah.

Ward No. 22.—Bounded on the north by Lower Circular Road, and the road leading from it to the Jeerat bridge; south by Ward No. 21; east by Ward No. 21; west by Tolly's Nullah.

Ward No. 23.—Bounded on the north by Tolly's Nullah; south by the Goragachee Road; east by Tolly's Nullah; west by Diamond Harbour Road.

Ward No. 24.—Bounded on the north by Komedan Bagan Lane and Circular Garden Reach Road; south by Goragachee Road; east by Diamond Harbour Road; west by some 3rd Lane and some 4th Lane.

Ward No. 25.—Bounded on the north by the river Hooghly; south by Ward No. 24; east by Tolly's Nullah and Diamond Harbour Road; and west by the Goragachee Road.

R. D'R. & others—Reg. No. 4177J—160—4-12-91.